Solutions Manual

ESSENTIAL CONCEPTS OF CHEMISTRY

SHARON J. SHERMAN
The College of New Jersey

ALAN SHERMAN
Middlesex County College

Houghton Mifflin Company Boston New York

HOUGHTON MIFFLIN COMPANY   BOSTON   NEW YORK

Senior Sponsoring Editor: Richard Stratton
Editorial Assistant: Katie Shutzer
Senior Manufacturing Coordinator: Sally Culler
Marketing Manager: Penny Hoblyn
Editorial Assistant: Joy Park

Printed in the U.S.A.

ISBN: 0-395-92129-5

123456789-SB-02 01 00 99 98

CONTENTS

PREFACE

As you study chemistry, you will solve numerous problems. To be sure that you understand what is involved in solving these problems, we have prepared this Solutions Manual for *Essential Concepts of Chemistry*. In this manual you will find answers to all exercises that have specific solutions. We have not included answers to exercises that lend themselves to discussion or that require you to offer an opinion.

Unlike the answers to selected exercises that appear at the end of the textbook, the Solutions Manual features step-by-step solutions to the exercises. These solutions can be used in two ways. As you study the material contained in the chapter, you may test your knowledge by completing the self-test exercises that are keyed to the learning goals in the textbook. The Solutions Manual will help you determine whether you have worked out the problems correctly. And it will help if you are "stuck" on a particular type of problem. When you study for an exam, you might choose to work out all of the self-test exercises to reinforce your knowledge. You can check your answers by using the Solutions Manual.

The key to achieving success in chemistry is practicing until you are secure and confident in your knowledge. The Solutions Manual is a tool that will help you in your studies. If you need further assistance, the Study Guide for *Essential Concepts of Chemistry*, written by James R. Braun, is also available as part of our total package.

S.J.S.
A.S.

1 THE ORIGINS OF CHEMISTRY: WHERE IT ALL BEGAN

SELF-TEST EXERCISES

2. The golden age of philosophy occurred between the years 600 B.C. and 400 B.C. in Greece. This period is considered the beginning of scientific thought because it represents the first time in recorded history that a culture began to study the fundamental structure of the world.

3. Empedocles thought that the world was composed of four elements: earth, air, fire, and water.

4. Thales thought the world was composed of water.

5. Democritus proposed the atomic theory.

6. Democritus established the concept of the atom.

7. Empedocles would probably have said that paper was composed of earth and fire. The reasoning would be that when you burn paper the fire comes out and earth (ash) is left behind.

8. If you have to choose among combinations of the four elements (earth, air, fire, and water) that made up the world (according to Greek thought), you might consider vegetation as being composed of earth and water. The logic behind this is that it takes earth and water to grow vegetation.

9. Some of the contributions of the early Egyptian civilizations to chemistry were processes involving the mining and purifying of the metals gold, silver, and copper. They also made embalming fluids and dyes.

10. False. The Egyptians mined and purified the metals gold, silver, and copper, not gold, silver, and antimony.

11. While the Greeks were studying philosophy and mathematics, the Egyptians were already practicing the art of chemistry, which they called *khemia*.

12. The art of *khemia* flourished until the seventh century A.D.

13. The aim of chemistry from A.D. 300 to A.D. 1600 was to *transmute* base metals into gold and to find the *elixir of life* and the *philosopher's stone*.

14. The alchemists tried to change metals like lead and iron into gold.

15. The people who tried to turn lead into gold were known as alchemists.

16. The *elixir of life* was supposed to be a potion that would extend life indefinitely if a person took it internally.

17. The main message of Boyle's book, *The Sceptical Chymist,* was that scientific theories had to be proved by experiment.

EXTRA EXERCISES

28. Chemistry is the science that deals with matter and the changes that matter undergoes.

29. According to Empedocles and the theory of the four elements (earth, air, fire, and water):
    (a) Copper would be made from earth.
    (b) Rain would be made from water.
    (c) Lightning would be made from fire.
    (d) Nitrogen would be made from air.

2

2 SYSTEMS OF MEASUREMENT

SELF-TEST EXERCISES

1. (a) 5   (b) 1   (c) 3   (d) 4   (e) 7

   (f) 2   (g) 1   (h) 4   (i) 3

2. (a) 6   (b) 3   (c) 4   (d) 2   (e) 4

   (f) 5   (g) 1   (h) 5

3. (a) 7   (b) 2   (c) 1   (d) 3   (e) 7

   (f) 3   (g) 6   (h) 4   (i) 6   (j) 4

4. (a) 7   (b) 3   (c) 1   (d) 3   (e) 3

   (f) 4   (g) 1   (h) 2

5. Perimeter = 4.234 cm + 3.8 cm + 5.67 cm + 4.00 cm
             = 17.7 cm (three significant figures)

6. Perimeter = 3.23 cm + 5.006 cm + 3 cm
             = 11.236 cm or 11 cm (to two significant figures)

7. Perimeter = 4.00 cm + 5.000 cm + 6.0 cm
             = 15.0 cm (to three significant figures)

8. $A = s^2 = (4.2 \text{ cm})^2 = 17.64 \text{ cm}^2$ or 18 cm^2 (to two significant figures)

9. Perimeter = 7.382 cm + 3.95 cm + 5.4342 cm + 3.83 cm
    = 20.60 cm

10. $A = l \times w$ = 10.12 cm × 10.25 cm
    = 103.73 cm^2 or 103.7 cm^2 (to four significant figures)

11. Area = 20.62 cm × 10.4 cm = 214 cm^2 (three significant figures)

12. $A = s^2 = (2.1$ cm$)^2 = 4.41$ cm^2 or 4.4 cm^2 (to two significant figures)

13. (a) 2   (b) 3   (c) 4   (d) 4   (e) 1

    (f) 2   (g) 3   (h) 4   (i) 4   (j) 3

14. Perimeter = 2.1 cm + 2.1 cm + 2.1 cm + 2.1 cm = 8.4 cm

15. (a) 6×10^2 (b) 6.00×10^2 (c) 6.000×10^2

    (d) 3.2×10^{11} (e) 2×10^{-3} (f) 3.007×10^{-4}

    (g) 1.5×10^{-7}

16. (a) 9×10^5 (b) 4.5×10^4 (c) 2.97×10^3

    (d) 2.546×10^6 (e) 6×10^{-5} (f) 1.22×10^{-2}

    (g) 5.6×10^{-2} (h) 2.00040×10^1

17. (a) $10{,}581 = 1.0581 \times 10^4$ (b) $0.00205 = 2.05 \times 10^{-3}$

    (c) $1{,}000{,}000 = 1 \times 10^6$ (d) $802 = 8.02 \times 10^2$

18. (a) 4.5×10^7 (b) 4.0×10^2 (c) 4.00×10^2

    (d) 4.000×10^2 (e) 4.25000×10^5

19. (a) $850{,}000{,}000 = 8.5 \times 10^8$ (b) $0.00000607 = 6.07 \times 10^{-6}$

    (c) $6{,}308{,}000 = 6.308 \times 10^6$ (d) $0.06005 = 6.005 \times 10^{-2}$

    (e) $500 = 5 \times 10^2$ (f) $5\overline{0}0 = 5.0 \times 10^2$

    (g) $5\overline{00} = 5.00 \times 10^2$ (h) $500.0 = 5.000 \times 10^2$

    (i) $23{,}\overline{0}00{,}000 = 2.300 \times 10^7$ (j) $0.0000000930 = 9.30 \times 10^{-8}$

20. (a) 1.23×10^{-1} (b) 6×10^{-3} (c) 6.01×10^{-3}

21. Area = (8.00 m)(3.00 m) = 24.0 m^2
    Volume = (8.00 m)(3.00 m)(4.00 m) = 96.0 m^3

22. Area A = 5.0 m × 4.0 m = $2\bar{0}$ m^2

23. Using a page size of 7.19 in. (18.3 cm) by 9.19 in. (23.3 cm)
    (a)   Area A = 18.3 cm × 23.3 cm = 426 cm^2
    (b)   Area A = 7.19 in. × 9.19 in. = 66.1 in.^{2}

24. Using a page size of 7.19 in. (18.3 cm) by 9.19 in. (23.3 cm)
    (a)   Area A = 0.183 m × 0.233 m = 0.0426 m^2

    (b)   Area $A = \dfrac{7.19 \text{ in.}}{12 \text{ in./ft}} \times \dfrac{9.19 \text{ in.}}{12 \text{ in./ft}} = 0.459$ ft^2

25. Area A = $3\bar{0}$ m × $2\bar{0}$ m = $6\bar{0}0$ m^2

26. Area A = 1.5 m × 2.0 m = 3.0 m^2

27. Volume V = 5.00 cm × 6.00 cm × 15.0 cm = $45\bar{0}$ cm^3

28. Volume V = 5.0 m × 4.0 m × 2.0 m = $4\bar{0}$ m^3

29. Volume of cylinder,
    $V = \pi r^2 h = 3.14 \times (15.0 \text{ cm})^2 \times 60.0 \text{ cm} = 42{,}400$ cm^3

30. Volume $V = \pi r^2 h = 3.14 \times (3.0 \text{ cm})^2 \times 25 \text{ cm} = 706$ cm^3 or 710 cm^3
    (to two significant figures)

31. Volume = (16.0 ft)(32.0 ft)(5.00 ft) = 2.560 ft^3

    Volume (cm^3) = $(2{,}560 \text{ ft}^3)\left(\dfrac{28{,}400 \text{ cm}^3}{1 \text{ ft}^3}\right) = 7.27 \times 10^7$ cm^3

32. ? cm^3 = $(2 \text{ m}^3)\left(\dfrac{1 \times 10^6 \, cm^3}{1 m^3}\right) = 2 \times 10^6$ cm^3

33. ? Liters = $(7.27 \times 10^7 \text{ cm}^3)\left(\dfrac{1.00 L}{1.00 \times 10^3 \, cm^3}\right) = 7.27 \times 10^4$ L

    ? gallons = $(7.27 \times 10^4 \text{ L})\left(\dfrac{1.06 \text{ quarts}}{1.00 \text{ L}}\right)\left(\dfrac{1.0 \text{ gallon}}{4.00 \text{ quarts}}\right) = 19{,}300$ gallons

34. $V = \pi r^2 h = 3.14 \times (5.0 \text{ cm})^2 \times 1\bar{0} \text{ cm} = 785 \text{ cm}^3$ or 790 cm^3
(to two significant figures)

35. $? \dfrac{\text{in.}^3}{\text{ft}^3} = \left(\dfrac{12 \text{ in.}}{1 \text{ ft}}\right)^3 = \dfrac{1,728 \text{ in.}^3}{\text{ft}^3}$

36. $V = l \times w \times h = 4\bar{0} \text{ cm} \times 25 \text{ cm} \times 15 \text{ cm} = 15,000 \text{ cm}^3$ or $1.5 \times 10^4 \text{ cm}^3$

37. (a) $? \text{ g} = 0.25 \text{ kg} \times \dfrac{1,000 \text{ g}}{1 \text{ kg}} = 250 \text{ g}$

   (b) $? \text{ dg} = 0.25 \text{ kg} \times \dfrac{1,000 \text{ g}}{1 \text{ kg}} \times \dfrac{10 \text{ dg}}{1 \text{ g}} = 2,500 \text{ dg}$

   (c) $? \text{ mg} = 0.25 \text{ kg} \times \dfrac{1,000 \text{ g}}{1 \text{ kg}} \times \dfrac{1,000 \text{ mg}}{1 \text{ g}} = 250,000 \text{ mg}$

   (d) $? \text{ μg} = (0.25 \text{ kg})\left(\dfrac{1,000 g}{1 kg}\right)\left(\dfrac{1 \times 10^6 \, mg}{1 g}\right) = 250,000,000 \text{ μg}$

38. (a) $? \text{ g} = (4.17 \text{ kg})\left(\dfrac{1,000 \text{ g}}{1 \text{ kg}}\right) = 4,170 \text{ g}$

   (b) $? \text{ dg} = (4,170 \text{ g})\left(\dfrac{10 \text{ dg}}{1 \text{ g}}\right) = 41,700 \text{ dg}$

   (c) $? \text{ mg} = (4,170 \text{ g})\left(\dfrac{1,000 \text{ mg}}{1 \text{ g}}\right) = 4,170,000 \text{ mg}$

   (d) $? \text{ μg} = (4,170 \text{ g})\left(\dfrac{1 \times 10^6 \, mg}{1 g}\right) = 4,170,000,000 \text{ μg}$

39. (a) $? \text{ dm} = 3.1 \text{ m} \times \dfrac{10 \text{ dm}}{1 \text{ m}} = 31 \text{ dm}$

   (b) $? \text{ cm} = 3.1 \text{ m} \times \dfrac{100 \text{ cm}}{1 \text{ m}} = 310 \text{ cm}$

   (c) $? \text{ mm} = 3.1 \text{ m} \times \dfrac{1,000 \text{ mm}}{1 \text{ m}} = 3,100 \text{ mm}$

40. (a) $? \text{ cm} = (35,000 \text{ mm})\left(\dfrac{1 \text{ cm}}{10 \text{ mm}}\right) = 3,500 \text{ cm}$

(b) $? \text{ dm} = (3{,}500 \text{ cm})\left(\dfrac{1 \text{ dm}}{10 \text{ cm}}\right) = 350 \text{ dm}$

(c) $? \text{ m} = (350 \text{ dm})\left(\dfrac{1 \text{ m}}{10 \text{ dm}}\right) = 35 \text{ m}$

(d) $? \text{ km} = (35 \text{ m})\left(\dfrac{1 \text{ km}}{1{,}000 \text{ m}}\right) = 0.035 \text{ km}$

41. (a) $? \text{ cm} = 149 \text{ mm} \times \dfrac{1 \text{ cm}}{10 \text{ mm}} = 14.9 \text{ cm}$

(b) $? \text{ m} = 149 \text{ mm} \times \dfrac{1 \text{ m}}{1{,}000 \text{ mm}} = 0.149 \text{ m}$

(c) $? \text{ km} = 149 \text{ mm} \times \dfrac{1 \text{ km}}{1{,}000{,}000 \text{ mm}} = 0.000149 \text{ km}$

42. (a) $? \text{ dm} = (5.5 \text{ m})\left(\dfrac{10 \text{ dm}}{1 \text{ m}}\right) = 55 \text{ dm}$

(b) $? \text{ cm} = (5.5 \text{ m})\left(\dfrac{100 \text{ cm}}{1 \text{ m}}\right) = 550 \text{ cm}$

(c) $? \text{ mm} = (5.5 \text{ m})\left(\dfrac{1{,}000 \text{ mm}}{1 \text{ m}}\right) = 5{,}500 \text{ mm}$

43. (a) $? \text{ mm} = 7.850 \text{ m} \times \dfrac{1{,}000 \text{ mm}}{1 \text{ m}} = 7.850 \times 10^3 \text{ mm}$

(b) $? \text{ cm} = 7.850 \text{ m} \times \dfrac{100 \text{ cm}}{1 \text{ m}} = 7.850 \times 10^2 \text{ cm}$

(c) $? \text{ dm} = 7.850 \text{ m} \times \dfrac{10 \text{ dm}}{1 \text{ m}} = 7.850 \times 10 \text{ dm}$

(d) $? \text{ km} = 7.850 \text{ m} \times \dfrac{1 \text{ km}}{1{,}000 \text{ m}} = 7.850 \times 10^{-3} \text{ km}$

44. (a) $? \text{ cm} = (125 \text{ mm})\left(\dfrac{1 \text{ cm}}{10 \text{ mm}}\right) = 12.5 \text{ cm}$

(b) $? \text{ m} = (125 \text{ mm})\left(\dfrac{1 \text{ m}}{1{,}000 \text{ mm}}\right) = 0.125 \text{ m}$

(c) $? \text{ km} = (0.125 \text{ m})\left(\dfrac{1 \text{ km}}{1{,}000 \text{ m}}\right) = 0.000125 \text{ km or } 1.25 \times 10^{-4} \text{ km}$

45. (a) $? \text{ m} = 0.34 \text{ km} \times \dfrac{1{,}000 \text{ m}}{1 \text{ km}} = 340 \text{ m}$

(b) $? \text{ dm} = 0.34 \text{ km} \times \dfrac{1{,}000 \text{ m}}{1 \text{ km}} \times \dfrac{10 \text{ dm}}{1 \text{ m}} = 3{,}400 \text{ dm}$

(c) $? \text{ cm} = 0.34 \text{ km} \times \dfrac{1{,}000 \text{ m}}{1 \text{ km}} \times \dfrac{100 \text{ cm}}{1 \text{ m}} = 34{,}000 \text{ cm}$

(d) $? \text{ mm} = 0.34 \text{ km} \times \dfrac{1{,}000 \text{ m}}{1 \text{ km}} \times \dfrac{1{,}000 \text{ mm}}{1 \text{ m}} = 340{,}000 \text{ mm}$

46. (a) $? \text{ mm} = (1.234 \text{ m})\left(\dfrac{1{,}000 \text{ mm}}{1 \text{ m}}\right) = 1{,}234 \text{ mm}$

(b) $? \text{ cm} = (1.234 \text{ m})\left(\dfrac{100 \text{ cm}}{1 \text{ m}}\right) = 123.4 \text{ cm}$

(c) $? \text{ dm} = (1.234 \text{ m})\left(\dfrac{10 \text{ dm}}{1 \text{ m}}\right) = 12.34 \text{ dm}$

(d) $? \text{ km} = (1.234 \text{ m})\left(\dfrac{1 \text{ km}}{1{,}000 \text{ m}}\right) = 0.001234 \text{ km or } 1.234 \times 10^{-3} \text{ km}$

47. (a) $? \text{ cg} = 2{,}185 \text{ mg} \times \dfrac{1 \text{ cg}}{10 \text{ mg}} = 218.5 \text{ cg}$

(b) $? \text{ dg} = 2{,}185 \text{ mg} \times \dfrac{1 \text{ dg}}{100 \text{ mg}} = 21.85 \text{ dg}$

(c) $? \text{ g} = 2{,}185 \text{ mg} \times \dfrac{1 \text{ g}}{1{,}000 \text{ mg}} = 2.185 \text{ g}$

(d) $? \text{ kg} = 2{,}185 \text{ mg} \times \dfrac{1 \text{ g}}{1{,}000 \text{ mg}} \times \dfrac{1 \text{ kg}}{1{,}000 \text{ g}} = 0.002185 \text{ kg}$

48. (a) $? \text{ m} = (7.5 \text{ km})\left(\dfrac{1{,}000 \text{ m}}{1 \text{ km}}\right) = 7{,}500 \text{ m}$

(b) $? \text{ dm} = (7{,}500 \text{ m})\left(\dfrac{10 \text{ dm}}{1 \text{ m}}\right) = 75{,}000 \text{ dm or } 7.5 \times 10^4 \text{ dm}$

(c)　$? \text{ cm} = (7,500 \text{ m})\left(\dfrac{100 \text{ cm}}{1 \text{ m}}\right) = 750,000 \text{ cm or } 7.5 \times 10^5 \text{ cm}$

49.　(a)　$? \text{ L} = 3.\overline{500} \text{ mL} \times \dfrac{1 \text{ L}}{1,000 \text{ mL}} = 3.500 \text{ L}$

　　　(b)　$? \text{ dL} = 3.500 \text{ L} \times \dfrac{10 \text{ dL}}{1 \text{ L}} = 35.00 \text{ dL}$

50.　(a)　$? \text{ L} = (1,\overline{500} \text{ mL})\left(\dfrac{1 \text{ L}}{1,000 \text{ mL}}\right) = 1.500 \text{ L}$

　　　(b)　$? \text{ dL} = (1.500 \text{ L})\left(\dfrac{10 \text{ dL}}{1 \text{ L}}\right) = 15.00 \text{ dL}$

51.　$? \dfrac{\text{cm}^3}{\text{m}^3} = \left(\dfrac{100 \text{ cm}}{1 \text{ m}}\right)^3 = 1.00 \times 10^6 \text{ cm}^3/\text{m}^3$

52.　(a)　$? \text{ cg} = (25,55\overline{0} \text{ mg})\left(\dfrac{1 \text{ cg}}{10 \text{ mg}}\right) = 2,555.0 \text{ cg}$

　　　(b)　$? \text{ dg} = (2,555.0 \text{ cg})\left(\dfrac{1 \text{ dg}}{10 \text{ cg}}\right) = 255.50 \text{ dg}$

　　　(c)　$? \text{ g} = (255.50 \text{ dg})\left(\dfrac{1 \text{ g}}{10 \text{ dg}}\right) = 25.550 \text{ g}$

　　　(d)　$? \text{ kg} = (25.550 \text{ g})\left(\dfrac{1 \text{ kg}}{1,000 \text{ g}}\right) = 0.025550 \text{ kg}$

53.　(a)　$? \text{ ft} = 25.0 \text{ m} \times \dfrac{3.28 \text{ ft}}{1 \text{ m}} = 82.0 \text{ ft}$

　　　(b)　$? \text{ in.} = 25.0 \text{ m} \times \dfrac{39.4 \text{ in.}}{1 \text{ m}} = 985 \text{ in.}$

54.　(a)　$? \text{ ft} = (100.0 \text{ m})\left(\dfrac{3.28 \text{ ft}}{1 \text{ m}}\right) = 328 \text{ ft}$

　　　(b)　$? \text{ in.} = (328 \text{ ft})\left(\dfrac{12 \text{ in.}}{1 \text{ ft}}\right) = 3,940 \text{ in.}$

55.　(a)　$? \text{ gal} = 1.2 \text{ L} \times \dfrac{1.06 \text{ qt}}{1 \text{ L}} \times \dfrac{1 \text{ gal}}{4 \text{ qt}} = 0.32 \text{ gal}$

(b) $? \text{qt} = (0.32 \text{ gal})\left(\dfrac{4 \text{ qt}}{1 \text{ gal}}\right) = 1.3 \text{ qt}$

56. (a) $? \text{gal} = (10.0 \text{ L})\left(\dfrac{1 \text{ gal}}{3.77 \text{ L}}\right) = 2.65 \text{ gal}$

    (b) $? \text{qt} = (2.65 \text{ gal})\left(\dfrac{4 \text{ qt}}{1 \text{ gal}}\right) = 10.6 \text{ qt}$

57. (a) $? \text{lb} = 5.00 \text{ g} \times \dfrac{1 \text{ lb}}{454 \text{ g}} = 0.0110 \text{ lb}$

    (b) $? \text{oz} = 0.0110 \text{ lb} \times \dfrac{16 \text{ oz}}{1 \text{ lb}} = 0.176 \text{ oz}$

58. (a) $? \text{lb} (100.0 \text{ kg})\left(\dfrac{2.2 \text{ lb}}{1 \text{ kg}}\right) = 220.0 \text{ lb}$

    (b) $? \text{tons} = (220.0 \text{ lb})\left(\dfrac{1 \text{ ton}}{2,000 \text{ lb}}\right) = 0.1100 \text{ ton}$

59. $? \text{ft}^3 = 1 \text{ m}^3 \times \dfrac{39.4 \text{ in.}}{1 \text{ m}} \times \dfrac{39.4 \text{ in.}}{1 \text{ m}} \times \dfrac{39.4 \text{ in.}}{1 \text{ m}} \times \dfrac{1 \text{ ft}}{12 \text{ in.}} \times \dfrac{1 \text{ ft}}{12 \text{ in.}} \times \dfrac{1 \text{ ft}}{12 \text{ in.}}$

     $= 35.40 \text{ ft}^3 \text{ or } 35.4 \text{ ft}^3 \text{ (to three significant figures)}$

60. (a) $? \text{yd} = (25\overline{0} \text{ m})\left(\dfrac{1 \text{ yd}}{0.914 \text{ m}}\right) = 274 \text{ yd}$

    (b) $? \text{ft} = (274 \text{ yd})\left(\dfrac{3 \text{ ft}}{1 \text{ yd}}\right) = 821 \text{ ft}$

61. (a) $? \text{yd} = 10\overline{0} \text{ m} \times \dfrac{3.28 \text{ ft}}{1 \text{ m}} \times \dfrac{1 \text{ yd}}{3 \text{ ft}} = 109 \text{ yd}$

    (b) $? \text{ft} = 10\overline{0} \text{ m} \times \dfrac{3.28 \text{ ft}}{1 \text{ m}} = 328 \text{ ft}$

62. $? \text{lb} = (2.50 \text{ g})\left(\dfrac{1 \text{ lb}}{454 \text{ g}}\right) = 5.51 \times 10^{-3} \text{ lb}$

63. $? \dfrac{\text{ft}^2}{\text{m}^2} = \left(\dfrac{3.28 \text{ ft}}{1 \text{ m}}\right)^2 = 10.8 \text{ ft}^2/\text{m}^2$

64. $? \text{gal} = (50.0 \text{ L})\left(\dfrac{1 \text{ gal}}{3.77 \text{ L}}\right) = 13.3 \text{ gal}$

66. (a) $? L = (2\bar{0}\ \cancel{gal})\left(\dfrac{3.77\ L}{1\ \cancel{gal}}\right) = 75\ L$

    (b) $? mL = (75\ \cancel{L})\left(\dfrac{1{,}000\ mL}{1\ \cancel{L}}\right) = 75{,}000\ mL$

68. (a) $? kg = (100.0\ \cancel{lb})\left(\dfrac{1\ kg}{2.200\ \cancel{lb}}\right) = 45.45\ kg$

    (b) $? g = (45.45\ \cancel{kg})\left(\dfrac{1{,}000\ g}{1\ \cancel{kg}}\right) = 45{,}450\ g$

69. (a) $? m = 1\bar{0}\ \cancel{ft} \times \dfrac{0.305\ m}{1\ \cancel{ft}} = 3.0\ m$

    (b) $? cm = 1\bar{0}\ \cancel{ft} \times \dfrac{12\ \cancel{in.}}{1\ \cancel{ft}} \times \dfrac{2.54\ cm}{1\ \cancel{in.}} = 3.0 \times 10^2\ cm$

    (c) $? mm = 3\bar{0}0\ \cancel{cm} \times \dfrac{10\ mm}{1\ \cancel{cm}} = 3.0 \times 10^3\ mm$

70. (a) $? m = (5.0\ \cancel{ft})\left(\dfrac{1\ m}{3.28\ \cancel{ft}}\right) = 1.5\ m$

    (b) $? cm = (1.5\ \cancel{m})\left(\dfrac{100\ cm}{1\ \cancel{m}}\right) = 150\ cm$

71. (a) $? m = 6.00\ \cancel{ft} \times \dfrac{1\ m}{3.28\ \cancel{ft}} = 1.83\ m$

    (b) $? cm = 6.00\ \cancel{ft} \times \dfrac{1\ \cancel{m}}{3.28\ \cancel{ft}} \times \dfrac{100\ cm}{1\ \cancel{m}} = 183\ cm$

72. (a) $? m = (25\ \cancel{ft})\left(\dfrac{1\ m}{3.28\ \cancel{ft}}\right) = 7.6\ m$

    (b) $? cm = (7.6\ \cancel{m})\left(\dfrac{100\ cm}{1\ \cancel{m}}\right) = 760\ cm$

73. (a) $? m = 10\bar{0}\ \cancel{yd} \times \dfrac{3\ \cancel{ft}}{1\ \cancel{yd}} \times \dfrac{1\ m}{3.28\ \cancel{ft}} = 91.5\ m$

    (b) $? cm = 10\bar{0}\ \cancel{yd} \times \dfrac{3\ \cancel{ft}}{1\ \cancel{yd}} \times \dfrac{1\ \cancel{m}}{3.28\ \cancel{ft}} \times \dfrac{100\ cm}{1\ \cancel{m}} = 9{,}150\ cm$

74. (a) $? \text{L} = (15 \text{ gal})\left(\dfrac{3.77 \text{ L}}{1 \text{ gal}}\right) = 57 \text{ L}$

    (b) $? \text{ mL} = (57 \text{ L})\left(\dfrac{1,000 \text{ mL}}{1 \text{ L}}\right) = 57,000 \text{ mL}$

75. (a) $? \text{ liters} = 5.00 \text{ gal} \times \dfrac{4 \text{ qt}}{1 \text{ gal}} \times \dfrac{1 \text{ liter}}{1.06 \text{ qt}} = 18.9 \text{ L}$

    (b) $? \text{ mL} = 5.00 \text{ gal} \times \dfrac{4 \text{ qt}}{1 \text{ gal}} \times \dfrac{1 \text{ liter}}{1.06 \text{ qt}} \times \dfrac{1,000 \text{ mL}}{1 \text{ liter}} = 18,900 \text{ mL}$

76. (a) $? \text{ kg} = (2\overline{2}0 \text{ lb})\left(\dfrac{1 \text{ kg}}{2.20 \text{ lb}}\right) = 1\overline{0}0 \text{ kg}$

    (b) $? \text{ g} = (1\overline{0}0 \text{ kg})\left(\dfrac{1,000 \text{ g}}{1 \text{ kg}}\right) = 100,000 \text{ g or } 1.00 \times 10^5 \text{ g}$

78. $V_{\text{cube}} = (6.00 \text{ cm})^3 = 216 \text{ cm}^3$

     $D = \dfrac{m}{V} = \dfrac{583 \text{ g}}{216 \text{ cm}^3} = 2.70 \text{ g/cm}^3$

79. $D = \dfrac{m}{V}$

    Given: $m = 600.0 \text{ g}$
               $V = (5.00 \text{ cm})^3 = 125 \text{ cm}^3$
               $D = ?$

               $D = \dfrac{m}{V} = \dfrac{600.0 \text{ g}}{125 \text{ cm}^3} = 4.80 \text{ g/cm}^3$

80. $V = \dfrac{m}{D} = \dfrac{274.5 \text{ g}}{2.70 \text{ g/cm}^3} = 102 \text{ cm}^3$

81.   Given: $D = 2.7 \text{ g/cm}^3$
               $m = 549 \text{ g}$
               $V = ?$

               $V = \dfrac{m}{D} = \dfrac{549 \text{ g}}{2.7 \text{ g/cm}^3} = 549 \text{ g} \times \dfrac{1.0 \text{ cm}^3}{2.7 \text{ g}} = 203 \text{ cm}^3 \text{ or } 2\overline{0}0 \text{ cm}^3$

    (for the proper number of significant figures)

82. $V_{block} = 2.0 \text{ cm} \times 3.0 \text{ cm} \times 4.0 \text{ cm} = 24 \text{ cm}^3$

$m = D \times V = (3.5 \text{ g/cm}^3)(24 \text{ cm}^3) = 84 \text{ g}$

83. Given: $D = 3.5 \text{ g/cm}^3$
$V = 1.0 \text{ cm} \times 3.0 \text{ cm} \times 5.0 \text{ cm} = 15 \text{ cm}^3$
$m = ?$

$D = \frac{m}{V}$ or $m = D \times V = 3.5 \text{ g/cm}^3 \times 15 \text{ cm}^3 = 52.5 \text{ g}$ or   53 g

(for the proper number of significant figures)

84. $V_{cube} = (1.5 \text{ cm})^3 = 3.4 \text{ cm}^3$

$m = D \times V = (2.50 \text{ g/cm}^3)(3.4 \text{ cm}^3) = 8.5 \text{ g}$

85. Given: $D = 0.177 \text{ g/liter}$

$V = \frac{4}{3} \pi r^3 = \frac{4}{3} \times 3.14 \times (3.0 \text{ cm})^3 = 113.0 \text{ cm}^3$ or   110 cm^3

(to two significant figures)
$m = ?$

$m = D \times V = 0.177 \text{ g/liter} \times 110 \text{ cm}^3 \times \dfrac{1 \text{ liter}}{1,000 \text{ cm}^3} = 0.019 \text{ g}$

86. $V = \dfrac{m}{D} = \dfrac{15.0 \text{ g}}{0.250 \text{ g/cm}^3} = 60.0 \text{ cm}^3$

87. Given: Total volume = 1.00 liter
Mass of Cs $= V \times D$
$= 6.00 \text{ cm}^3 \times 1.90 \text{ g/cm}^3$
$= 11.4 \text{ g}$

Mass of Fe = 14.0 g

Volume of Fe $= \dfrac{m}{D} = \dfrac{14 \text{ g}}{7.86 \text{ g/cm}^3} = 1.78 \text{ cm}^3$

Mass of Hg $= 5\overline{00} \text{ cm}^3 \times 13.6 \text{ g/cm}^3 = 6,8\overline{0}0 \text{ g}$
Total volume of Cs + Fe + Hg = 508 cm^3
Volume of air = 1,000 cm^3 – 508 cm^3 = 492 cm^3

Mass of air $= V \times D$
$= 4.92 \times 10^2 \text{ cm}^3 \times 1.18 \times 10^{-3} \text{ g/cm}^3$
$= 0.580 \text{ g}$

$$\text{Av. density} = \frac{\text{total mass}}{\text{total volume}} = \frac{6{,}830 \text{ g}}{1{,}000 \text{ cm}^3} = 6.83 \text{ g/cm}^3$$

88. $V_{\text{sphere}} = 20.0 \text{ cm}^3 - 10.0 \text{ cm}^3 = 10.0 \text{ cm}^3$

$$D = \frac{m}{V} = \frac{75.0 \text{ g}}{10.0 \text{ cm}^3} = 7.50 \text{ g/cm}^3$$

89.   Given: Total volume of tank $= 1.50 \text{ ft} \times 1.00 \text{ ft} \times 0.500 \text{ ft}$
$$= 0.750 \text{ ft}^3$$
$$= 21{,}300 \text{ cm}^3$$

Total mass of fish $= 2.00 \text{ g} \times 2 + 2.50 \text{ g} + 9.80 \text{ g}$
$$= 16.30 \text{ g}$$

Volume of gravel $= \frac{1}{8} \times 21{,}300 \text{ cm}^3 = 2{,}660 \text{ cm}^3$

Mass of gravel $= V \times D$
$$= 2{,}660 \text{ cm}^3 \times 3.00 \text{ g/cm}^3$$
$$= 7{,}980 \text{ g}$$

Volume of $H_2O = 21{,}300 \text{ cm}^3 - 2{,}660 \text{ cm}^3 = 18{,}600 \text{ cm}^3$

Mass of $H_2O = V \times D$
$$= 18{,}600 \text{ cm}^3 \times 1.00 \text{ g/cm}^3 = 18{,}600 \text{ g}$$

$$\text{Average density} = \frac{\text{Total mass of contents}}{\text{volume of tank}}$$

$$= \frac{16.3 \text{ g} + 7{,}980 \text{ g} + 18{,}600 \text{ g}}{21{,}300 \text{ cm}^3}$$

$$= 1.25 \text{ g/cm}^3$$

90. $V_{\text{solid}} = 8.0 \text{ cm} \times 2.0 \text{ cm} \times 3.0 \text{ cm} = 48 \text{ cm}^3$

$$D = \frac{m}{V} = \frac{192.0 \text{ g}}{48 \text{ cm}^3} = 4.0 \text{ g/cm}^3$$

91.   Given: $D = 1.61 \text{ g/cm}^3$
$$V = (4.1 \text{ cm})^3 = 69 \text{ cm}^3$$
$$m = ?$$
$$m = V \times D = 1.61 \text{ g/cm}^3 \times 69 \text{ cm}^3 = 111 \text{ g} \quad \text{or} \quad 110 \text{ g}$$

92. $V_{sphere} = \dfrac{4}{3}\,\pi r^3 = \dfrac{4}{3}(3.14)(1.06\text{ cm})^3 = 4.99\text{ cm}^3$

$D = \dfrac{m}{V} = \dfrac{9.80\text{ g}}{4.99\text{ cm}^3} = 1.96\text{ g/cm}^3$

93. Total mass = total volume × average density
$$= 250\text{ cm}^3 \times 2.00\text{ g/cm}^3 = 500\text{ g}$$

Volume of milk products = $0.900 \times 250\text{ cm}^3 = 225\text{ cm}^3$

Mass of milk products = $V \times D$
$$= 225\ \cancel{\text{cm}}^3 \times 1.50\text{ g/}\cancel{\text{cm}}^3$$
$$= 338\text{ g}$$

Mass of chocolate powder = 500 g – 338 g = 162 g

94. $V = \dfrac{m}{D} = \dfrac{672\ \cancel{\text{g}}}{10.5\ \cancel{\text{g}}/\text{cm}^3} = 64.0\text{ cm}^3$

$S = (64.0\text{ cm}^3)^{1/3} = 4.00\text{ cm}$

95. Given: $D = ?$
$V = (3.50\text{ cm})^3 = 42.9\text{ cm}^3$
$m = 400\text{ g}$

$D = \dfrac{m}{V} = \dfrac{400\text{ g}}{42.9\text{ cm}^3} = 9.32\text{ g/cm}^3$

96. $V_{cylinder} = \pi r^2 h = (3.14)(2.00\text{ cm})^2(10.00\text{ cm}) = 126\text{ cm}^3$

$m = D \times V = (8.92\text{ g/}\cancel{\text{cm}}^3)(126\ \cancel{\text{cm}}^3) = 1{,}120\text{ g}$

97. Given: $D = 18.9\text{ g/cm}^3$
$V = 30.0\text{ cm} \times 10.0\text{ cm} \times 5.00\text{ cm} = 1{,}500\text{ cm}^3$
$m = ?$
$m = D \times V = 18.9\text{ g/}\cancel{\text{cm}}^3 \times 1{,}500\ \cancel{\text{cm}}^3 = 28{,}400\text{ g}$

98. Mass of liquid = 488 g – 80.00 g = 408 g

$D = \dfrac{m}{V} = \dfrac{408\text{ g}}{30.0\text{ cm}^3} = 13.6\text{ g/cm}^3$

The element must be mercury—the only liquid element with a density of 13.6 g/cm^3.

99.   Given: $D = 11.3 \text{ g/cm}^3$
      $V = ?$
      $m = 250 \text{ g}$

$$V = \frac{m}{D} = \frac{250 \text{ g}}{11.3 \text{ g/cm}^3} = 22.1 \text{ cm}^3$$

100. Given: $D_{stone} = ?$
      $m = 21.06 \text{ g}$
      $V_i = \text{(water in cylinder)} = 10.0 \text{ cm}^3$
      $V_f = \text{(water in cylinder with stone)} = 16.0 \text{ cm}^3$

$$V_{stone} = V_f - V_i = 16.0 \text{ cm}^3 - 10.0 \text{ cm}^3 = 6.0 \text{ cm}^3$$

$$D_{stone} = \frac{m}{V} = \frac{21.06 \text{ g}}{6.0 \text{ cm}^3} = 3.5 \text{ g/cm}^3$$

The density of diamond given in the *Handbook of Chemistry and Physics* is 3.5 g/cm^3. Therefore this stone could be a diamond.

101. Given: $D = ?$
      $V = 40.0 \text{ mL} - 25.0 \text{ mL} = 15.0 \text{ mL}$
      $m = 55.0 \text{ g}$

$$D = \frac{m}{V} = \frac{55.0 \text{ g}}{15.0 \text{ mL}} = 3.67 \text{ g/mL}$$

102. $V_{Cu} = \dfrac{m}{D} = \dfrac{120.0 \text{ g}}{8.92 \text{ g/cm}^3} = 13.5 \text{ cm}^3$

$$V_{Ag} = \frac{m}{D} = \frac{200.0 \text{ g}}{10.5 \text{ g/cm}^3} = 19.0 \text{ cm}^3$$

$$\text{Average density} = \frac{m_{Cu} + m_{Ag}}{V_{Cu} + V_{Ag}} = \frac{120.0 \text{ g} + 200.0 \text{ g}}{13.5 \text{ cm}^3 + 19.0 \text{ cm}^3} = 9.85 \text{ g/cm}^3$$

103. Given: $D = 0.800 \text{ g/cm}^3$

$$V = \frac{4}{3} \pi r^3 = \frac{4}{3} \times 3.14 \times (18.0 \text{ cm})^3 = 24{,}400 \text{ cm}^3$$

$m = ?$
$m = D \times V = 0.800 \text{ g/cm}^3 \times 24{,}400 \text{ cm}^3 = 19{,}500 \text{ g}$

$$m = D \times V = 0.800 \text{ g/cm}^3 \times 24{,}400 \text{ cm}^3 = 19{,}500 \text{ g}$$

104. $1 \text{ gal} = 3.77 \text{ L} = 3{,}770 \text{ cm}^3$
$$m = D \times V = (0.56 \text{ g/cm}^3)(3{,}770 \text{ cm}^3) = 2{,}100 \text{ g}$$

105. Given: $D = 0.500 \text{ g/cm}^3$
$V = ?$
$m = 25.0 \text{ g}$

$$V = \frac{m}{D} = \frac{25.0 \text{ g}}{0.500 \text{ g/cm}^3} = 50.0 \text{ cm}^3$$

106. $V_{Al} = \dfrac{m}{D} = \dfrac{100 \text{ g}}{2.70 \text{ g/cm}^3} = 37.0 \text{ cm}^3$

$$m_{Pb} = D \times V = (11.3 \text{ g/cm}^3)(37.0 \text{ cm}^3) = 418 \text{ g}$$

107. $? \text{ °C} = \dfrac{°F - 32}{1.8} = \dfrac{100.0 - 32}{1.8} = \dfrac{68.0}{1.8} = 37.8 \text{ °C}$

108. $? \text{ °C} = \dfrac{°F - 32}{1.8} = \dfrac{2{,}200 - 32}{1.8} = \dfrac{2{,}168}{1.8} = 1{,}204 \text{ °C}$

109. $? \text{ °C} = \dfrac{°F - 32}{1.8} = \dfrac{-40 - 32}{1.8} = \dfrac{-72}{1.8} = -40 \text{ °C}$

−40 °F is equivalent to −40 °C.

110. $? \text{ °C} = \dfrac{°F - 32}{1.8} = \dfrac{-20.0 - 32}{1.8} = \dfrac{-52.0}{1.8} = -28.9 \text{ °C}$

111. Each 1 °C increase equals a 1.8 °F increase. Therefore a 3 °C increase equals a 3 × 1.8 or 5.4 °F increase. Normal body temperature is 98.6 °F. Therefore this individual's temperature is 98.6 °F + 5.4 °F or 104.0 °F.

112. $? \text{ °F} = (1.8 \times \text{ °C}) + 32 = (1.8 \times 23.0) + 32 = 41.4 + 32 = 73.4 \text{ °F}$

113. (a) $? \text{ °C} = \dfrac{°F - 32}{1.8} = \dfrac{50 - 32}{1.8} = \dfrac{18}{1.8} = 10 \text{ °C}$

(b) $? \text{ °C} = \dfrac{°F - 32}{1.8} = \dfrac{-94 - 32}{1.8} = \dfrac{-126}{1.8} = -70 \text{ °C}$

(c) $? \text{ °C} = \dfrac{°F - 32}{1.8} = \dfrac{419 - 32}{1.8} = 215 \text{ °C}$

(d) $?\,°C = \dfrac{°F - 32}{1.8} = \dfrac{-130 - 32}{1.8} = -90\ °C$

114. $9\ °C = 5\ °F - 160$

$?\ °F = \dfrac{9°C + 160}{5} = \dfrac{9(-20.0) + 160}{5} = -4.00\ °F$

115. (a) $?\ °F = (1.8 \times\ °C) + 32 = (1.8 \times 95.0) + 32$
$= 171 + 32 = 203\ °F$

(b) $?\ °F = (1.8 \times\ °C) + 32 = [1.8 \times (-80.0)] + 32$
$= -144 + 32 = -112\ °F$

(c) $?\ °F = (1.8 \times\ °C) + 32 = (1.8 \times 80.0) + 32$
$= 144 + 32 = 176\ °F$

(d) $?\ °F = (1.8 \times\ °C) + \underline{32} = (1.8 \times 210) + 32$
$= 378 + 32 = 4\underline{1}0\ °F$

116. $9\ °C = 5\ °F - 160$

$?\ °F = \dfrac{9°C + 160}{5} = \dfrac{9(15.0) + 160}{5} = 59.0\ °F$

EXTRA EXERCISES

117. The answer to this question is "no." Although the *mass* of an object is constant wherever it is, the weight of an object is dependent on the gravitational force with which a planet attracts an object. The closer to the center of the planet, the greater the force and therefore the weight. An object weighs more in Death Valley, which is 86 m (282 ft) below sea level, than it would weigh on the top of Mount McKinley, which is 6,198 m (20,330 ft) above sea level.

118. No, he did not fill out the application correctly.

$?\ \text{ft tall} = 4.00\ \cancel{m} \times \dfrac{3.28\ \text{ft}}{1.00\ \cancel{m}} = 13.1\ \text{ft}$

$?\ \text{lb} = 200.0\ \cancel{kg} \times \dfrac{2.20\ \text{lb}}{1.00\ \cancel{kg}} = 4\overline{4}0\ \text{lb}$

119. Given: $D = 1.0$ g/mL
     $m = 48$ g
     $V = ?$

$$V = \frac{m}{D} = \frac{48 \text{ g}}{1.0 \text{ g/mL}} = 48 \text{ mL}$$

120. $9 \,^{\circ}C = 5 \,^{\circ}F - 160$

$$^{\circ}C = \frac{5\,^{\circ}F - 160}{9} = \frac{(5)(425) - 160}{9} = 218 \,^{\circ}C$$

122. (a) 10^3 g = 1 kg   (b) 10^{-3} kg = 1 g   (c) 10^6 µg = 1 g

     (d) 10^3 mg = 1 g

123. 8.2×10^2

124. $^{\circ}C = \dfrac{5\,^{\circ}F - 160}{9} = \dfrac{(5)(16.0) - 160}{9} = -8.89 \,^{\circ}C$

125. (a) $^{\circ}F = \dfrac{9\,^{\circ}C + 160}{5} = \dfrac{(9)(16) + 160}{5} = 61 \,^{\circ}F$

     (b) $^{\circ}F = \dfrac{(9)(2\overline{00}) + 160}{5} = 392 \,^{\circ}F$

126. (a) $^{\circ}C = \dfrac{(5)(3\overline{00}) - 160}{9} = 149 \,^{\circ}C$

     (b) $^{\circ}C = \dfrac{(5)(-15\overline{0}) - 160}{9} = -101\infty C$

127. ? miles per hour $= \dfrac{10\overline{0} \text{ m}}{9.90 \text{ s}} \times \dfrac{3,6\overline{00} \text{ s}}{1.00 \text{ hr}} \times \dfrac{3.28 \text{ ft}}{1.00 \text{ m}} \times \dfrac{1.00 \text{ mi}}{5,280 \text{ ft}}$

     $= 22.6$ mph

3 MATTER AND ENERGY, ATOMS AND MOLECULES

SELF-TEST EXERCISES

1. A *hypothesis* expresses a tentative explanation of a series of observations. A *scientific theory* is a tested model that explains some basic phenomenon of nature. Theories are always subject to modification and change as scientists gather more evidence. A *scientific law* is a factual statement about the behavior of nature derived from extensive experimentation. It may sometimes be expressed in mathematical terms. There are no known exceptions to such a law.

2. Check the text and follow the steps of the scientific method to create a scheme for evaluating the effectiveness of the drug.

3. The universe is composed of matter and energy. The universe "works" by matter changing into new matter, energy changing into new forms of energy, and matter and energy being interconverted. The sum total of matter and energy in the universe is constant. However, on earth we take concentrated forms of energy (high-quality energy), use this energy to do work, and allow it to dissipate into the environment as low-quality energy.

4. The significance of the *Law of Conservation of Mass and Energy* is that it says that during all chemical changes, nothing is created or destroyed, just "shifted" around. You should be able to account for all of the reactants and products in a chemical reaction.

5. (a) 2   (b) 5   (c) 3   (d) 4   (e) 1

20

6. (a) *Elements* are the basic building blocks of matter. *Compounds* are chemical combinations of two or more elements. *Mixtures* are materials that consist of two or more substances, each substance retaining its own characteristic properties.
   (b) Solutions, compounds, and elements are uniform (homogeneous) throughout.
   (c) Heterogeneous mixtures are not uniform throughout.

7. (a) Shredding paper is a physical process.
   (b) Burning paper is a chemical process.
   (c) Cooking an egg is a chemical process.
   (d) Mixing egg whites with egg yolks is a physical process.
   (e) Digesting food is a chemical process.
   (f) Toasting bread is a chemical process.

8. (a) Ice melting is a physical process.
   (b) Sugar dissolving is a physical process.
   (c) Milk souring is a chemical process.
   (d) Eggs becoming rotten is a chemical process.
   (e) Water boiling is a physical process.
   (f) The cooking of a hard-boiled egg is a chemical process.

9. An *atom* is the smallest part of an element that retains the physical and chemical properties of that element. A *molecule* is the smallest part of a compound that retains the physical and chemical properties of that compound.

10. (a) The smallest particle of matter that can enter into chemical combination is an atom.
    (b) The smallest particle of a compound that can enter into chemical combination is a molecule.

11. (a) Ba is a metal.
    (b) Si is a metalloid.
    (c) O is a nonmetal.
    (d) Hg is a metal.
    (e) Ge is a metalloid.
    (f) In is a metal.
    (g) U is a metal.

12. (a) Mn is a metal.
    (b) Nd is a metal.
    (c) Al is a metal.
    (d) At is a metalloid.
    (e) Pt is a metal.
    (f) Cl is a nonmetal.
    (g) Ra is a metal.

13. Co is the symbol for the element cobalt.
CO is the chemical formula for carbon monoxide.

14. Si is the symbol for silicon.
SI is the chemical formula for sulfur iodide.

15. The percent H and the percent O are the same in each experiment. The percent H is 11.1% by weight and the percent O is 88.9% by weight.

17. (a) There are 12 atoms of C, 22 atoms of H, and 11 atoms of O.
(b) There are 2 atoms of K, 1 atom of Cr, and 4 atoms of O.
(c) There are 8 atoms of H, 2 atoms of N, 3 atoms of O, and 2 atoms of S.
(d) There is 1 atom of Zn, 2 atoms of N, and 6 atoms of O.

18. (a) There are 2 atoms of H, 1 atom of Se, and 4 atoms of O.
(b) There are 21 atoms of C, 27 atoms of H, 1 atom of F, and 6 atoms of O.
(c) There are 3 atoms of N, 12 atoms of H, 1 atom of P, and 4 atoms of O.
(d) There are 3 atoms of Fe, 2 atoms of As, and 8 atoms of O.

19. *Atomic mass* is the mass of an atom of an element in atomic mass units.
Formula mass is the sum of the atomic masses of all atoms that make up a formula unit of a compound.
Molecular mass is the sum of the atomic masses of all of the atoms that make up a molecule of a compound.

20. (a) Molecular mass   (b) Formula mass   (c) Atomic mass
(d) Molecular mass   (e) Molecular mass   (f) Formula mass
(g) Atomic mass   (h) Formula mass

21. The atomic mass of sulfur would be 2.

22. The atomic mass of bromine would be 4.

23. The atomic masses are:
(a) Rb = 85.5   (b) Cr = 52.0   (c) U = 238.0
(d) Se = 79.0   (e) As = 74.9

24. (a) The atomic mass of S from the periodic table is 32.1.
(b) The atomic mass of N from the periodic table is 14.0.
(c) The atomic mass of Li from the periodic table is 6.9.
(d) The atomic mass of Cs from the periodic table is 132.9.
(e) The atomic mass of Au from the periodic table is 197.0.

25. The molecular or formula masses are:
    (a) FeO = 71.8   (b) Fe_2O_3 = 159.6   (c) CuI_2 = 317.3
    (d) Na_3PO_4 = 164.0 (e) $Mg(OH)_2$ = 58.3   (f) $NiBr_2$ = 218.5
    (g) $Hg_3(PO_4)_2$ = 791.8 (h) $(NH_4)_2CO_3$ = 96.0

26. (a) The molecular mass of H_2O is 18.0.
    (b) The molecular mass of H_2SO_4 is 98.1.
    (c) The molecular mass of NaCl is 58.5.
    (d) The molecular mass of $Ca_3(PO_4)_2$ is 310.3.
    (e) The molecular mass of P_2O_5 is 142.0.
    (f) The molecular mass of $SrSO_4$ is 183.7.
    (g) The molecular mass of C_2H_6O is 46.0.
    (h) The molecular mass of SO_2 is 64.1.

27. The molecular or formula masses are:
    (a) 60.1   (b) 82.1   (c) 121.6   (d) 104.5   (e) 187.5
    (f) 218.7   (g) 149.0   (h) 60.0

28. The molecular or formula masses are:
    (a) 23.9   (b) 106.0   (c) 129.9   (d) 102.9   (e) 80.1
    (f) 30.0   (g) 54.0   (h) 116.1

EXTRA EXERCISES

29.(a) Two atoms of hydrogen and 1 atom of oxygen per molecule of water.
   (b) Six atoms of carbon, 12 atoms of hydrogen, and 6 atoms of oxygen per
        molecule of glucose.
   (c) One calcium atom, two oxygen atoms, and one hydrogen atom per formula
        unit of calcium hydroxide.
   (d) Two atoms of hydrogen in a hydrogen molecule.

35. (a) Magnesium and chlorine
    (b) Nitrogen and oxygen
    (c) Nitrogen, hydrogen, sulfur, and oxygen
    (d) Hydrogen, phosphorus, and oxygen

36. (a) NO_2 (b) Na_2S (c) K_3AsO_4 (d) P_2O_5

37. (a) Gold is an element.
    (b) Air is a mixture.
    (c) Carbon dioxide is a compound.

(d) Wine is a mixture.

(e) Table salt is a compound.

38. (a) Toasting bread involves a chemical change.

(b) Water freezing involves a physical change.

(c) Tearing paper involves a physical change.

(d) Burning wood involves a chemical change.

39. The molecular masses are:

(a) 254.2   (b) 63.0   (c) 89.8   (d) 601.9

40. Hf is the symbol for the element hafnium.

HF is the chemical formula for hydrogen fluoride.

4 ATOMIC THEORY, PART 1: WHAT'S IN AN ATOM?

SELF-TEST EXERCISES

3. The major points of Dalton's atomic theory were as follows:
   (a) All elements are composed of tiny indivisible particles called atoms. This idea was similar to the idea of Democritus. Both men believed that there is an ultimate particle—that all matter was composed of tiny indestructible and indivisible spheres.
   (b) All matter is composed of combinations of these atoms. In Chapter 3 we discussed how the atoms of different elements combine to form molecules of compounds. For example, two atoms of hydrogen and one atom of oxygen combine to form a water molecule.
   (c) Atoms of different elements are different. Dalton believed that gold was different from silver because somehow the atoms of gold were different from the atoms of silver.
   (d) Atoms of the same element have the same size, mass, and form. Dalton believed that all gold atoms, for example, were the same as all other gold atoms in every respect.

   Experiments performed after the publication of Dalton's theory indicated that atoms are divisible and that there are differences among atoms of the same element (isotopes).

4. Both Dalton and Democritus believed that atoms were the smallest particles of matter of which all things were composed.

5. The Thomson model of the atom, called the plum-pudding model, had the electrons embedded symmetrically in a sea of positive charge. The Rutherford model of the atom, called the nuclear model, had the protons in the center of the atom (the nucleus) and the electrons outside the nucleus.

6. A Crookes tube has two pieces of metal, one on each end, called electrodes. The tube is evacuated; in other words, the air in the tube is removed. A zinc sulfide screen may be placed in the tube to make it possible to observe the phenomena that occur when electricity is applied to the electrodes.

9. ? electrons $= \dfrac{1.672 \times 10^{24} \, g}{9.107 \times 10^{28} \, g} = 1{,}836$ electrons

10. The subatomic particle with the greatest mass is the neutron.
     The subatomic particle with the least mass is the electron.

11. The three major subatomic particles are:
     Proton, charge of +1, approximate mass of 1 amu
     Electron, charge of –1, approximate mass of 0.0005 amu
     Neutron, charge of 0, approximate mass of 1 amu

13. (a) $^{244}_{94}$ Pu has 94p, 94e, 150n.   (b) $^{48}_{22}$ Ti has 22p, 22e, 26n.

     (c) $^{262}_{103}$ Lr has 103p, 103e, 159n.

14. (a) $^{75}_{33}$ As has 33p, 33e, 42n.   (b) $^{266}_{109}$ Mt has 109p, 109e, 157n.

     (c) $^{222}_{86}$ Rn has 86p, 86e, 136n.

15. (a) $^{16}_{8}$ O has 8 protons, 8 electrons, and 8 neutrons.

     (b) $^{17}_{8}$ O has 8 protons, 8 electrons, and 9 neutrons.

     (c) $^{18}_{8}$ O has 8 protons, 8 electrons, and 10 neutrons.

     (d) $^{20}_{10}$ Ne has 10 protons, 10 electrons, and 10 neutrons.

     (e) $^{21}_{10}$ Ne has 10 protons, 10 electrons, and 11 neutrons.

     (f) $^{22}_{10}$ Ne has 10 protons, 10 electrons, and 12 neutrons.

16. (a) $^{31}_{15}$ P has 15p, 15e, 16n.   (b) $^{22}_{10}$ Ne has 10p, 10e, 12n.

     (c) $^{24}_{12}$ Mg has 12p, 12e, 12n.

17. The atoms are (a) $^{16}_{8}$O, (b) $^{15}_{7}$N, (c) $^{17}_{8}$O. Therefore (b) is not an isotope of the others.

18. The atoms shown are:

    (a) 12p, 12e, 14n, which is $^{26}_{12}$Mg   (b) 12p, 12e, 12n, which is $^{24}_{12}$Mg

    (c) 13p, 13e, 12n, which is $^{25}_{13}$Al

    Therefore (a) and (b) are isotopes of each other and (c) is not an isotope of the other two.

19. (a) $^{57}_{25}$Mn has 25 protons, 25 electrons, and 32 neutrons.

    (b) $^{60}_{27}$Co has 27 protons, 27 electrons, and 33 neutrons.

    (c) $^{80}_{36}$Kr has 36 protons, 36 electrons, and 44 neutrons.

    (d) $^{128}_{52}$Te has 52 protons, 52 electrons, and 76 neutrons.

20. (a) $^{35}_{16}$X has 16p, 16e, 19n.   (b) $^{300}_{90}$Y has 90p, 90e, 210n.

21. Remove 3 protons, 3 electrons, and 8 neutrons.

22. The atoms shown are:

    (a) 14p, 14e, 15n, which is $^{29}_{14}$Si   (b) 15p, 15e, 14n, which is $^{29}_{15}$P

    (c) 15p, 15e, 15n, which is $^{30}_{15}$P

    Therefore (b) and (c) are isotopes of each other and (a) is not an isotope of the other two.

23.

Symbol	Protons	Electrons	Neutrons	Mass number	Atomic number
$^{174}_{70}$Yb	70	70	104	174	70
$^{141}_{59}$Pr	59	59	82	141	59
$^{104}_{44}$Ru	44	44	60	104	44
$^{45}_{21}$Sc	21	21	24	45	21
$^{50}_{22}$Ti	22	22	28	50	22

$^{25}_{12}$Mg   12   12   13   25   12

24. $^{42}_{20}$Ca has 20p, 20e, 22n.

25. (a) Two different isotopes of a particular element cannot have the same mass number because they have to contain different numbers of neutrons, and the same number of protons.
     (b) Atoms of two different elements can have the same mass number if the number of protons and neutrons in each atom add to the same sum.

26. Atoms of an element with the same number of electrons and protons, but different numbers of neutrons, are called *isotopes*.

27. Isotopes are atoms with the same number of *protons* and *electrons* but different numbers of *neutrons*.

28. (a) The number of protons in an atom is called the *atomic number* of that element.
     (b) The sum of the numbers of protons and neutrons in an isotope is called the *mass number* of that isotope.

29. (a) $^{200}_{80}$Hg   (b) $^{15}_{7}$N   (c) $^{27}_{13}$Al   (d) $^{262}_{107}$Bh

30. (a) The standard notation for 3p, 3e, 3n is $^{6}_{3}$Li.

     (b) The standard notation for 9p, 9e, 10n is $^{19}_{9}$F.

     (c) The standard notation for 14p, 14e, 16n is $^{30}_{14}$Si.

31. Atomic mass of Ga = $(68.9257 \times 0.6016) + (70.9249 \times 0.3984)$
                        = 69.72

32. Atomic mass of C = $(12.0000)(0.9889) + (13.003)(0.0111)$
                       = 12.01

33. Atomic mass of Cl = $(34.9689 \times 0.7553) + (36.9659 \times 0.2447)$
                        = 35.46

34. Atomic mass of Mg = $(23.9850)(0.7870) + (24.9858)(0.1013) + (25.8826)(0.1117)$
                        = 24.31

35. Atomic mass of Cr = $(49.9461 \times 0.0431) + (51.9405 \times 0.8376)$

$$+ (52.9407 \times 0.0955) + (53.9389 \times 0.0238)$$
$$= 52.00$$

36. Atomic mass of Cu = $(62.9296)(0.6909) + (64.9278)(0.3091)$
$$= 63.55$$

37. Let x = relative abundance of ^{79}Br
$1 - x$ = relative abundance of ^{81}Br
$79.90 = 78.9183x + 80.9163(1 - x)$
$x = 0.509$ or 50.9% of ^{79}Br
$1 - x = 0.491$ or 49.1% of ^{81}Br

38. Let x = relative abundance of ^{11}B
$1 - x$ = relative abundance of ^{10}B
$11.009x + 10.013(1 - x) = 10.81$
$$x = 0.800$$
Therefore, $^{11}B = 80.0\%$ abundance and $^{10}B = 20.0\%$ abundance

39. Let x = relative abundance of ^{121}Sb
$1 - x$ = relative abundance of ^{123}Sb
$121.75 = 120.9038x + 122.9041(1 - x)$
$x = 0.577$ or 57.7% of ^{121}Sb
$1 - x = 0.423$ or 42.3% of ^{123}Sb

40. Let x = relative abundance of ^{37}Cl
$1 - x$ = relative abundance of ^{35}Cl
Therefore, $36.9659x + 34.9689(1 - x)$ $= 35.453$
$$x = 0.242$$
Therefore, $^{37}Cl = 24.2\%$ and $^{35}Cl = 75.8\%$

41. ^{22}Ne has a natural abundance of 8.82%. In 1.00×10^9 Ne atoms there are

$(1.00 \times 10^9)(0.0882) = 8.82 \times 10^7$ ^{22}Ne atoms.

42. ^{29}Si atoms have a natural abundance of 4.70%. In 5.00×10^6 Si atoms there are

$(5.00 \times 10^6)(0.0470) = 2.35 \times 10^5$ ^{29}Si atoms.

43. From Table 4.2, the natural abundance of ^{17}O is 0.037%. Therefore,

$$\text{Number of O atoms} = \frac{7,400 \ ^{17}O \text{ atoms}}{0.00037} = 2.0 \times 10^7 \text{ O atoms}$$

44. From Table 4.2, the natural abundance of ^{18}O is 0.204%. Therefore,

$$\text{Number of O atoms} = \frac{102 \; ^{18}\text{O atoms}}{0.00204} = \overline{50,000} \text{ O atoms}$$

45. From Table 4.2, percent natural abundance of ^{6}Li = 7.42%.

$$\text{Number } ^6\text{Li atoms} = \left(\frac{0.0742 \, ^6\text{Li atom}}{1 \, \text{Li atom}}\right)(1\times10^{\,8}\,\text{Li atoms})$$

$$= 7.42 \times 10^6 \text{ atoms of } ^6\text{Li}$$

46. From Table 4.2, the natural abundance of ^{7}Li = 92.58%.

$$\text{Number of } ^7\text{Li atoms} = (0.9258)(1,000 \text{ Li atoms})$$
$$= 926 \text{ atoms of } ^7\text{Li}$$

47. From Table 4.2, the percent natural abundance of ^{26}Mg = 11.17%.

$$? \; ^{26}\text{Mg atoms} = \left(\frac{0.1117 \, ^{26}\text{Mg atom}}{1 \, \text{Mg atom}}\right)(5.00\times10^6\,\text{Mg atoms})$$

$$= 5.59 \times 10^5 \text{ atoms of } ^{26}\text{Mg}$$

48. From Table 4.2, the natural abundance of ^{14}N atoms = 99.63%.

$$\text{Number of } ^{14}\text{N atoms} = (0.9963)(1,000 \times 10^{14} \text{ N atoms})$$
$$= 9.963 \times 10^{13} \text{ atoms of } ^{14}\text{N}$$

49. From Table 4.2, the percent natural abundance of ^{13}C = 1.11%.

$$? \; ^{13}\text{C atoms} = \left(\frac{0.0111 \, ^{13}\text{C atom}}{1 \, \text{C atom}}\right)(2.00\times10^4\,\text{C atoms})$$

$$= 2.22 \times 10^2 \text{ atoms of } ^{13}\text{C}$$

50. From Table 4.2, the percent natural abundance of ^{22}Ne = 8.82%.

$$? \; ^{22}\text{Ne atoms} = \left(\frac{0.0882 \, ^{22}\text{Ne atom}}{1 \, \text{Ne atom}}\right)(1\times10^6\,\text{Ne atoms})$$

$$= 8.82 \times 10^4 \; ^{22}\text{Ne atoms} \quad \text{or} \quad 9 \times 10^4 \; ^{22}\text{Ne atoms}$$

(to one significant figure)

51. From Table 4.2, the percent natural abundance of ^{15}N = 0.37%.

$$? \, ^{15}\text{N atoms} = \left(\frac{0.0037 \, ^{15}\text{N atom}}{1 \, \text{N atom}} \right) (1.0 \times 10^{15} \, \text{N atoms})$$

$$= 3.7 \times 10^{12} \text{ atoms of } ^{15}\text{N}$$

52. From Table 4.2, the natural abundance of ^{6}Li is 7.42%.

    Number of ^{6}Li atoms = (0.0742)(1,000 Li atoms) = 74

53. From Table 4.2, the natural abundance of ^{2}H is 0.015%.

$$? \, \text{H atoms} = \left(\frac{1 \, \text{H atom}}{0.00015 \, ^{2}\text{H atom}} \right) (150,000 \, ^{2}\text{H atoms})$$

$$= 1.0 \times 10^{9} \text{ H atoms}$$

54. From Table 4.2, the natural abundance of ^{14}N is 99.63%.

$$? \, ^{14}\text{N atoms} = \left(\frac{0.9963 \, ^{14}\text{N atoms}}{1 \, \text{N atom}} \right) (1 \times 10^{8} \, \text{N atoms})$$

$$= 9.963 \times 10^{7} \, ^{14}\text{N atoms}$$

EXTRA EXERCISES

55. With regard to chemical properties, isotopes of a particular element behave the same.

56. Given: $^{200}_{84}\text{A}$ $^{208}_{82}\text{B}$ $^{222}_{86}\text{C}$ $^{184}_{74}\text{D}$

    (a) The atom with the most electrons is C because it has the highest atomic number.
    (b) The atom with the least neutrons is D, with 110 neutrons.
    (c) The mass number of atom C is 222.
    (d) The atom with the least protons is D because it has the lowest atomic number.
    (e) Atom A's atomic number identifies it as the element Po (polonium).

57. In a neutral atom, the atomic number and the number of electrons are the same.

59. The experiment that proved that the atoms of all elements contain electrons was the *photoelectric effect* experiment performed by Philip Lenard in 1902.

60. (a) $^{13}_{6}C$ (b) $^{10}_{5}B$

        Electrons = protons = 6   Electrons = protons = 5
        Neutrons = 13 – 6 = 7   Neutrons = 10 – 5 = 5

    (c) $^{14}_{7}N$

        Electrons = protons = 7
        Neutrons = 14 – 7 = 7

61. The problem with Dalton's statement that the atoms of a particular element are identical in every respect was that he did not know about the existence of isotopes.

62. Percent natural abundance of neon-21 = 0.257

$$\text{Number neon-21 atoms} = (10^6 \ \cancel{\text{Ne atoms}})\left(\frac{0.00257 \text{ neon-21 atoms}}{1 \ \cancel{\text{Ne atom}}}\right)$$

$$= 2.57 \times 10^3$$

63. 1 electron = 0.0005486 amu
    1 proton = 1.0073 amu

$$\text{Number of electrons} = \frac{1.0073}{0.0005486} = 1{,}836$$

64. The atomic number is equal to the number of protons, whereas the mass number is the sum of the protons and the neutrons. Therefore the atomic number of an element cannot exceed its mass number.

66. The three isotopes of hydrogen are ^1H, ^2H, and ^3H. The three isotopes of oxygen are ^{16}O, ^{17}O, and ^{18}O. The possible combinations of molecules and molecular masses are as follows:

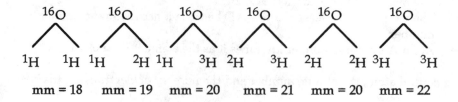

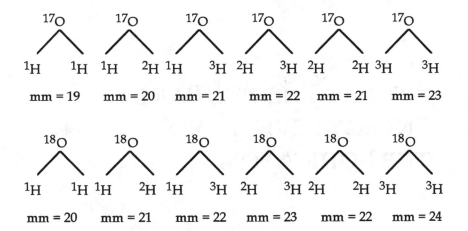

5 ATOMIC THEORY, PART 2: ENERGY LEVELS AND THE BOHR ATOM

SELF-TEST EXERCISES

1. A *continuous spectrum* is a spectrum in which one color of light merges into the next color when viewed on a screen or photographic film. A *line spectrum* occurs when a distinct set of brightly colored lines is seen when viewed on a screen or photographic film.

2. A spectrum is the band of colors formed when radiant energy is broken up. The visible spectrum is formed when white light is passed through a prism, resulting in a rainbow of colors. The visible spectrum is a small portion of the electromagnetic spectrum that extends from high-energy gamma rays to low-energy, long radio waves.

3. By examining the line spectrum of an extraterrestrial body with a spectro-scope, scientists can determine which elements are present.

4. Violet has the highest energy and red has the longest wavelength.

5. Helium comes from the Greek word *helios,* which means "sun."

6. Each element has its own unique line spectrum. Line spectra can be used to identify specific elements that make up a compound.

7. The *Thomson model of the atom,* commonly referred to as the "plum-pudding" model, has the electrons embedded symmetrically in a sea of positive electricity (the protons). The *Rutherford model of the atom,* commonly referred to as the "nuclear" model, pictures the atom as a sphere that has a

small but densely packed center called the nucleus, wherein the protons (and neutrons) reside, and an empty outer area where the electrons reside. The *Bohr model of the atom,* commonly referred to as the "solar system" model, retains the concept of the nucleus and has the electrons moving about the nucleus in specific shells or energy levels.

8. The electrons of an atom are in the *ground state* when they are in their lowest energy levels. The electrons of an atom are in the *excited state* when they have gained energy and have temporarily moved to higher energy levels.

9. Energy levels in atoms

10. According to the Bohr model of the atom, electrons jump between energy levels. This gives rise to line spectra. If electrons spiraled their way from one energy level to the next, continuous spectra would result.

11. Electrons

12. The farther away an energy level is from the nucleus, the *higher* the energy of an electron in that level.

13. Seven energy levels, K, L, M, N, O, P, Q or 1, 2, 3, 4, 5, 6, 7, respectively. Energy levels or shells are areas in an atom in which electrons are located at various distances from the nucleus.

14. The theoretical maximum number of electrons that can populate each of the first three energy levels are 2, 8, and 18, as determined by using the $2n^2$ rule where $n =$ 1, 2, and 3.

15. The electrons of an atom are in the ground state when they are in their lowest energy levels. The electrons of an atom are in the excited state when they have gained energy and have moved temporarily to higher energy levels.

16. The ground state of a lithium atom has two electrons in the K level and 1 electron in the L level. If the lithium atom was in an excited state, the K and/or L electrons would have jumped to higher energy levels.

17. Excited state

18. A magnesium atom that has the configuration K has 2e, L has 8e, and M has 2e, is in the ground state.

19. The *Bohr model of the atom* relies on subatomic particles following classical physical laws. The situation is more complex. Therefore, the quantum mechanical model of the atom was needed to refine the Bohr model.

20. The laws of quantum mechanics

21. De Broglie explained how electrons in motion had the properties of waves and also had mass.

22. Schrödinger developed a mathematical equation that described electrons as having both particle and wave properties.

23. (a) Energy level one has one sublevel.
    (b) Energy level two has two sublevels.
    (c) Energy level three has three sublevels.
    (d) Energy level four has four sublevels.

24. Energy level seven has seven sublevels. They are the *s, p, d, f, g, h,* and *i* sublevels.

25. The number of electrons in an energy level is the sum of the electrons in the sublevels.

26. Energy level three has three sublevels, the *s* sublevel that holds two electrons, the *p* sublevel that holds six electrons, and the *d* sublevel that holds ten electrons.

27. Energy level six has six sublevels, the *s* sublevel, *p* sublevel, *d* sublevel, *f* sublevel, *g* sublevel, and *h* sublevel. The sixth energy level can hold a maximum of 72 electrons.

28. Energy level four has four sublevels, the *s* sublevel, *p* sublevel, *d* sublevel, and *f* sublevel. The fourth energy level can hold a maximum of 32 electrons.

30. The region of "highest probability" is the distance from the nucleus at which the electron is most likely to be found.

31. The *s* sublevel in any energy level has one orbital, and the *p* sublevel in any energy level has three orbitals. Therefore, the *s* and *p* sublevels have a total of four orbitals.

32. The *s* sublevel has one orbital, the *p* sublevel has three orbitals, and the *d* sublevel has five orbitals, for a total of nine orbitals.

33. Figure 5.12 in the text shows the relationship of the 1*s*, 2*s*, and 3*s* orbitals to each other. The 4*s* orbital would be further from the nucleus of the atom.

34. See Figure 5.11 in the text for the shape of the *p* orbitals.

35. There are no 2*d* or 2*f* sublevels.

36. There is no $3f$ sublevel.

37. (a) $_7$N: $1s^22s^22p^3$

    (b) $_{23}$V: $1s^22s^22p^63s^23p^64s^23d^3$

    (c) $_{54}$Xe: $1s^22s^22p^63s^23p^64s^23d^{10}4p^65s^24d^{10}5p^6$

    (d) $_{51}$Sb: $1s^22s^22p^63s^23p^64s^23d^{10}4p^65s^24d^{10}5p^3$

38. (a) $1s^22s^22p^63s^23p^64s^23d^{10}4p^65s^24d^{10}5p^2$

    (b) $1s^22s^22p^63s^23p^64s^23d^7$

    (c) $1s^22s^22p^63s^23p^64s^23d^{10}4p^65s^24d^{10}5p^66s^24f^{14}5d^{10}6p^6$

    (d) $1s^22s^22p^63s^23p^64s^23d^{10}4p^5$

39. (a) $_{56}$Ba   (b) $_{20}$Ca   (c) $_{38}$Sr   (d) $_4$Be

40. (a) 2 electrons: He   (b) 7 electrons: N
    (b) 29 electrons: Cu   (d) 34 electrons: Se

41. (a) 31   (b) 8   (c) 13   (d) 10   (e) 31

42. K has 2e, L has 8e, M has 18e, and N has 2e. Therefore,

K	L		M			N
s	s	p	s	p	d	s
2	2	6	2	6	10	2

    (a) The atomic number of this element is 30.
    (b) The total number of s electrons is 8.
    (c) The total number of p electrons is 12.
    (d) The total number of d electrons is 10.
    (e) The number of protons is 30.

43. Elements 6 and 14 in Group IVA.
    Elements 17 and 35 in Group VIIA.
    Elements 3 and 19 in Group IA.

44. Atomic no. 5 $1s^22s^22p^1$
                          3 outer electrons

    Atomic no. 18 $1s^22s^22p^63s^23p^6$
                          8 outer electrons

Atomic no. 16 $1s^2 2s^2 2p^6 3s^2 3p^4$
6 outer electrons

Atomic no. 36 $1s^2 2s^2 2p^6 3s^2 3p^6 4s^2 3d^{10} 4p^6$
8 outer electrons

Atomic no. 10 $1s^2 2s^2 2p^6$
8 outer electrons

Atomic no. 13 $1s^2 2s^2 2p^6 3s^2 3p^1$
3 outer electrons

Elements 5 and 13 are in the same group.
Elements 10, 18, and 36 are in the same group.

45. For energy level Q, $n = 7$ and $2n^2 = 98$.

46. For the N energy level, which is also known as the fourth energy level, the maximum number of electrons $= 2n^2 = 2(4)^2 = 32$.

47. (a) $_{31}$Ga $1s^2 2s^2 2p^6 3s^2 3p^6 4s^2 3d^{10} 4p^1$

     (b) $_{51}$Sb $1s^2 2s^2 2p^6 3s^2 3p^6 4s^2 3d^{10} 4p^6 5s^2 4d^{10} 5p^3$

     (c) $_{82}$Pb $1s^2 2s^2 2p^6 3s^2 3p^6 4s^2 3d^{10} 4p^6 5s^2 4d^{10} 5p^6 6s^2 4f^{14} 5d^{10} 6p^2$

     (d) $_{88}$Ra $1s^2 2s^2 2p^6 3s^2 3p^6 4s^2 3d^{10} 4p^6 5s^2 4d^{10} 5p^6 6s^2 4f^{14} 5d^{10} 6p^6 7s^2$

48. (a) $_3$Li $1s^2 2s^1$

     (b) $_{12}$Mg $1s^2 2s^2 2p^6 3s^2$

     (c) $_{56}$Ba $1s^2 2s^2 2p^6 3s^2 3p^6 4s^2 3d^{10} 4p^6 5s^2 4d^{10} 5p^6 6s^2$

49. (a) $_{12}$Mg   (b) $_{38}$Sr   (c) $_{70}$Yb   (d) $_{81}$Tl

50. (a) Atomic no. 11 is Na.
     (b) Atomic no. 68 is Er.
     (c) Atomic no. 70 is Yb.
     (d) Atomic no. 86 is Rn.

51. (a) The atomic no. is 60.
     (b) The total number of s electrons is 12.
     (c) The total number of p electrons is 24.
     (d) The total number of d electrons is 20.
     (e) The total number of f electrons is 4.
     (f) The number of protons is 60.

52. (a) The atomic no. is 71.
    (b) The total number of s electrons is 12.
    (c) The total number of p electrons is 24.
    (d) The total number of d electrons is 21.
    (e) The total number of f electrons is 14.
    (f) The number of protons is 71.

53. Electrons in the outermost energy level of an atom determine its chemical properties.

54. The number of electrons in the outermost shell or energy level determines the chemical properties of an element.

55. Group VIIIA elements tend to be chemically unreactive.

56. Elements in the same vertical column of the periodic table exhibit similar chemical properties. Therefore, the similar groups are as follows: Li, K, Rb, Na, and Cs are similar. Ne, Kr, Rn, and Xe are similar.

EXTRA EXERCISES

57. Electron configurations for elements 1–20 may be found in Table 5.3 of the textbook.

58. The elements beryllium ($_4$Be) and calcium ($_{20}$Ca) are isoelectronic with $_{12}$Mg. An atom of $_4$Be has two electrons in the K level and 2 electrons in the L level. An atom of $_{20}$Ca has 2 electrons in the K level, 8 electrons in the L level, 8 electrons in the M level, and 2 electrons in the N level.

60. The line spectrum of an element is sometimes referred to as its fingerprint, because each element produces a unique array of emission lines that is its line spectrum.

61. Electrons produce line spectra when they fall back to their ground-state energy levels after they have absorbed energy to reach their excited states.

64. If an electron absorbs too much energy it can jump out of the atom completely. This is known as the *process of ionization*.

65. The atomic number would be 280.

6 THE PERIODIC TABLE: KEEPING TRACK OF THE ELEMENTS

SELF-TEST EXERCISES

2. When scientists discovered a new element, they could see if it had properties predicted by the periodic law.

4. Mendeleev based his periodic table on having elements with similar chemical properties in the same chemical family. He adhered to this practice even if it meant putting heavier elements before lighter ones in the table.

5. The lanthanide series and the actinide series of elements are usually shown apart from the rest of the table for convenience. To fit these series into the table where they belong would extend the table's width and make it awkward in size.

6. (a) Döbereiner discovered that some elements with similar chemical properties came in groups of three.
   (b) Newlands's table was based on atomic weight and on having sets of eight elements.
   (c) Mendeleev's table was based on placing elements with similar chemical properties in the same chemical family.

7. (a) Ga   (b) S   (c) Hg   (d) Bh

8. In the periodic table a horizontal row is called a *period*. A vertical column is called a *group* or *family*.

9. The atoms of elements within the same group have the same number of electrons in their outermost energy levels.

40

10. Elements in the B groups show somewhat similar chemical behavior because their inner electron shells are filled in the same manner.

11. The group number reflects the number of electrons in the outermost energy level for the A-group elements.

12. (a)   Period 2 has 8 elements.   (b)   Period 3 has 8 elements.
    (c)   Period 4 has 18 elements   (d)   Period 5 has 18 elements.
    (e)   Period 6 has 32 elements   (f)   Period 7 has 23 elements.

13. The representative elements are also known as the *A-group* elements. The transition metals are also known as the *B-group* elements.

14. The statement is true for A and B groups. Elements in the same group have the same number of electrons in the outermost energy level.

15. On the basis of periodic trends, the elements in order of increasing ionization potential are Ba, Sr, Te, I, Br.

16. An angstrom is a unit of length equal to 1×10^{-10} m.

17. On the basis of periodic trends, the elements in order of increasing atomic radius are P, As, I, Sb, In.

18. In the periodic table, the atomic radius increases as we move from top to bottom.

19. *Electron affinity* is the energy released when an additional electron is added to a neutral atom.

20. In the periodic table, the atomic radius decreases as we move from left to right.

21. After you had removed an electron from a neutral atom, you would need more energy to remove the second electron.

22. The elements in order of increasing atomic radius are H, F, S, In, Tl.

23. (a)   Elements with the highest electron affinity are found in Group VIIA.
    (b)   Elements with the lowest ionization potential are found in Group IA.
    (c)   The most unreactive elements are found in Group VIIIA, which consists of the noble gases.

24. The energy needed to pull an electron away from an isolated atom is the *ionization potential*.

25. (a) The ionization potential *decreases* as one moves down a group of elements.
    (b) The ionization potential *increases* as one moves from left to right across a period of elements.
    (c) The atomic radius *decreases* as one moves from left to right across a period of elements.

26. It is more difficult to remove an electron from an atom at the top of a group of elements than it is to remove an electron from an atom at the bottom of a group of elements, because the atom of an element at the top of a group of elements has its outermost electrons closer to the nucleus than the atom of an element at the bottom of a group of elements.

27. On the basis of periodic trends, the elements in order of increasing atomic radius are Cl, S, Ca, Sr, Rb.

28. Because a chlorine atom is smaller than a sodium atom, the electrons in a chlorine atom are closer to the nucleus. Therefore, there is a greater force exerted on the electrons in the chlorine atom. As a result, more energy is required to remove an electron from a chlorine atom.

29. On the basis of periodic trends, the elements in order of increasing ionization potential are Sb, I, As, P.

30. The elements in order of increasing ionization potential are Cs, Ge, Se, Br, F.

31. Answer d: A positive ion is an atom or group of atoms that has *lost an electron*.

32. The quantity that depends on the attraction between an electron and the nucleus of an atom is called *electron affinity*.

33. Answer c: A Cl^{1-} ion is a Cl atom that has gained an electron.

34. Electron affinity *decreases* as one moves down a group of elements.

35. Answer d: An Mg^{2+} ion is an Mg atom that has *lost two electrons*.

36. Electron affinity *increases* as one moves from left to right across the periodic table.

EXTRA EXERCISES

37. (a)   A bromine atom is smaller than a potassium atom because the increased
nuclear charge of the protons in the bromine atom causes the energy levels to
be pulled closer to the nucleus of the atom.

(b)   The ionization potential for a sodium atom is greater than the ionization
potential for a rubidium atom because the outermost electron in sodium (the
$3s^1$ electron) is closer to the nucleus than the outermost electron in rubidium
(the $5s^1$ electron).

38.   Elements in the same group have similar chemical properties. This relationship
does not generally hold true for elements in the same period.

39. (a) $_{11}Na$, $1s^2 2s^2 2p^6 3s^1$

(b) $_{13}Al$, $1s^2 2s^2 2p^6 3s^2 3p^1$

(c) $_8O$, $1s^2 2s^2 2p^4$

(d) $_{16}S$, $1s^2 2s^2 2p^6 3s^2 3p^4$

(e) $_5B$, $1s^2 2s^2 2p^1$

(f) $_3Li$, $1s^2 2s^1$

The similar pairs based on electron configuration are: $_3Li$ and $_1Na$, $_5B$ and $_{13}Al$, $_8O$
and $_{16}S$.

40. (a) $_1H$, $1s^1$

(b) $_3Li$, $1s^2 2s^1$

(c) $_4Be$, $1s^2 2s^2$

(d) $_{12}Mg$, $1s^2 2s^2 2p^6 3s^2$

(e) $_{20}Ca$, $1s^2 2s^2 2p^6 3s^2 3p^6 4s^2$

The similar pairs based on electron configuration are: $_1H$ and $_3Li$; $_4Be$, $_{12}Mg$, and
$_{20}Ca$.

41.   The noble gas that follows radon would have the atomic number 118.

42.   Group IA forms 1+ ions and Group VIIA forms 1– ions.

43.   A chlorine atom has 17 protons and 17 electrons. A chloride ion has 17 protons and
18 electrons.

44. (a) K has a larger radius than Br, because atomic radius decreases across a period.
    (b) K has a larger radius than Na, because atomic radius increases moving down a group.
    (c) K has a larger radius than K^{1+}, because K^{1+} has lost its outermost electron.

45. For A-group elements, the group number is the number of electrons in the outermost energy level. Therefore, Na in group IA has one electron in its outermost energy level. Carbon in group IVA has four electrons in its outermost energy level. Nitrogen in group VA has five electrons in its outermost energy level.

46. Mg has the higher ionization potential because ionization potential decreases as we move down a group of elements.

47. (a) 2   (b) 8   (c) 8   (d) 18   (e) 18
    (f) 32

48. (a) K is lower than Ca.   (b) Se is lower than O.

49. (a) K has a larger radius than Ca.   (b) Se has a larger radius than O.

50. Group IVA

51. The atomic weight of the most stable isotope is listed.

53. False. The group number reveals the number of electrons in the outermost energy level for A-group elements.

54. The statement is true.

55. Elements 15 and 33 in Group VA
    Elements 38 and 56 in Group IIA
    Elements 14 and 50 in Group IVA

56. Atomic no. 16 $1s^2 2s^2 2p^6 3s^2 3p^4$
    6 outer electrons

    Atomic no. 36 $1s^2 2s^2 2p^6 3s^2 3p^6 4s^2 3d^{10} 4p^6$
    8 outer electrons

    Atomic no. 39 $1s^2 2s^2 2p^6 3s^2 3p^6 4s^2 3d^{10} 4p^6 5s^2 4d^1$
    2 outer electrons

Atomic no. 8 $1s^2 2s^2 2p^4$
                  6 outer electrons

Atomic no. 34 $1s^2 2s^2 2p^6 3s^2 3p^6 4s^2 3d^{10} 4p^4$
                  6 outer electrons

The elements of atomic numbers 8, 16, and 34 are in the same chemical group because they have the same number of electrons in their outermost energy levels.

7 CHEMICAL BONDING: HOW ATOMS COMBINE

SELF-TEST EXERCISES

1. (a) $\cdot\overset{\displaystyle\cdot\cdot}{\underset{\displaystyle\cdot}{As}}\cdot$ (b) $\cdot\overset{\displaystyle\cdot\cdot}{\underset{\displaystyle\cdot\cdot}{Cl}}:$ (c) $\overset{\displaystyle\cdot}{Ra}\cdot$ (d) $\overset{\displaystyle\cdot}{Cs}$ (e) $:\overset{\displaystyle\cdot\cdot}{\underset{\displaystyle\cdot\cdot}{Rn}}:$

2. (a) $\cdot\overset{\displaystyle\cdot\cdot}{\underset{\displaystyle\cdot\cdot}{F}}:$ (b) $Ca\cdot$ (c) $\overset{\displaystyle\cdot}{K}$ (d) $\cdot\overset{\displaystyle\cdot}{\underset{\displaystyle\cdot}{C}}\cdot$ (e) $\overset{\displaystyle\cdot}{\underset{\displaystyle\cdot}{B}}\cdot$

3. (a) $\cdot\overset{\displaystyle\cdot\cdot}{\underset{\displaystyle\cdot}{O}}:$ (b) $:\overset{\displaystyle\cdot\cdot}{\underset{\displaystyle\cdot\cdot}{O}}:^{2-}$

4. (a) $\cdot\overset{\displaystyle\cdot\cdot}{\underset{\displaystyle\cdot\cdot}{Br}}:$ (b) $:\overset{\displaystyle\cdot\cdot}{\underset{\displaystyle\cdot\cdot}{F}}:^{1-}$

5. (a) $Mg\cdot$ (b) Mg^{2+}

6. (a) $\overset{\displaystyle\cdot}{Ba}\cdot$ (b) Ba^{2+}

7. Some examples of ions that are isoelectronic with Ar atom are

   $:\overset{\displaystyle\cdot\cdot}{\underset{\displaystyle\cdot\cdot}{Cl}}:^{1-}$, $:\overset{\displaystyle\cdot\cdot}{\underset{\displaystyle\cdot\cdot}{S}}:^{2-}$ or K^{1+}, Ca^{2+}

46

8. (a) $\cdot \overset{\displaystyle .}{\underset{\displaystyle .}{Si}} \cdot$ (b) $\cdot \overset{\displaystyle ..}{\underset{\displaystyle .}{Te}} :$ (c) $\cdot \overset{\displaystyle ..}{\underset{\displaystyle ..}{At}} :$

9. (a) Mg^{2+} (b) Na^{1+} (c) Al^{3+}

10. (a) Calcium ion, Ca^{2+} (b) Cesium ion, Cs^{1+}

   (c) Boron ion, B^{3+}

11. Examples of two ions that are isoelectronic with Ca^{2+} ion are

   $: \overset{\displaystyle ..}{\underset{\displaystyle ..}{Cl}} :^{1-}$ or K^{1+}

12. (a) Sulfide ion, $: \overset{\displaystyle ..}{\underset{\displaystyle ..}{S}} :^{2-}$ (b) Telluride ion, $: \overset{\displaystyle ..}{\underset{\displaystyle ..}{Te}} :^{2-}$

   (c) Nitride ion, $: \overset{\displaystyle ..}{\underset{\displaystyle ..}{N}} :^{3-}$

13. Covalent bonds are called electron-sharing bonds because typically each atom donates electrons to form the bond. The donated electrons are shared by the two atoms forming the bond.

14. A *coordinate covalent bond* is a bond in which one atom donates the electrons to form the bond.

15. When each atom donates *two* electrons to form a covalent bond, the type of bond formed is a *double covalent bond*.

16. When each atom donates *three* electrons to form a covalent bond, the type of bond formed is a *triple covalent bond*.

17. $H_2, O_2, N_2, Cl_2, Br_2, I_2, F_2$

18. Hydrogen, chlorine, bromine, iodine, and fluorine are diatomic elements that contain single covalent bonds. Oxygen atoms contain double covalent bonds, and nitrogen atoms contain triple covalent bonds.

19. (a)

```
          ..
        : Br :
          |      ..
  H  –   C  –  Br :
          |      ..
        : Br :
          ..
```

(b) H – C ≡ C – H

(c)

```
        ..
  H  –  P  –  H
        |
        H
```

(d) H – C ≡ N̈

20. (a)

```
          ..
  H  –  Cl :
          ..
```

(b)

```
                ..
              : Br :
        ..      |      ..
    : Br  –   C   –  Br :
        ..      |      ..
              : Br :
                ..
```

(c)

```
      ..              ..
    : O  ←  S  →  O :
      ..      ||      ..
            : O
              ..
```

(d)

```
      ..      ..      ..
    : Cl  –  Sb  –  Cl :
      ..      |      ..
            : Cl :
              ..
```

21. (a)

```
              ..
            : F :
        ..    |    ..
    : F  –   C   –  F :
        ..    |    ..
            : F :
              ..
```

(b)

```
    H  –  C  =  C  –  H
          |      |
          H      H
```

(c)

```
          ..
  H  –  As  –  H
          |
          H
```

(d)

```
          ..
  H  –  S :
          |
          H
```

22. (a)

```
      ..              ..
    : S  =  C  =  S :
```

(b)

```
      ..              ..
    : O  =  C  =  O :
```

(c)
$$\ddot{O}$$
$$\diagup \; \diagdown$$
$$:\ddot{Cl}: \quad \ddot{Cl}:$$

(d)
$$\begin{array}{ccc} H & H & H \\ | & | & | \\ H - C - C - C - H \\ | & | & | \\ H & H & H \end{array}$$

23.

$$\begin{array}{c} :\ddot{Cl} \quad :\ddot{Cl}: \\ \diagdown \; \diagup \\ P - \ddot{Cl}: \\ \diagup \; \diagdown \\ :\ddot{Cl} \quad :\ddot{Cl}: \end{array}$$

There are ten electrons surrounding the P atom in PCl₅.

24.

$$:\ddot{F} - B - \ddot{F}:$$
$$|$$
$$:\ddot{F}:$$

Six electrons surround the boron atom in BF₃.

25. (a)
$$\begin{array}{c} O = N - \ddot{O} - H \\ \downarrow \\ :\ddot{O}: \end{array}$$

(b)
$$\begin{array}{c} :\ddot{O}: \\ \uparrow \\ H - \ddot{O} - S - \ddot{O} - H \end{array}$$

26.
$$\begin{array}{c} :\ddot{O} \leftarrow \ddot{Cl} - \ddot{O} - H \\ \downarrow \\ :\ddot{O}: \end{array}$$

27. An *ionic bond* is a bond formed by the transfer of electrons from one atom to another. The atoms are always of different elements.

28. The formation of ionic bonds involves the transfer of electrons from one atom to another. The formation of covalent bonds involves the sharing of electrons between atoms.

29. (a) Ionic   (b) Covalent   (c) Covalent
    (d) Covalent

30. (a) Ionic   (b) Ionic   (c) Ionic
    (d) Ionic   (e) Covalent

31.

	Compound	Electronegativity difference	Percentage ionic	Percentage covalent
(a)	CH_4	0.4	4	96
(b)	N_2	0.0	0	100
(c)	FeO	1.7	51	49
(d)	Al_2O_3	2.0	63	37

32.

	Compound	Electronegativity difference	Percentage ionic	Percentage covalent
(a)	HCl	0.9	19.0	81.0
(b)	NH_3	0.9	19.0	81.0
(c)	KI	1.7	51.0	49.0
(d)	CS_2	0.0	0.0	100.0

33.

Compound	Electronegativity difference	Percentage covalent
HI	0.4	96.0
HBr	0.7	88.0
HCl	0.9	81.0
HF	1.9	41.0

HI   HBr   HCl   HF

Most covalent $\rightarrow$ Least covalent

34.

Compound	Electronegativity difference	Percentage covalent
Br_2	0.0	100.0
SO_2	1.0	78.0
NH_3	0.9	81.0
HCl	0.9	81.0

Br_2 NH_3 HCl SO_2

Most
covalent   →   Least
covalent

35.

	Compound	Electronegativity difference	Percentage ionic	Percentage covalent
(a)	CF_4	1.5	43.0	57.0
(b)	AsH_3	0.1	0.5	99.5
(c)	CsCl	2.3	74.0	26.0
(d)	CuO	1.6	47.0	53.0

36.

	Compound	Electronegativity difference	Percentage ionic	Percentage covalent
(a)	CO_2	1.0	22.0	78.0
(b)	F_2	0.0	0.0	100.0
(c)	$MgCl_2$	1.8	55.0	45.0
(d)	BaF_2	3.1	91.0	9.0

37.

Compound	Electronegativity difference	Percentage covalent
H_2O	1.4	61.0
H_2S	0.4	96.0
H_2Se	0.3	98.0
H_2Te	0.0	100.0

H_2O H_2S H_2Se H_2Te

Least covalent $\rightarrow$ Most covalent

38.

Compound	Electronegativity difference	Percentage covalent
HF	1.9	41.0
NH_3	0.9	81.0
BH_3	0.1	99.5
CH_4	0.4	96.0
H_2O	1.4	61.0

HF H_2O NH_3 CH_4 BH_3

Least covalent $\rightarrow$ Most covalent

39.

Compound	Electronegativity difference	Percentage ionic
LiCl	2.0	63.0
NaCl	2.1	67.0
KCl	2.2	70.0
RbCl	2.2	70.0
CsCl	2.3	74.0

The most ionic compound is CsCl.

40.

Compound	Electronegativity difference	Percentage ionic
HF	1.9	59.0
HCl	0.9	19.0
HBr	0.7	12.0
HI	0.4	4.0

The most ionic compound is HF.

41. (a) Covalent   (b) Covalent   (c) Ionic
    (d) Covalent

42. (a) Covalent   (b) Covalent
    (c) Covalent (using electronegativity)   (d) Covalent

43. *Polar molecules* seem to have a positive side and a negative side because of the electronegativities of the atoms forming polar bonds and because of the shape of the molecule itself. In *nonpolar molecules,* the bond polarities (if they exist) cancel each other out because of the shape of the molecule.

44. (a) H_2 has nonpolar bonds.
    (b) NO has polar bonds.
    (c) HCl has polar bonds.

45. (a) The bonds and the molecule are polar.
    (b) The bonds and the molecule are polar.
    (c) The bonds and the molecule are polar.
    (d) The bonds and the molecule are nonpolar.

46. (a) The bonds are polar; the molecule is nonpolar.
    (b) The bonds and the molecule are polar.
    (c) The bonds are polar; the molecule is nonpolar.
    (d) The bond and the molecule are nonpolar.

47. (a) The C–H bonds are polar; the molecule is nonpolar.
    (b) The bonds and the molecule are polar.
    (c) The bonds are polar; the molecule is nonpolar.
    (d) The bond and the molecule are nonpolar.

48. (a) The bond and the molecule are nonpolar.
    (b) The bonds are polar; the molecule is nonpolar.

(c)   The bonds are polar; the molecule is nonpolar.
(d)   The bonds and the molecule are polar.

EXTRA EXERCISES

49. The statement "electron deficiencies are satisfied" means that the octet rule is obeyed.

50. (a)

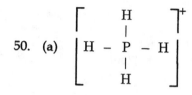

(b)

$$: \overset{..}{O} = C = \overset{..}{O} :$$

(c)

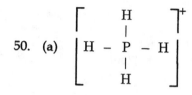

51. The formula for sodium chloride is NaCl, because a sodium atom wants to lose *one* electron and a chlorine atom wants to gain *one* electron. The formula for calcium chloride is $CaCl_2$, because a calcium atom wants to lose *two* electrons and requires *two* chlorine atoms for bonding, each of which wants to gain one electron.

52. The following are differences in electronegativity among the atoms forming each bond.

3.5 3.5	3.0 3.5	2.5 3.5
O=O	N–O	C–O
Difference = 0	Difference = 0.5	Difference = 1.0

Therefore the least polar bond is the O=O bond; it is followed by the N–O bond, and the C–O bond is the most polar.

53. The following are the differences in electronegativity among the atoms forming each bond.

2.5 2.1	2.5 3.5	3.0 3.5
C–H	C–O	N–O
Difference = 0.4	Difference = 1.0	Difference = 0.5

   2.5   2.5

   C–S

Difference = 0

Therefore the most covalent bond (the least polar) is C–S.

54. (a)
$$\left[\begin{array}{c} H \\ | \\ H - N - H \\ | \\ H \end{array} \right]^{+}$$
    (b) $: \overset{..}{\underset{..}{Cl}} - \overset{..}{\underset{..}{Br}} :$

55. (a) MgO   (b) Al_2O_3 (c) Cs_2S

56. (a) The Al atom wants to give up *three* electrons. Each Cl atom wants *one* electron. Therefore, three Cl atoms combine with one Al atom.

 (b) Each Na atom wants to give up *one* electron. The O atom wants *two* electrons. Therefore, two Na atoms combine with an O atom.

 (c) Each Mg atom wants to give up *two* electrons. Each N atom wants *three* electrons. Therefore, three Mg atoms combine with two N atoms.

57. A molecule may have polar bonds, but be nonpolar if the center of positive charge on the molecule coincides with the center of negative charge; in other words, the molecule is nonpolar if the molecular dipoles cancel.

58. (a) K_2S (b) $CaBr_2$ (c) Li_2O (d) $AlCl_3$

59. There is no way that the duet rule can be satisfied for a molecule containing three hydrogen atoms.

60. (a)   CF$_4$

$$:\overset{\displaystyle ..}{\underset{\displaystyle ..}{F}} - \overset{\displaystyle :\overset{..}{F}:}{\underset{\displaystyle :\overset{..}{F}:}{C}} - \overset{\displaystyle ..}{\underset{\displaystyle ..}{F}}:$$

(b)   AsCl$_3$

$$:\overset{..}{\underset{..}{Cl}} - \overset{..}{As} - \overset{..}{\underset{..}{Cl}}:$$
$$:\overset{..}{\underset{..}{Cl}}:$$

(c)   ICl

$$:\overset{..}{\underset{..}{I}} - \overset{..}{\underset{..}{Cl}}:$$

(d)   H$_2$Te

$$\overset{.. \, ..}{Te}$$
$$\diagup \quad \diagdown$$
$$H \quad \ H$$

8 CHEMICAL NOMENCLATURE: THE NAMES AND FORMULAS OF CHEMICAL COMPOUNDS

SELF-TEST EXERCISES

1. The rules that govern the systematic names are developed by the *International Union of Pure and Applied Chemistry (IUPAC)*. This gives order to the millions of compounds that exist. There are no rules that govern the common names of compounds. Most common names have been derived from common usage or just handed down through chemical history.

3. The systematic name for water is hydrogen oxide or dihydrogen oxide.

4. The common name of CO_2 is dry ice. The systematic name is carbon dioxide.

5. (a) hepta- is 7   (b) di- is 2   (c) tri- is 3
    (d) octa- is 8   (e) mono- is 1

6. (a) 3 is tri-   (b) 7 is hepta-   (c) 2 is di-
    (d) 9 is nona-

7. (a) P_2S_5 (b) ClO_2 (c) N_2O_4 (d) Cl_2O_7

8. (a) CCl_4 (b) P_4O_{10} (c) PBr_5 (d) SeO_2

9. (a) Al_2S_3 (b) Li_2O (c) Na_3N (d) Sr_3P_2 (e) $AgBr$
    (f) ZnO

10. (a) LiI (b) CaO (c) $SrBr_2$ (d) K_3P (e) Rb_2S
    (f) Ba_3N_2

11. (a) 9 is IX   (b) 8 is VIII   (c) 7 is VII
    (d) 6 is VI

12. (a) III is 3   (b) VIII is 8   (c) VI is 6
    (d) IV is 4

13. (a) *-ic* is the metal ion with the higher charge
    (b) *-ous* is the metal ion with the lower charge
    (c) *-ide* is the suffix for the atom or ion that has a negative charge in a chemical compound

14. (a) Ferrous is Fe^{2+} and ferric is Fe^{3+}
    (b) Cuprous is Cu^{1+} and cupric is Cu^{2+}
    (c) Cobaltous is Co^{2+} and cobaltic is Co^{3+}
    (d) Stannous is Sn^{2+} and stannic is Sn^{4+}

15. (a) Cu_2S (b) $HgCl_2$ (c) FeO (d) SnI_2 (e) $CoBr_3$
    (f) Hg_3N_2

16. (a) UF_6 (b) FeN (c) $MnCl_2$ (d) FeS (e) Cu_2O
    (f) Hg_2Cl_2

17. (a) $(NH_4)^{1+}$ (b) $(OH)^{1-}$ (c) $(BO_3)^{3-}$
    (d) $(HCO_3)^{1-}$ (e) $(C_2O_4)^{2-}$ (f) $(SO_3)^{2-}$

18. (a) $(CN)^{1-}$ (b) $(ClO_2)^{1-}$ (c) $(ClO_3)^{1-}$
    (d) $(CrO_4)^{2-}$ (e) $(Cr_2O_7)^{2-}$ (f) $(PO_4)^{3-}$

19. (a) Arsenate   (b) Permanganate   (c) Sulfite
    (d) Ammonium   (e) Hydrogen sulfite   (f) Acetate

20. (a) Nitrite   (b) Nitrate   (c) Perchlorate
    (d) Cyanide   (e) Borate   (f) Hypochlorite

21. (a) $Hg_3(PO_4)_2$ (b) $Sn_3(AsO_4)_2$ (c) $Fe(C_2H_3O_2)_3$
    (d) Li_3PO_4 (e) $Al_2(SO_3)_3$ (f) $Zn(NO_2)_2$

22. (a) $CsOH$ (b) Cu_3AsO_4 (c) $(NH_4)_2SO_4$
    (d) K_2CO_3 (e) $Fe(CN)_3$ (f) Cu_2SO_4

23. (a) $PbSO_4$ (b) $CO_3(PO_4)_2$ (c) $(NH_4)_2Cr_2O_7$

    (d) CaC_2O_4 (e) $Sn(NO_3)_2$ (f) $Mg(HSO_4)_2$

24. (a) $KClO_3$ (b) $Zn(OH)_2$ (c) $Zn_3(PO_4)_2$

    (d) $AgNO_2$ (e) $Hg(NO_3)_2$ (f) Cu_2SO_3

25. (a) Diphosphorus pentasulfide   (b) Carbon monoxide
    (c) Silicon dioxide   (d) Chlorine dioxide

26. (a) Dinitrogen monoxide   (b) Nitrogen dioxide
    (c) Sulfur trioxide   (d) Dinitrogen pentoxide

27. (a) Aluminum oxide   (b) Sodium iodide
    (c) Zinc chloride   (d) Magnesium nitride
    (e) Silver sulfide   (f) Lithium iodide

28. (a) Cesium oxide   (b) Aluminum sulfide
    (c) Barium iodide   (d) Gallium chloride
    (e) Potassium oxide   (f) Magnesium sulfide

29. (a) 1–   (b) 2.67+   (c) 4+   (d) 5+   (e) 1–

30. (a) 1+   (b) 3+   (c) 5+   (d) 7+

31. (a) 5+   (b) 1+   (c) 1+   (d) 15+   (e) 3–
    (f) 1–

32. (a) 3+   (b) 5+   (c) 5+   (d) 3+   (e) 1–
    (f) 1–

33. (a) Osmium(VIII) oxide
    (b) Mercury(I) phosphide or mercurous phosphide
    (c) Iron(II) sulfide or ferrous sulfide
    (d) Cobalt(II) chloride or cobaltous chloride
    (e) Copper(I) nitride or cuprous nitride
    (f) Copper(I) oxide or cuprous oxide

34. (a) Copper(II) sulfide or cupric sulfide
    (b) Gold(III) bromide
    (c) Iron(II) oxide or ferrous oxide
    (d) Copper(II) phosphide or cupric phosphide
    (e) Vanadium(V) oxide
    (f) Manganese(IV) oxide

35. (a) Silver carbonate
    (b) Mercury(II) phosphate or mercuric phosphate
    (c) Iron(III) sulfate or ferric sulfate
    (d) Sodium nitrate
    (e) Copper(II) chromate or cupric chromate
    (f) Zinc hydroxide

36. (a) Calcium carbonate
    (b) Sodium nitrite
    (c) Sodium hydroxide
    (d) Magnesium hydroxide
    (e) Potassium dichromate
    (f) Ammonium iodide

37. (a) Calcium sulfate
    (b) Potassium cyanide
    (c) Aluminum phosphate
    (d) Copper(I) oxalate or cuprous oxalate
    (e) Iron(III) chromate or ferric chromate
    (f) Copper(II) nitrite or cupric nitrite

38. (a) Rubidium sulfate
    (b) Iron(II) acetate or ferrous acetate
    (c) Magnesium borate
    (d) Potassium permanganate
    (e) Bismuth(III) sulfate
    (f) Ammonium oxalate

39. (a) $HClO$ (b) HBr (c) HNO_3

    (d) $HClO_2$ (e) $HBrO_4$ (f) H_2SO_4

40. (a) $HC_2H_3O_2$ (b) H_2SO_3 (c) $HClO_3$

    (d) HF (e) H_3PO_4 (f) HNO_2

41. (a) Hydrocyanic acid   (b) Hydrosulfuric acid
    (c) Bromic acid   (d) Sulfuric acid
    (e) Hypochlorous acid   (f) Bromous acid

42. (a) Periodic acid   (b) Chloric acid
    (c) Hydrobromic acid   (d) Hydrofluoric acid
    (e) Chlorous acid   (f) Hypoiodous acid

43. (a)   Milk of magnesia is $Mg(OH)_2$

    (b)   Oil of vitriol is H_2SO_4

    (c)   Saltpeter is $NaNO_3$

    (d)   Laughing gas is N_2O

44. (a)   Epsom salts is $MgSO_4 \cdot 7H_2O$

    (b)   Muriatic acid is HCl

    (c)   Marble is $CaCO_3$

    (d)   Table salt is $NaCl$

45. (a) CaO is quicklime

    (b) $CaCO_3$ is marble or limestone

    (c) $CaSO_4 \cdot 2H_2O$ is gypsum

    (d) H_2SO_4 is oil of vitriol

46. (a)   Dry ice is carbon dioxide

    (b)   Saltpeter is sodium nitrate

    (c)   Baking soda is sodium hydrogen carbonate

    (d)   Borax is sodium tetraborate decahydrate

EXTRA EXERCISES

47. (a) SrO (b) AlN (c) Rb_2S

48. (a) AlN (b) V_2O_5 (c) $Fe(OH)_3$ (d) $(NH_4)_2S$

49. (a)   Aluminum nitride
    (b)   Vanadium(V) oxide
    (c)   Iron(III) hydroxide or ferric hydroxide
    (d)   Ammonium sulfide

50. (a) SnS (b) Cu_3PO_4 (c) $Fe(NO_2)_3$

    (d) $Mg(C_2H_3O_2)_2$

51.

Metal ion	Nonmetal ion		
	Bromide	*Sulfate*	*Phosphate*
Sodium	NaBr	Na_2SO_4	Na_3PO_4
Calcium	$CaBr_2$	$CaSO_4$	$Ca_3(PO_4)_2$
Aluminum	$AlBr_3$	$Al_2(SO_4)_3$	$AlPO_4$

52. (a) Potassium chlorite
    (b) Iron(III) cyanide or ferric cyanide
    (c) Diphosphorus pentasulfide
    (d) Carbon tetrachloride
    (e) Acetic acid
    (f) Tin(IV) oxide or stannic oxide

53. (a) GaF_3 (b) $Pd(NO_3)_2$ (c) AuP

    (d) $La(C_2H_3O_2)_3$ (e) PuO_2 (f) RuO_4

9 CALCULATIONS INVOLVING CHEMICAL FORMULAS

SELF-TEST EXERCISES

2. (a) A mole is 6.02×10^{23}.
    (b) 602,000,000,000,000,000,000,000

3. Au has an atomic mass of 197.0.

    $? \text{ moles Au} = (19.7 \text{ g})\left(\dfrac{1 \text{ mole}}{197.0 \text{ g}}\right) = 0.100 \text{ mole Au}$

4. $? \text{ moles Si atoms} = (5.62 \text{ g})\left(\dfrac{1 \text{ mole}}{28.1 \text{ g}}\right) = 0.200 \text{ mole}$

5. $\dfrac{\text{dollars}}{\text{mg U}} = \dfrac{0.01 \text{ dollar}}{10^8 \text{ atoms U}} \times \dfrac{1 \text{ mole U atoms}}{238.0 \text{ g U}} \times \dfrac{1 \text{ g}}{1{,}000 \text{ mg}} \times \dfrac{6.02 \times 10^{23} \text{ atoms U}}{1 \text{ mole U atoms}}$

    $= \$2.53 \times 10^8 \text{ or } \$3 \times 10^8$

6. $? \text{ moles S atoms} = (0.963 \text{ g})\left(\dfrac{1 \text{ mole}}{32.1 \text{ g}}\right) = 0.0300 \text{ mole}$

7. (a) $? \text{ moles Al atoms} = 16.2 \text{ g Al} \times \dfrac{1 \text{ mole Al atoms}}{27.0 \text{ g Al}} = 0.600 \text{ mole}$

    (b) $? \text{ moles Ti atoms} = 239.5 \text{ g Ti} \times \dfrac{1 \text{ mole Ti atoms}}{47.9 \text{ g Ti}} = 5.00 \text{ mole}$

63

(c)   ? moles Mg atoms = 0.06075 g Mg $\times$ $\dfrac{1 \text{ mole Mg atoms}}{24.3 \text{ g Mg}}$ = 0.00250 mole

(d)   ? moles U atoms = 3,570.0 g U $\times$ $\dfrac{1 \text{ mole U atoms}}{238.0 \text{ g U}}$ = 15.00 mole

8. (a)   ? moles Cu atoms = $(2,397.0 \text{ g})\left(\dfrac{1 \text{ mole}}{63.5 \text{ g}}\right)$ = 37.7 moles

   (b)   ? moles W atoms = $(13.79 \text{ g})\left(\dfrac{1 \text{ mole}}{183.9 \text{ g}}\right)$ = 0.07499 mole

   (c)   ? mole Ar atoms = $(0.00399 \text{ g})\left(\dfrac{1 \text{ mole}}{39.9 \text{ g}}\right)$ = 1.00×10^{-4} mole

   (d)   ? mole Ag atoms = $(16.19 \text{ g})\left(\dfrac{1 \text{ mole}}{107.9 \text{ g}}\right)$ = 0.1500 mole

9. ? g Hg = $(0.250 \text{ mole})\left(\dfrac{200.6 \text{ g}}{1 \text{ mole}}\right)$ = 50.2 g

10. ? g Rb = $(1.50 \text{ moles})\left(\dfrac{85.5 \text{ g}}{1 \text{ mole}}\right)$ = 128 g

11. ? g Co = $(0.750 \text{ mole})\left(\dfrac{58.9 \text{ g}}{1 \text{ mole}}\right)$ = 44.2 g

12. ? g Cr = $(0.0250 \text{ mole})\left(\dfrac{52.0 \text{ g}}{1 \text{ mole}}\right)$ = 1.30 g

13. (a)   ? grams Ni = 4.600 moles Ni atoms $\times$ $\dfrac{58.7 \text{ g Ni}}{1 \text{ mole Ni atoms}}$ = $27\bar{0}$ g

    (b)   ? grams Br$_2$ = 0.00300 mole Br$_2$ $\times$ $\dfrac{159.8 \text{ g}}{1 \text{ mole Br}_2}$ = 0.479 g

    (c)   ? grams Ca = 200.0 moles Ca atoms $\times$ $\dfrac{40.1 \text{ g Ca}}{1 \text{ mole Ca atoms}}$ = 8,020 g

    (d)   ? grams S = 0.04000 mole S atoms $\times$ $\dfrac{32.1 \text{ g S}}{1 \text{ mole S atoms}}$ = 1.28 g

14. (a)   ? g Rn = $(0.400 \text{ mole})\left(\dfrac{222 \text{ g}}{1 \text{ mole}}\right)$ = 88.8 g

(b) $? \text{ g } F_2 = (19.0 \text{ moles})\left(\dfrac{38.0 \text{ g}}{1 \text{ mole}}\right) = 722 \text{ g}$

(c) $? \text{ g } Hg = (0.0350 \text{ mole})\left(\dfrac{200.6 \text{ g}}{1 \text{ mole}}\right) = 7.02 \text{ g}$

(d) $? \text{ g } Yb = (7.200 \text{ mole})\left(\dfrac{173.0 \text{ g}}{1 \text{ mole}}\right) = 1{,}246 \text{ g}$

15. $? \text{ atoms } Al = (2.00 \text{ g})\left(\dfrac{1 \text{ mole}}{27.0 \text{ g}}\right)\left(\dfrac{6.02 \times 10^{23} \text{ atoms}}{1 \text{ mole}}\right) = 4.46 \times 10^{22} \text{ atoms}$

16. One mole of Na atoms = 23.0 g. Therefore,

$$? \text{ mole Na atoms } = (13.8 \text{ g})\left(\dfrac{1 \text{ mole}}{23.0 \text{ g}}\right) = 0.600 \text{ mole}$$

$$? \text{ atoms of Na } = (0.600 \text{ mole})\left(\dfrac{6.02 \times 10^{23} \text{ atoms}}{1 \text{ mole}}\right)$$

$$= 3.61 \times 10^{23} \text{ atoms}$$

17. $? \dfrac{\text{dollars}}{\text{C atom}} = \dfrac{\$1{,}800}{2 \text{ carats}} \times \dfrac{1 \text{ carat}}{0.2 \text{ g C}} \times \dfrac{12.0 \text{ g C}}{6.02 \times 10^{23} \text{ atoms C}} = \$9 \times 10^{-20}$

18. One mole H_2O = 18.0 g. Therefore

$$? \text{ mole } H_2O = (1{,}8\overline{00} \text{ g})\left(\dfrac{1 \text{ mole}}{18.0 \text{ g}}\right) = 1\overline{00} \text{ moles}$$

$$? \, H_2O \text{ molecules } = (1\overline{00} \text{ moles})\left(\dfrac{6.02 \times 10^{23} \text{ molecules}}{1 \text{ mole}}\right)$$

$$= 6.02 \times 10^{25} \text{ molecules}$$

$$? \text{ atoms } = (6.02 \times 10^{25} \text{ molecules})\left(\dfrac{3 \text{ atoms}}{1 \text{ molecule}}\right)$$

$$= 1.81 \times 10^{26} \text{ atoms}$$

19. $? \text{ miles } = 0.1 \text{ mole Ag atoms} \times \dfrac{6.02 \times 10^{23} \text{ atoms Ag}}{1 \text{ mole Ag atoms}}$

$$\times \frac{2.68 \ \overset{\circ}{\text{A}}}{1 \ \text{atom Ag}} \times \frac{10^{-8} \ \text{cm}}{1 \ \overset{\circ}{\text{A}}} \times \frac{1 \ \text{ft}}{30.5 \ \text{cm}} \times \frac{1 \ \text{mile}}{5,280 \ \text{ft}} = 1 \times 10^{10} \ \text{miles}$$

20. One mole of Cl_2 = 71.0 g. Therefore

$$? \ \text{mole} \ Cl_2 \ = \ (\overset{-}{350} \ \text{g}) \left(\frac{1 \ \text{mole}}{71.0 \ \text{g}} \right) = 4.93 \ \text{moles}$$

$$? \ \text{molecules} \ Cl_2 \ = \ (4.93 \ \text{moles}) \left(\frac{6.02 \times 10^{23} \ \text{molecules}}{1 \ \text{mole}} \right)$$

$$= 2.97 \times 10^{24} \ \text{molecules}$$

$$? \ \text{atoms} \ Cl_2 \ = \ (2.97 \times 10^{24} \ \text{molecules}) \left(\frac{2 \ \text{atoms}}{1 \ \text{molecule}} \right)$$

$$= 5.94 \times 10^{24} \ \text{atoms}$$

21. In 100 g of compound there are 39.6 g Na and 60.4 g Cl.

$$? \ \text{moles Na atoms} = 39.6 \ \text{g Na} \times \frac{1 \ \text{mole Na atoms}}{23.0 \ \text{g Na}} = 1.72 \ \text{moles}$$

$$? \ \text{moles Cl atoms} \ = 60.4 \ \text{g Cl} \times \frac{1 \ \text{mole Cl atoms}}{35.5 \ \text{g Cl}} = 1.70 \ \text{moles}$$

$Na_{1.7}Cl_{1.7}$ or NaCl, table salt

22. $? \ \text{mole Al} = (15.8 \ \text{g}) \left(\dfrac{1 \ \text{mole}}{27.0 \ \text{g}} \right) = 0.585 \ \text{mole}$

$? \ \text{mole S} \ = (28.2 \ \text{g}) \left(\dfrac{1 \ \text{mole}}{32.1 \ \text{g}} \right) = 0.879 \ \text{mole}$

$? \ \text{mole O} \ = (56.1 \ \text{g}) \left(\dfrac{1 \ \text{mole}}{16.0 \ \text{g}} \right) = 3.51 \ \text{mole}$

$$\frac{Al_{0.585} \ S_{0.879} \ O_{3.51}}{0.585 \quad 0.585 \quad 0.585}$$

$Al_1 S_{1.5} O_6$ or $Al_2 S_3 O_{12}$, which chemists usually write as $Al_2(SO_4)_3$

23. ? moles C atoms $= \dfrac{0.840 \text{ g C}}{\text{g compound}} \times 386 \text{ g compound} \times \dfrac{1 \text{ mole C atoms}}{12.0 \text{ g C}}$

$= 27.0 \text{ moles}$

? moles H atoms $= \dfrac{0.119 \text{ g H}}{\text{g compound}} \times 386 \text{ g compound} \times \dfrac{1 \text{ mole H atoms}}{1.0 \text{ g H}}$

$= 46 \text{ moles}$

? moles O atoms $= \dfrac{0.041 \text{ g O}}{\text{g compound}} \times 386 \text{ g compound} \times \dfrac{1 \text{ mole O atoms}}{16.0 \text{ g O}}$

$= 1.0 \text{ mole}$

The molecular formula is $C_{27}H_{46}O$.

24. ? mole Ca $= (24.2 \text{ g})\left(\dfrac{1 \text{ mole}}{40.1 \text{ g}}\right) = 0.603 \text{ mole}$

? mole N $= (17.1 \text{ g})\left(\dfrac{1 \text{ mole}}{14.0 \text{ g}}\right) = 1.22 \text{ moles}$

? mole O $= (58.5 \text{ g})\left(\dfrac{1 \text{ mole}}{16.0 \text{ g}}\right) = 3.66 \text{ moles}$

$Ca_{\frac{0.603}{0.603}} N_{\frac{1.22}{0.603}} O_{\frac{3.66}{0.603}}$

$Ca_1N_2O_6$, which is more commonly written as $Ca(NO_3)_2$, calcium nitrate

25. In 100 g of compound there are 80.0 g C and 20.0 g H.

? moles C atoms $= 80.0 \text{ g C} \times \dfrac{1 \text{ mole C atoms}}{12.0 \text{ g C}} = 6.67 \text{ moles}$

? moles H atoms $= 20.0 \text{ g H} \times \dfrac{1 \text{ mole H atoms}}{1.0 \text{ g H}} = 2\bar{0} \text{ moles}$

The empirical formula is $C_{6.67}H_{20.0}$ or CH_3.

The empirical formula mass is 15.

The molecular mass is $\overline{30}$, or twice the empirical formula mass.

The molecular formula is thus C_2H_6.

26. $? \text{ mole C } = (60.56 \text{ g})\left(\dfrac{1 \text{ mole}}{12.01 \text{ g}}\right) = 5.042 \text{ moles}$

$? \text{ mole H} = (11.18 \text{ g})\left(\dfrac{1 \text{ mole}}{1.008 \text{ g}}\right) = 11.09 \text{ moles}$

$? \text{ mole N} = (28.26 \text{ g})\left(\dfrac{1 \text{ mole}}{14.01 \text{ g}}\right) = 2.017 \text{ moles}$

$C_{\frac{5.042}{2.017}} H_{\frac{11.09}{2.017}} O_{\frac{2.017}{2.017}}$

$C_{2.5}H_{5.5}N_1$, which is $C_5H_{11}N_2$

27. In 100 g of compound there are 54.55 g C, 9.09 g H, and 36.36 g O.

$? \text{ moles C atoms } = 54.55 \text{ g C} \times \dfrac{1 \text{ mole C atoms}}{12.0 \text{ g C}} = 4.55 \text{ moles}$

$? \text{ moles H atoms } = 9.09 \text{ g H} \times \dfrac{1 \text{ mole H atoms}}{1.0 \text{ g H}} = 9.1 \text{ moles}$

$? \text{ moles O atoms } = 36.36 \text{ g O} \times \dfrac{1 \text{ mole O atoms}}{16.0 \text{ g O}} = 2.27 \text{ moles}$

The empirical formula is $C_{4.55}H_{9.1}O_{2.27} = C_2H_4O$.

The empirical formula mass is 44.

The molecular mass is 88, or twice the empirical formula mass.

The molecular formula is thus $C_4H_8O_2$.

28. $? \text{ mole C} = (64.81 \text{ g})\left(\dfrac{1 \text{ mole}}{12.0 \text{ g}}\right) = 5.40 \text{ moles}$

$? \text{ mole H} = (13.60 \text{ g})\left(\dfrac{1 \text{ mole}}{1.01 \text{ g}}\right) = 13.5 \text{ moles}$

$? \text{ mole O} = (21.59 \text{ g})\left(\dfrac{1 \text{ mole}}{16.0 \text{ g}}\right) = 1.35 \text{ moles}$

$$\frac{C_{5.40}}{1.35} \frac{H_{13.5}}{1.35} \frac{O_{1.35}}{1.35} = C_4H_{10}O_1, \text{ usually written as } C_4H_{10}O$$

29. $Ba_3(PO_4)_2$ has a mol. mass of 601.9. Therefore

$$? \text{ moles} = (451.4 \text{ g})\left(\frac{1 \text{ mole}}{601.9 \text{ g}}\right) = 0.7500 \text{ mole}$$

30. $CaSO_4$ has a mol. mass of 136.2. Therefore

$$? \text{ moles} = (0.1705 \text{ g})\left(\frac{1 \text{ mole}}{136.2 \text{ g}}\right) = 1.252 \times 10^{-3} \text{ mole}$$

31. HCl has a mol. mass of 36.5. Therefore

$$? \text{ moles} = (100.0 \text{ g})\left(\frac{1 \text{ mole}}{36.5 \text{ g}}\right) = 2.74 \text{ moles}$$

32. O_2 has a mol. mass of 32.0. Therefore

$$? \text{ moles} = (6.40 \text{ g})\left(\frac{1 \text{ mole}}{32.0 \text{ g}}\right) = 0.200 \text{ mole}$$

33. N_2O has a mol. mass of 44.0. Therefore

$$? \text{ moles} = (2.20 \text{ g})\left(\frac{1 \text{ mole}}{44.0 \text{ g}}\right) = 0.0500 \text{ mole}$$

34. $Mg(OH)_2$ has a formula mass of 58.3. Therefore

$$? \text{ moles} = (2.00 \text{ g})\left(\frac{1 \text{ mole}}{58.3 \text{ g}}\right) = 3.43 \times 10^{-2} \text{ moles}$$

35. (a) $? \text{ g } CH_4 = (2.50 \text{ mole})\left(\frac{16.0 \text{ g}}{1 \text{ mole}}\right) = 40.0 \text{ g}$

   (b) $? \text{ g } SO_3 = (0.0400 \text{ mole})\left(\frac{80.1 \text{ g}}{1 \text{ mole}}\right) = 3.20 \text{ g}$

   (c) $? \text{ g } Al_2(SO_4)_3 = (0.00600 \text{ mole})\left(\frac{342.3 \text{ g}}{1 \text{ mole}}\right) = 2.05 \text{ g}$

   (d) $? \text{ g } (NH_4)_3PO_4 = (0.020 \text{ mole})\left(\frac{149.0 \text{ g}}{1 \text{ mole}}\right) = 3.0 \text{ g}$

36. H_2O has a mol. mass of 18.0. Therefore

$$? \text{ g} = (10.0 \text{ moles})\left(\frac{18.0 \text{ g}}{1 \text{ mole}}\right) = 18\bar{0} \text{ g}$$

37. SO_2 has a mol. mass of 64.1. Therefore

$$? \text{ g} = (0.20 \text{ mole})\left(\frac{64.1 \text{ g}}{1 \text{ mole}}\right) = 13 \text{ g}$$

38. H_2SO_4 has a mol. mass of 98.1. Therefore

$$? \text{ g} = (4.00 \text{ moles})\left(\frac{98.1 \text{ g}}{1 \text{ mole}}\right) = 392 \text{ g}$$

39. C_3H_8 has a mol. mass of 44.0. Therefore

$$? \text{ g} = (51.6 \text{ moles})\left(\frac{44.0 \text{ g}}{1 \text{ mole}}\right) = 2{,}270 \text{ g}$$

This is 5.00 pounds of propane.

40. $NaHCO_3$ has a formula mass of 84.0. Therefore

$$? \text{ g} = (5.40 \text{ moles})\left(\frac{84.0 \text{ g}}{1 \text{ mole}}\right) = 454 \text{ g}$$

This is one pound of baking soda.

41. CO_2 has a mol. mass of 44.0. Therefore

$$? \text{ molecules} = (198.0 \text{ g})\left(\frac{1 \text{ mole}}{44.0 \text{ g}}\right)\left(\frac{6.02 \times 10^{23} \text{ molecules}}{1 \text{ mole}}\right)$$

$$= 2.71 \times 10^{24} \text{ molecules}$$

42. SO_2 has a mol. mass of 64.1. Therefore

$$? \text{ molecules} = (6.40 \text{ g})\left(\frac{1 \text{ mole}}{64.1 \text{ g}}\right)\left(\frac{6.02 \times 10^{23} \text{ molecules}}{1 \text{ mole}}\right)$$

$$= 6.01 \times 10^{22} \text{ molecules}$$

43. NaCl has a formula mass of 58.5. Therefore

$$? \text{ formula units } = (14.6 \text{ g})\left(\frac{1 \text{ mole}}{58.5 \text{ g}}\right)\left(\frac{6.02 \times 10^{23} \text{ formula units}}{1 \text{ mole}}\right)$$

$$= 1.50 \times 10^{23} \text{ formula units}$$

44. $? \text{ molecules of } C_3H_8 = (51.6 \text{ moles})\left(\frac{6.02 \times 10^{23} \text{ molecules}}{1 \text{ mole}}\right)$

$$= 3.11 \times 10^{25} \text{ molecules}$$

45. ? formula units of $NaHCO_3$

$$= (5.40 \text{ moles})\left(\frac{6.02 \times 10^{23} \text{ formula units}}{1 \text{ mole}}\right)$$

$$= 3.25 \times 10^{24} \text{ formula units}$$

46. Mg_3N_2 has a formula mass of 100.9. Therefore

$$? \text{ formula units } = (20.2 \text{ g})\left(\frac{1 \text{ mole}}{100.9 \text{ g}}\right)\left(\frac{6.02 \times 10^{23} \text{ formula units}}{1 \text{ mole}}\right)$$

$$= 1.21 \times 10^{23} \text{ formula units}$$

47. The empirical formula is $C_3H_4O_3$, giving a formula mass of 88.0
    The molecular mass is 176.0, or twice the formula mass.
    The molecular formula is $C_6H_8O_6$.

48. The formula mass of HF = 20.0.   40.0/20.0 = 2.   Therefore the molecular formula is $(HF)_2$ or H_2F_2.

49. The empirical formula mass is 13.0. The molecular formula mass is six times this value. Thus the molecular formula is C_6H_6.

50. The formula mass of CHO = 29.0.   116.0/29.0 = 4.   Therefore the molecular formula is $(CHO)_4$ or $C_4H_4O_4$.

51. The empirical formula mass is 42.0. The molecular formula mass of melamine is three times this value. Thus the molecular formula of melamine is $C_3H_6N_6$.

52. The formula mass of C_6H_6N = 92.0.   184.0/92.0 = 2.   Therefore the molecular formula is $(C_6H_6N)_2$ or $C_{12}H_{12}N_2$.

53. The empirical formula mass of CH_2O is 30.0. The molecular mass of dextrose is 180.0, and that is six times the empirical mass of CH_2O. Therefore the molecular formula of dextrose is $(CH_2O)_6$, or $C_6H_{12}O_6$.

    The molecular mass of acetic acid is 60.0, and that is twice the empirical mass of CH_2O. Therefore the molecular formula of acetic acid is $(CH_2O)_2$, or $C_2H_4O_2$.

54. Given: The formula mass of the compound is 208.0 and its empirical formula is Fe_2S_3.

    The formula mass of Fe_2S_3 is 208. Therefore the empirical formula and the molecular formula are one and the same.

55. The formula mass of K_2CrO_4 is 194.2.

    $$\text{Percent K} = \frac{78.2}{194.2} \times 100 = 40.3\%$$

    $$\text{Percent Cr} = \frac{52.0}{194.2} \times 100 = 26.8\%$$

    $$\text{Percent O} = \frac{64.0}{194.2} \times 100 = 33.0\%$$

56. (a) $$\text{Percent C} = \frac{24.0}{30.0} \times 100 = 80.0\%$$

    $$\text{Percent H} = \frac{6.0}{30.0} \times 100 = \overline{2}0\% \text{ in } C_2H_6$$

    (b) $$\text{Percent N} = \frac{14.0}{46.0} \times 100 = 30.4\%$$

    $$\text{Percent O} = \frac{32.0}{46.0} \times 100 = 69.6\% \text{ in } NO_2$$

    (c) $$\text{Percent C} = \frac{12.0}{44.0} \times 100 = 27.3\%$$

    $$\text{Percent O} = \frac{32.0}{44.0} \times 100 = 72.7\% \text{ in } CO_2$$

57. (a)   The formula mass of BF_3 is 67.8.

$$\text{Percent B} = \frac{10.8}{67.8} \times 100 = 15.9\%$$

$$\text{Percent F} = \frac{57.0}{67.8} \times 100 = \underline{84.1\%}$$

$$\text{Total percent} \quad 100.0$$

(b) The formula mass of UF_6 is 352.

$$\text{Percent U} = \frac{238.0}{352.0} \times 100 = 67.61\%$$

$$\text{Percent F} = \frac{114.0}{352.0} \times 100 = \underline{32.39\%}$$

$$\text{Total percent} \quad 100.00$$

(c) The molecular weight of $C_3H_8O_3$ is 92.0.

$$\text{Percent C} = \frac{36.0}{92.0} \times 100 = 39.1\%$$

$$\text{Percent H} = \frac{8.0}{92.0} \times 100 = 8.7\%$$

$$\text{Percent O} = \frac{48.0}{92.0} \times 100 = \underline{52.2\%}$$

$$\text{Total percent} \quad 100.0$$

58. (a) $\text{Percent O} = \dfrac{16.0}{18.0} \times 100 = 88.9\%$ for H_2O

(b) $\text{Percent O} = \dfrac{16.0}{28.0} \times 100 = 57.1\%$ for CO

(c) $\text{Percent O} = \dfrac{64.0}{98.1} \times 100 = 65.2\%$ for H_2SO_4

59. Let x = mass of salt. Then $50 - x$ = mass of sugar.

$$\frac{35.5}{58.5} \; x = \text{mass of Cl in mixture}$$

$$\frac{35.5}{58.5} \ x = \frac{0.20 \text{ g Cl}}{1 \text{ g mixture}} \times 50 \text{ g mixture}$$

$$x = 16 \text{ g salt and } 34 \text{ g sugar}$$

60.   ? moles $NH_3 = (1,\overline{700} \text{ g})\left(\frac{1 \text{ mole}}{17.0 \text{ g}}\right) = 1\overline{00} \text{ moles}$

? moles N atoms $= (1\overline{00} \text{ moles } NH_3)\left(\frac{1 \text{ mole N}}{1 \text{ mole } NH_3}\right)$

$$= 1\overline{00} \text{ moles N atoms (or 50.0 moles } N_2 \text{ gas)}$$

61.   (a)   The molecular mass of SO_2 is 64.1.

Percent S $= \dfrac{32.1}{64.1} \times 100 = 50.1\%$

Percent O $= \dfrac{32.0}{64.1} \times 100 = \underline{49.9\%}$

Total percent   100.0

(b)   The molecular mass of CH_4 is 16.0.

Percent C $= \dfrac{12.0}{16.0} \times 100 = 75.0\%$

Percent H $= \dfrac{4.0}{16.0} \times 100 = \underline{25\%}$

Total percent $\overline{100}$

(c)   The molecular mass of $C_{12}H_{22}O_{11}$ is 342.0.

Percent C $= \dfrac{144.0}{342.0} \times 100 = 42.11\%$

Percent H $= \dfrac{22.0}{342.0} \times 100 = 6.43\%$

Percent O $= \dfrac{176.0}{342.0} \times 100 = \underline{51.46\%}$

Total percent   100.00

(d) The formula mass of $CaCO_3$ is 100.1.

$$\text{Percent Ca} = \frac{40.1}{100.1} \times 100 = 40.1\%$$

$$\text{Percent C} = \frac{12.0}{100.1} \times 100 = 12.0\%$$

$$\text{Percent O} = \frac{48.0}{100.1} \times 100 = \underline{48.0\%}$$

$$\text{Total percent} \qquad 100.1$$

62. $\text{Percent H} = \dfrac{2.0}{18.0} \times 100 = 11\%$ in H_2O

Therefore grams of hydrogen = $(0.11)(18\overline{0}$ g) = 20 g.

63. The formula mass of CuO is 79.5.

$$\text{Percent Cu} = \frac{63.5}{79.5} \times 100 = 79.9\%$$

? grams Cu = $1,60\overline{0}$ g CuO $\times$ 0.799 = 1,280 g Cu

64. $\text{Percent O} = \dfrac{32.1}{64.1} \times 100 = 50.0\%$ in SO_2

Therefore grams of oxygen = $(0.500)(320.0)$ = $16\overline{0}$ g.

65. The formula mass of Fe_2O_3 is 159.6.

$$\text{Percent Fe} = \frac{111.6}{159.6} \times 100 = 69.92\%$$

? grams Fe = 350.0 g Fe_2O_3 $\times$ 0.6992 = 244.7 g Fe

66. $\text{Percent S} = \dfrac{32.1}{34.1} \times 100 = 94.1\%$ in H_2S

67. From Exercise 61(a).

$$\text{Percent O} = 49.9 \text{ or } \frac{49.9 \text{ g O}}{50.1 \text{ g S}}$$

$$? \text{ grams O} = 2\overline{0}0 \text{ g S} \times \frac{49.9 \text{ g O}}{50.1 \text{ g S}} = 199 \text{ g}$$

68. $\text{Percent H} = \dfrac{4.0}{32.0} \times 100 = 13 \text{ percent H in CH}_3\text{OH}$

69.   Let x = grams Na$_2$S. Then

$$\frac{32.1}{78.1} \, x = \text{grams S} = 5\overline{0}0 \text{ g mixture} \times \frac{25.0 \text{ g S}}{100.0 \text{ g mixture}}$$

$$x = 304$$

Therefore 304 g Na$_2$S and 196 g Fe$_2$O$_3$

70. $\text{Percent N} = \dfrac{14.0}{63.0} \times 100 = 22.2\% \text{ in HNO}_3$

EXTRA EXERCISES

71. $? \text{ yr} = \$6.02 \times 10^{23} \times \dfrac{1 \text{ sec}}{\$1} \times \dfrac{1 \text{ hr}}{3{,}600 \text{ sec}} \times \dfrac{1 \text{ day}}{24 \text{ hr}} \times \dfrac{1 \text{ yr}}{365 \text{ days}} = 1.9 \times 10^{16} \text{ yr}$

72.   In $1\overline{0}0$ g of compound there are 24.3 g C, 4.1 g H, and 71.6 g Cl.

$$? \text{ moles C atoms} = 24.3 \text{ g C} \times \frac{1 \text{ mole C atoms}}{12.0 \text{ g C}} = 2.03 \text{ moles}$$

$$? \text{ moles H atoms} = 4.1 \text{ g H} \times \frac{1 \text{ mole H atoms}}{1.0 \text{ g H}} = 4.1 \text{ moles}$$

$$? \text{ moles Cl atoms} = 71.6 \text{ g Cl} \times \frac{1 \text{ mole Cl atoms}}{35.5 \text{ g Cl}} = 2.02 \text{ moles}$$

The simplest formula is CH$_2$Cl.

73.   The empirical formula mass is 49.5, which is half the molecular mass. The molecular formula is C$_2$H$_4$Cl$_2$.

74. $? \text{ grams Fe}_3\text{O}_4 = 1\overline{0}0 \text{ g O} \times \dfrac{231.4 \text{ g Fe}_3\text{O}_4}{64.0 \text{ g O}} = 362 \text{ g}$

75. $? \text{ atoms C} = 1.75 \ \cancel{\text{carats}} \times \dfrac{\overline{200} \ \cancel{\text{mg}}}{1.00 \ \cancel{\text{carat}}} \times \dfrac{1 \ \cancel{\text{g}}}{1{,}000 \ \cancel{\text{mg}}} \times \dfrac{6.02 \times 10^{23} \ \text{atoms C}}{12.0 \ \cancel{\text{g C}}}$

$= 1.76 \times 10^{22} \text{ atoms}$

76. $\text{Percent Fe in Fe}_2\text{O}_3 = \dfrac{111.6 \text{ g Fe}}{159.6 \text{ g Fe}_2\text{O}_3} \times 100 = 69.92\%$

$\text{Percent Fe in Fe}_3\text{O}_4 = \dfrac{167.4 \text{ g Fe}}{231.4 \text{ g Fe}_3\text{O}_4} \times 100 = 72.34\%$

77. Take $\overline{100}$ g of each ore.

		Grams	Atoms	Empirical formula
Ore A	Cu	63.3	1	
	Fe	11.1	0.2	Cu$_5$FeS$_4$
	S	25.6	0.8	
Ore B	Cu	34.6	0.54	
	Fe	30.4	0.54	CuFeS$_2$
	S	34.9	1.1	

78. $\text{Percent O} = \dfrac{32.0 \text{ g O}}{64.1 \text{ g SO}_2} \times 100 = 49.9\% \text{ in O}$

$\text{Percent S} = \dfrac{32.1 \text{ g S}}{64.1 \text{ g SO}_2} \times 100 = 50.1\% \text{ in S}$

79. $? \text{ grams} = 10 \ \cancel{\text{atoms Ag}} \times \dfrac{107.9 \text{ g Ag}}{6.02 \times 10^{23} \ \cancel{\text{atoms Ag}}}$

$= 1.79 \times 10^{-21} \text{ g}$

80. $? \text{ moles H}_3\text{PO}_4 = (392 \ \cancel{\text{g}})\left(\dfrac{1 \text{ mole}}{98.0 \ \cancel{\text{g}}}\right) = 4.00 \text{ moles H}_3\text{PO}_4$

$? \text{ moles P} = (4.00 \ \cancel{\text{moles H}_3\text{PO}_4})\left(\dfrac{1 \text{ mole P}}{1 \ \cancel{\text{mole H}_3\text{PO}_4}}\right) = 4.00 \text{ moles P}$

81. $? \text{ g P} = (4.00 \text{ moles P})\left(\dfrac{31.0 \text{ g}}{1 \text{ mole}}\right) = 124 \text{ g}$

82.   1 amu = (1/12) mass of C–12

$? \text{ grams} = 1 \text{ amu} \times \dfrac{1 \text{ atom C-12}}{12.0 \text{ amu}} \times \dfrac{12.0 \text{ g C}}{6.02 \times 10^{23} \text{ atoms C}^{12}} = 1.66 \times 10^{-24} \text{ g}$

83.   The molecular formula of ethyl alcohol is C_2H_6O, and the molecular mass is 46.0.

(a) $? \text{ moles } C_2H_6O = 9.2 \text{ g alcohol} \times \dfrac{1 \text{ mole alcohol}}{46.0 \text{ g alcohol}} = 0.20 \text{ mole}$

(b) $? \text{ molecules } C_2H_6O$

$= 0.20 \text{ mole alcohol} \times \dfrac{6.02 \infty 10^{23} \text{ molecule}}{1 \text{ mole alcohol}} = 1.2 \times 10^{23} \text{ molecules}$

(c) $? \text{ moles C atoms} = 0.20 \text{ mole alcohol} \times \dfrac{2 \text{ moles C atoms}}{1 \text{ mole alcohol}} = 0.40 \text{ mole}$

(d) $? \text{ moles H atoms} = 0.20 \text{ mole alcohol} \times \dfrac{6 \text{ moles H atoms}}{1 \text{ mole alcohol}} = 1.2 \text{ moles}$

(e) $? \text{ moles O atoms} = 0.20 \text{ mole alcohol} \times \dfrac{1 \text{ mole O atoms}}{1 \text{ mole alcohol}} = 0.20 \text{ mole}$

(f) $? \text{ atoms C} = 0.40 \text{ mole C atoms} \times \dfrac{6.02 \times 10^{23} \text{ atoms C}}{1 \text{ mole C atoms}} = 2.4 \times 10^{23} \text{ atoms}$

(g) $? \text{ atoms H} = 1.2 \text{ moles H atoms} \times \dfrac{6.02 \times 10^{23} \text{ atoms H}}{1 \text{ mole H atoms}} = 7.2 \times 10^{23} \text{ atoms}$

(h) $? \text{ atoms O} = 0.20 \text{ mole O atoms} \times \dfrac{6.02 \times 10^{23} \text{ atoms O}}{1 \text{ mole O atoms}} = 1.2 \times 10^{23} \text{ atoms}$

84.   Mol. mass of $CH_3OH = 32.0$.

(a) $? \text{ mole } CH_3OH = (3.2 \text{ g})\left(\dfrac{1 \text{ mole}}{32.0 \text{ g}}\right) = 0.10 \text{ mole}$

(b)   ? molecules CH_3OH = $(0.10 \text{ mole})\left(\dfrac{6.0 \times 10^{23} \text{ molecules}}{1 \text{ mole}}\right)$

$= 6.0 \times 10^{22}$ molecules

(c)   ? mole C = $(0.10 \text{ mole } CH_3OH)\left(\dfrac{1 \text{ mole C}}{1 \text{ mole } CH_3OH}\right)$ = 0.10 mole C

(d)   ? mole H = $(0.10 \text{ mole } CH_3OH)\left(\dfrac{4 \text{ mole H}}{1 \text{ mole } CH_3OH}\right)$ = 0.40 mole H

(e)   ? mole O = $(0.10 \text{ mole } CH_3OH)\left(\dfrac{1 \text{ mole O}}{1 \text{ mole } CH_3OH}\right)$ = 0.10 mole O

(f)   ? C atoms = $(0.10 \text{ mole C})\left(\dfrac{6.0 \times 10^{23} \text{ atoms}}{1 \text{ mole C}}\right)$ = 6.0×10^{22} C atoms

(g)   ? H atoms = $(0.40 \text{ mole H})\left(\dfrac{6.0 \times 10^{23} \text{ atoms}}{1 \text{ mole H}}\right)$ = 2.4×10^{23} H atoms

(h)   ? O atoms = $(0.10 \text{ mole O})\left(\dfrac{6.0 \times 10^{23} \text{ atoms}}{1 \text{ mole O}}\right)$ = 6.0×10^{22} O atoms

85. (a)   ? moles H_2O = $7.20 \text{ g } H_2O \times \dfrac{1 \text{ mole } H_2O}{18.0 \text{ g } H_2O}$ = 0.400 mole

(b)   ? moles MnO_2 = $260.7 \text{ g } MnO_2 \times \dfrac{1 \text{ mole } MnO_2}{86.9 \text{ g } MnO_2}$ = 3.00 moles

(c)   ? moles N_2 = $0.070 \text{ g } N_2 \times \dfrac{1 \text{ mole } N_2}{28.0 \text{ g } N_2}$ = 0.0025 mole

(d)   ? moles $(NH_4)_2SO_4$

$= 1,980.0 \text{ g } (NH_4)_2SO_4 \times \dfrac{1 \text{ mole } (NH_4)_2SO_4}{132.1 \text{ g } (NH_4)_2SO_4}$ = 14.99 moles

86. (a)   Mol. mass of NH_3 = 17.0

? mole = $(0.34 \text{ g})\left(\dfrac{1 \text{ mole}}{17.0 \text{ g}}\right)$ = 0.020 mole

(b)   Mol. mass of MnO_2 = 86.9

$$? \text{ mole} = (1{,}335.0 \text{ g})\left(\frac{1 \text{ mole}}{86.9 \text{ g}}\right) = 15.4 \text{ moles}$$

87. The molecular mass of glycine, $C_2H_5O_2N$, is 75.0.

(a) $? \text{ moles } C_2H_5O_2N = 300.0 \text{ g } C_2H_5O_2N \times \dfrac{1 \text{ mole } C_2H_5O_2N}{75.0 \text{ g } C_2H_5O_2N} = 4.00 \text{ moles}$

(b) $? \text{ molecules } C_2H_5O_2N$

$$= 4.00 \text{ moles } C_2H_5O_2N \times \frac{6.02 \times 10^{23} \text{ molecules } C_2H_5O_2N}{1 \text{ mole } C_2H_5O_2N}$$

$$= 2.41 \times 10^{24} \text{ molecules}$$

(c) $? \text{ moles C atoms} = 4.00 \text{ moles } C_2H_5O_2N \times \dfrac{2 \text{ moles C atoms}}{1 \text{ mole } C_2H_5O_2N} = 8.00 \text{ moles}$

(d) $? \text{ moles H atoms} = 4.00 \text{ moles } C_2H_5O_2N \times \dfrac{5 \text{ moles H atoms}}{1 \text{ mole } C_2H_5O_2N} = 20.0 \text{ moles}$

(e) $? \text{ moles O atoms} = 4.00 \text{ moles } C_2H_5O_2N \times \dfrac{2 \text{ moles O atoms}}{1 \text{ mole } C_2H_5O_2N} = 8.00 \text{ moles}$

(f) $? \text{ moles N atoms} = 4.00 \text{ moles } C_2H_5O_2N \times \dfrac{1 \text{ mole N atoms}}{1 \text{ mole } C_2H_5O_2N} = 4.00 \text{ moles}$

(g) $? \text{ grams C} = 8.00 \text{ moles C atoms} \times \dfrac{12.0 \text{ g C}}{1 \text{ mole C atoms}} = 96.0 \text{ g}$

(h) $? \text{ grams H} = 20.0 \text{ moles H atoms} \times \dfrac{1.0 \text{ g H}}{1 \text{ mole H atoms}} = 2\bar{0} \text{ g}$

(i) $? \text{ grams O} = 8.00 \text{ moles O atoms} \times \dfrac{16.0 \text{ g O}}{1 \text{ mole O atoms}} = 128 \text{ g}$

(j) $? \text{ grams N} = 4.00 \text{ moles N atoms} \times \dfrac{14.0 \text{ g N}}{1 \text{ mole N atoms}} = 56.0 \text{g}$

(k)   Both should equal 300.0 g.

88. (a)   Mol. mass of H_2O = 18.0 g

$$? \text{ moles} = (72\bar{0} \text{ g})\left(\frac{1 \text{ mole}}{18.0 \text{ g}}\right) = 40.0 \text{ moles}$$

(b)   Mol. mass of MnO_2 = 86.9 g

$$? \text{ moles} = (13.35 \text{ g})\left(\frac{1 \text{ mole}}{86.9 \text{ g}}\right) = 0.154 \text{ mole}$$

10 THE CHEMICAL EQUATION: RECIPE FOR A REACTION

SELF-TEST EXERCISES

1. (a) $2K + 2H_2O \rightarrow 2KOH + H_2$

   (b) $2HC_2H_3O_2 + Ca(OH)_2 \rightarrow Ca(C_2H_3O_2)_2 + 2H_2O$

   (c) $Mg + Cu(NO_3)_2 \rightarrow Mg(NO_3)_2 + Cu$

   (d) $Na_2O + H_2O \rightarrow 2NaOH$

   (e) $2ZnS + 3O_2 \rightarrow 2ZnO + 2SO_2$

   (f) $3KOH + Al(NO_3)_3 \rightarrow Al(OH)_3 + 3KNO_3$

2. (a) $3Ca(OH)_2 + 2H_3PO_4 \rightarrow Ca_3(PO_4)_2 + 6H_2O$

   (b) $2Sr + O_2 \rightarrow 2SrO$

   (c) $Mg(ClO_3)_2 \rightarrow MgCl_2 + 3O_2$

   (d) $Fe(OH)_3 + 3HCl \rightarrow FeCl_3 + 3H_2O$

   (e) $4K + O_2 \rightarrow 2K_2O$

   (f) $2P + 3Br_2 \rightarrow 2PBr_3$

3. (a) $4Fe + 3O_2 \rightarrow 2Fe_2O_3$

   (b) $3H_2SO_4 + 2Al(OH)_3 \rightarrow Al_2(SO_4)_3 + 6H_2O$

   (c) $2AgNO_3 + BaCl_2 \rightarrow 2AgCl + Ba(NO_3)_2$

(d) $Cu_2S + O_2 \rightarrow 2Cu + SO_2$

4. (a) $2H_2 + O_2 \rightarrow 2H_2O$

   (b) $KOH + HC_2H_3O_2 \rightarrow KC_2H_3O_2 + H_2O$

   (c) $N_2 + 3H_2 \rightarrow 2NH_3$

   (d) $2KClO_3 \rightarrow 2KCl + 3O_2$

5. (a)   Combination   (b)   Decomposition
   (c)   Double-replacement   (d)   Single-replacement
   (e)   Double-replacement

6. (a)   Combination   (b)   Decomposition
   (c)   Single-replacement   (d)   Double-replacement
   (e)   Combination   (f)   Double-replacement

7. (a)   Decomposition   (b)   Decomposition
   (c)   Decomposition   (d)   Combination
   (e)   Combination   (f)   Single-replacement
   (g)   No reaction   (h)   Double-replacement

8. (a)   Decomposition   (b)   Combination
   (c)   Combination   (d)   Double-replacement
   (e)   Decomposition   (f)   Combination
   (g)   Single-replacement   (h)   Decomposition

9. (a)   Combination   (b)   Double-replacement
   (c)   Double-replacement   (d)   Single-replacement

10. (a)   Double-replacement   (b)   Combination
    (c)   Decomposition   (d)   Double-replacement
    (e)   Combination   (f)   Combination

11. (a) $H_2 + Br_2 \rightarrow 2HBr$ (b) $BaO + H_2O \rightarrow Ba(OH)_2$

    (c) $2Na + Cl_2 \rightarrow 2NaCl$ (d) $N_2 + 2O_2 \rightarrow 2NO_2$

    (e) $CaCO_3 \rightarrow CaO + CO_2$ (f) $2KOH \rightarrow K_2O + H_2O$

    (g) $Hg(ClO_3)_2 \rightarrow HgCl_2 + 3O_2$ (h) $PbCl_2 \rightarrow Pb + Cl_2$

    (i) $2Li + 2H_2O \rightarrow 2LiOH + H_2$ (j) $Zn + H_2SO_4 \rightarrow ZnSO_4 + H_2$

    (k) $Ni + Al(NO_3)_3 \rightarrow$ no reaction

(l) $2Al + 3Hg(C_2H_3O_2)_2 \rightarrow 2Al(C_2H_3O_2)_3 + 3Hg$

(m) $H_2SO_4 + 2NH_4OH \rightarrow (NH_4)_2SO_4 + 2H_2O$

(n) $2AgNO_3 + BaCl_2 \rightarrow 2AgCl \ (s) + Ba(NO_3)_2$

(o) $3H_2SO_3 + 2 \ Al(OH)_3 \rightarrow Al_2(SO_3)_3 + 6 \ H_2O$

(p) $NaNO_3 \ (aq) + KCl \ (aq) \rightarrow$ no reaction

12. (a) $Cu + S = CuS$ (b) $CaO + H_2O \rightarrow Ca(OH)_2$

     (c) $2Na + F_2 \rightarrow 2NaF$ (d) $2P + 3I_2 \rightarrow 2PI_3$

     (e) $MgCO_3 \xrightarrow{\text{heat}} MgO + CO_2$ (f) $2LiOH \rightarrow Li_2O + H_2O$

     (g) $Mg(ClO_3)_2 \rightarrow MgCl_2 + 3O_2$ (h) $Mg_3N_2 \rightarrow 3Mg + N_2$

     (i) $2Al + 2H_3PO_4 \rightarrow 2AlPO_4 + 3H_2$ (j) $Zn + Pb(NO_3)_2 \rightarrow Zn(NO_3)_2 + Pb$

     (k) $Cl_2 + 2KBr \rightarrow 2KCl + Br_2$ (l) $Br_2 + NaCl \rightarrow$ no reaction

     (m) $AgNO_3 + H_2S \rightarrow Ag_2S + 2HNO_3$

     (n) $BaCl_2 + (NH_4)_2CO_3 \rightarrow 2NH_4Cl + BaCO_3$

     (o) $3CaCO_3 + 2H_3PO_4 \rightarrow Ca_3(PO_4)_2 + 3H_2CO_3$

     (p) $2AgNO_3 + MgCl_2 \rightarrow Mg(NO_3)_2 + 2AgCl$

13. (a) $2N_2O \xrightarrow{\Delta} 2N_2 + O_2$ (b) $H_2CO_3 \rightarrow H_2O + CO_2$

     (c) $2NaNO_3 \rightarrow 2NaNO_2 + O_2$ (d) $H_2 + F_2 \rightarrow 2HF$

     (e) $N_2 + 3H_2 \rightarrow 2NH_3$ (f) $Ca + 2HCl \rightarrow CaCl_2 + H_2$

     (g) $Cu + NiCl_2 \rightarrow$ no reaction

     (h) $3AgNO_3 + K_3AsO_4 \rightarrow Ag_3AsO_4(s) + 3KNO_3$

14. (a) $2Na_2O \rightarrow 4Na + O_2$ (b) $H_2 + I_2 \rightarrow 2HI$

     (c) $4P + 3O_2 \rightarrow 2P_2O_3$

     (d) $2K_3PO_4 + 3BaCl_2 \rightarrow Ba_3(PO_4)_2(s) + 6KCl$

     (e) $2KClO_3 \rightarrow 2KCl + 3O_2$ (f) $2Ca + O_2 \rightarrow 2CaO$

     (g) $Cl_2 + 2NH_4I \rightarrow 2NH_4Cl + I_2$ (h) $2Ag_2O \rightarrow 4Ag + O_2$

15. (a) $2K + Cl_2 \rightarrow 2KCl$ (b) $K_2O + H_2O \rightarrow 2KOH$

    (c) $MgO + H_2O \rightarrow Mg(OH)_2$ (d) $CaO + CO_2 \rightarrow CaCO_3$

    (e) $2NH_3 \rightarrow N_2 + 3H_2$ (f) $SrCO_3 \rightarrow SrO + CO_2$

    (g) $2NaClO_3 \rightarrow 2NaCl + 3O_2$ (h) $Mg(OH)_2 \rightarrow MgO + H_2O$

16. (a) $2K + Br_2 \rightarrow 2KBr$ (b) $Li_2O + H_2O \rightarrow 2LiOH$

    (c) $BaO + H_2O \rightarrow Ba(OH)_2$ (d) $MgO + CO_2 \rightarrow MgCO_3$

    (e) $MgCO_3 \rightarrow MgO + CO_2$ (f) $Cu_2S \rightarrow 2Cu + S$

    (g) $Cr_2(CO_3)_3 \rightarrow Cr_2O_3 + 3CO_2$ (h) $2Al(ClO_3)_3 \rightarrow 2AlCl_3 + 9O_2$

17. (a) $HCl + NaOH$ (b) $H_2SO_4 + KOH$ (c) $HNO_3 + Al(OH)_3$

18. (a) $KOH + HCl$ (b) $Mg(OH)_2 + H_2SO_4$ (c) $Fe(OH)_3 + H_2SO_4$

19. (a) $Zn + 2HNO_2 \rightarrow Zn(NO_2)_2 + H_2$ (b) $Ag + NiCl_2 \rightarrow$ no reaction

    (c) $Zn + 2AgNO_3 \rightarrow Zn(NO_3)_2 + 2Ag$ (d) $2Cs + 2H_2O \rightarrow 2CsOH + H_2$

    (e) $3HCl + Al(OH)_3 \rightarrow AlCl_3 + 3H_2O$ (f) $KNO_3 + ZnCl_2 \rightarrow$ no reaction

    (g) $Al(NO_3)_3 + 3NaOH \rightarrow Al(OH)_3(s) + 3NaNO_3$

    (h) $K_2CrO_4 + Pb(NO_3)_2 \rightarrow PbCrO_4(s) + 2KNO_3$

20. (a) $Cu + 2\,AgCl \rightarrow CuCl_2 + 2\,Ag$ (b) $Cl_2 + KF \rightarrow$ no reaction

    (c) $Zn + 2HNO_3 \rightarrow Zn(NO_3)_2 + H_2$ (d) $Cu + HCl \rightarrow$ no reaction

    (e) $3NH_4NO_3 + H_3PO_4 \rightarrow$ no reaction

    (f) $ZnCl_2 + 2KOH \rightarrow Zn(OH)_2(s) + 2KCl$

    (g) $Ni_3(PO_4)_2 + HCl \rightarrow$ no reaction   (h) $AgNO_3 + KCl \rightarrow AgCl(s) + KNO_3$

21. (a) *Oxidation* is the loss of electrons by an atom undergoing reaction.
    (b) *Reduction* is the gain of electrons by an atom undergoing reaction.
    (c) An *oxidizing agent* is a substance that causes something else to be oxidized while it, itself, is reduced.
    (d) A *reducing agent* is a substance that causes something else to be reduced while it, itself, is oxidized.

22. (a) The loss of electrons is called *oxidation*.
    (b) The gain of electrons is called *reduction*.
    (c) A substance that causes something else to be oxidized is called an *oxidizing agent*.
    (d) A substance that causes something else to be reduced is called a *reducing agent*.

23. (a) $2K + Cl_2 \rightarrow 2KCl$
         The K is oxidized, and the Cl is reduced.

    (b) $2NH_3 \rightarrow N_2 + 3H_2$
         The N is oxidized, and the H is reduced.

    (c) $CuO + H_2 \rightarrow Cu + H_2O$
         The H is oxidized, and the Cu is reduced.

    (d) $Sn + 2Cl_2 \rightarrow SnCl_4$
         The Sn is oxidized, and the Cl is reduced.

24. (a) $2Na + F_2 \rightarrow 2NaF$
         The Na is oxidized and the F is reduced.

    (b) $4Al + 3C \rightarrow Al_4C_3$
         The Al is oxidized and the C is reduced.

    (c) $Cu + S \rightarrow CuS$
         The Cu is oxidized and the S is reduced.

    (d) $2Ag_2O \rightarrow 4Ag + O_2$
         The O is oxidized and the Ag is reduced.

25. (1) Cl_2 is the oxidizing agent; K is the reducing agent.
    (2) NH_3 is the reducing agent; NH_3 is the oxidizing agent.
    (3) CuO is the oxidizing agent; H_2 is the reducing agent.
    (4) Sn is the reducing agent; Cl_2 is the oxidizing agent.

26. (a) The Na is the reducing agent, and the F_2 is the oxidizing agent.
    (b) The Al is the reducing agent, and the C is the oxidizing agent.
    (c) The Cu is the reducing agent, and the S is the oxidizing agent.
    (d) The Ag_2O is both the reducing agent and the oxidizing agent.

27. (a) Zn is the reducing agent; HNO_2 is the oxidizing agent.
    (b) There is no reaction.
    (c) Zn is the reducing agent; $AgNO_3$ is the oxidizing agent.
    (d) Cs is the reducing agent; H_2O is the oxidizing agent.

28. (a)   The Cu is the reducing agent, and the AgCl is the oxidizing agent.
    (b)   No reduction.
    (c)   The Zn is the reducing agent, and the HNO_3 is the oxidizing agent.
    (d)   No reduction.

EXTRA EXERCISES

29. $5Zn^0 + V_2^{5+} + O_5^{2-} \rightarrow 5Zn^{2+}O^{2-} + 2V^0$

The Zn is oxidized and the V is reduced. The V_2O_5 is the oxidizing agent, and the Zn is the reducing agent.

30. $MgCO_3 \xrightarrow{\Delta} MgO + CO_2$ $CaCO_3 \xrightarrow{\Delta} CaO + CO_2$

31. (a)   Not balanced: $N_2 + 3H_2 \rightarrow 2NH_3$

(b)   Not balanced: $3Fe + 4H_2O \rightarrow Fe_3O_4 + 4H_2$

(c)   Balanced

32. The answer is wrong because the true formula for calcium chloride is $CaCl_2$ and the formula for calcium hydroxide is $Ca(OH)_2$.

33. (a) $2C + O_2 \rightarrow 2CO$ (b) $H_2 + Cl_2 \rightarrow 2HCl$

(c) $2Na + 2H_2O \rightarrow 2NaOH + H_2$ (d)   No reaction

34. (a)   No reaction   (b) $Mg + Zn(NO_3)_2 \rightarrow Mg(NO_3)_2 + Zn$

(c)   No reaction   (d) $Zn + Cu(NO_3)_2 \rightarrow Zn(NO_3)_2 + Cu$

35. An oxidizing agent typically gains electrons and therefore, it is reduced.

36. (a) $Ca(OH)_2 + 2HCl \rightarrow CaCl_2 + 2H_2O$ (double-replacement)

(b) $Zn + H_2SO_4 \rightarrow ZnSO_4 + H_2$ (single-replacement)

(c) $2Ba + O_2 \rightarrow 2BaO$ (combination)

(d) $Cs_2O + H_2O \rightarrow 2CsOH$ (combination)

37. $4NH_3 (g) + 7O_2 (g) \rightarrow 2N_2O_4 (g) + 6H_2O (g)$

38. For the reaction

    $$(Cr_2^{6+}O_7^{2-})^{2-} + 14H^{1+} + 6Fe^{2+} \rightarrow 2Cr^{3+} + 7H_2^4O^{2-} + 6Fe^{3+}$$

    (a)   The Fe^{2+} is oxidized.   (b)   The Cr^{6+} is reduced.

    (c)   The $(Cr_2O_7)^{2-}$ is the oxidizing agent.

    (d)   The Fe^{2+} is the reducing agent.

39.   12Na + P_4 $\rightarrow$ $4Na_3P$
       Sodium Phosphorus   Sodium
                              phosphide

40. $Mg(OH)_2 + 2HCl \rightarrow MgCl_2 + 2H_2O$ or $Mg + Cl_2 \rightarrow MgCl_2$

41. $LiOH + HCl \rightarrow LiCl + H_2O$

42. Yes, single-replacement reactions are redox reactions. An example is

    $$\overset{0}{Mg} + \overset{1+1-}{2HCl} \rightarrow \overset{2+1-}{MgCl_2} + \overset{0}{H_2}$$

    In this reaction the magnesium is oxidized and the hydrogen is reduced.

43. $C + O_2 \rightarrow CO_2$ or $CaCO_3 \overset{\Delta}{\longrightarrow} CaO + CO_2$

44. $3Zn(OH)_2 + 2H_3PO_4 \rightarrow Zn_3(PO_4)_2 + 6H_2O$

11 STOICHIOMETRY: THE QUANTITIES IN REACTIONS

SELF-TEST EXERCISES

1. (a) $2Na_2S_2O_3 + AgBr \rightarrow Na_3Ag(S_2O_3)_2 + NaBr$
        ?grams   46.95g   ?grams   ?grams

    (b) Moles AgBr = $(46.95 \text{ g AgBr})\left(\dfrac{1 \text{ mole}}{187.8 \text{ g}}\right)$ = 0.2500 mole AgBr

    Moles $Na_2S_2O_3$ = $(0.2500 \text{ mole AgBr})\left(\dfrac{2 \text{ moles } Na_2S_2O_3}{1 \text{ mole AgBr}}\right)$

    = 0.500 mole $Na_2S_2O_3$

    Grams $Na_2S_2O_3$ = $(0.500 \text{ mole})\left(\dfrac{158.2 \text{ g}}{1 \text{ mole}}\right)$ = 79.10 g

    (c) Moles $Na_3Ag(S_2O_3)_2$ = $(0.2500 \text{ mole AgBr})\left(\dfrac{1 \text{ mole } Na_3Ag(S_2O_3)_2}{1 \text{ mole AgBr}}\right)$

    = 0.2500 mole $Na_3Ag(S_2O_3)_2$

    Grams $Na_3Ag(S_2O_3)_2$ = $(0.2500 \text{ mole})\left(\dfrac{401.3 \text{ g}}{1 \text{ mole}}\right)$ = 100.3 g

$$\text{Moles NaBr} = (0.2500 \ \cancel{\text{mole AgBr}})\left(\frac{1 \text{ mole NaBr}}{1 \ \cancel{\text{mole AgBr}}}\right) = 0.2500 \text{ mole NaBr}$$

$$\text{Grams NaBr} = (0.2500 \ \cancel{\text{mole}})\left(\frac{102.9 \text{ g}}{1 \ \cancel{\text{mole}}}\right) = 25.73 \text{ g}$$

2. (a) $2Na + Cl_2 \rightarrow 2NaCl$
            4.60g ?grams ?grams

    (b) $\text{Moles Na} = (4.60 \text{ g Na})\left(\frac{1 \text{ mole}}{23.0 \text{ g}}\right) = 0.200 \text{ mole Na}$

          $\text{Moles NaCl} = (0.200 \ \cancel{\text{mole Na}})\left(\frac{2 \text{ moles NaCl}}{2 \ \cancel{\text{moles Na}}}\right) = 0.200 \text{ mole NaCl}$

          $\text{Grams NaCl} = (0.200 \ \cancel{\text{mole}})\left(\frac{58.5 \text{ g}}{1 \ \cancel{\text{mole}}}\right) = 11.7 \text{ g}$

    (c) $\text{Moles Cl}_2 = (0.200 \ \cancel{\text{mole Na}})\left(\frac{1 \text{ mole Cl}_2}{2 \ \cancel{\text{mole Na}}}\right) = 0.100 \text{ Cl}_2$

          $\text{Grams Cl}_2 = (0.100 \ \cancel{\text{mole}})\left(\frac{71.0 \text{ g}}{1 \ \cancel{\text{mole}}}\right) = 7.10 \text{ g}$

3. (a) $NH_4NO_3 \rightarrow N_2O + 2H_2O$
            ?grams   2.2g   ?grams

    (b) $\text{Moles N}_2\text{O} = 2.2 \ \cancel{\text{g N}_2\text{O}} \times \frac{1 \text{ mole N}_2\text{O}}{44.0 \ \cancel{\text{g N}_2\text{O}}} = 0.050 \text{ mole N}_2\text{O}$

          $\text{Moles NH}_4\text{NO}_3 = 0.050 \ \cancel{\text{mole N}_2\text{O}} \times \frac{1 \text{ mole NH}_4\text{NO}_3}{1 \ \cancel{\text{mole N}_2\text{O}}}$

          $= 0.050 \text{ mole NH}_4\text{NO}_3$

          $\text{Grams NH}_4\text{NO}_3 = 0.050 \ \cancel{\text{mole NH}_4\text{NO}_3} \times \frac{8\bar{0} \text{ g NH}_4\text{NO}_3}{1 \ \cancel{\text{mole NH}_4\text{NO}_3}}$

          $= 4.0 \text{ g NH}_4\text{NO}_3$

    (c) $\text{Moles H}_2\text{O} = 0.050 \ \cancel{\text{mole N}_2\text{O}} \times \frac{2 \text{ moles H}_2\text{O}}{1 \ \cancel{\text{mole N}_2\text{O}}} = 0.10 \text{ mole H}_2\text{O}$

$$\text{Grams } H_2O \ = 0.10 \text{ mole } H_2O \times \frac{18.0 \text{ g } H_2O}{1 \text{ mole } H_2O} = 1.8 \text{ g } H_2O$$

4. (a) $H_3PO_4 + 3LiOH \rightarrow Li_3PO_4 + 3H_2O$

        ?g   168g   ?g   ?g

   (b) $\text{Moles LiOH} = 168.0 \text{ g} \times \frac{1 \text{ mole}}{23.9 \text{ g}} = 7.03 \text{ moles LiOH}$

   $$\text{Moles } Li_3PO_4 = 7.03 \text{ moles LiOH} \times \frac{1 \text{ mole } Li_3PO_4}{3 \text{ moles LiOH}} = 2.34 \text{ moles } Li_3PO_4$$

   $$\text{Grams } Li_3PO_4 = 2.34 \text{ moles} \times \frac{115.7 \text{ g}}{\text{mole}} = 271 \text{ g } Li_3PO_4$$

   (c) $\text{Moles } H_3PO_4 = 7.03 \text{ moles LiOH} \times \frac{1 \text{ mole } H_3PO_4}{3 \text{ moles LiOH}} = 2.34 \text{ moles } H_3PO_4$

   $$\text{Grams } H_3PO_4 = 2.34 \text{ moles} \times \frac{98.0 \text{ g}}{\text{mole}} = 229 \text{ g } H_3PO_4$$

   $$\text{Moles } H_2O = 7.03 \text{ moles LiOH} \times \frac{3 \text{ moles } H_2O}{3 \text{ moles LiOH}} = 7.03 \text{ moles } H_2O$$

   $$\text{Grams } H_2O = 7.03 \text{ moles} \times \frac{18.0 \text{ g}}{\text{mole}} = 127 \text{ g } H_2O$$

5. (a) $C_7H_8 + 3HNO_3 \rightarrow C_7H_5N_3O_6 + 3H_2O$

       ?grams   1000g   ?g

   $$\text{Moles TNT} = 1,\overline{0}00 \text{ g TNT} \times \frac{1 \text{ mole TNT}}{227.0 \text{ g TNT}} = 4.41 \text{ moles TNT}$$

   (b) $\text{Moles } C_7H_8 = 4.41 \text{ moles TNT} \times \frac{1 \text{ mole } C_7H_8}{1 \text{ mole TNT}} = 4.41 \text{ moles } C_7H_8$

   $$\text{Grams } C_7H_8 = 4.41 \text{ moles } C_7H_8 \times \frac{92.0 \text{ g } C_7H_8}{1 \text{ mole } C_7H_8} = 405 \text{ g } C_7H_8$$

   $$\text{Moles } HNO_3 = 4.41 \text{ moles TNT} \times \frac{3 \text{ moles } HNO_3}{1 \text{ mole TNT}} = 13.2 \text{ moles } HNO_3$$

$$\text{Grams HNO}_3 = 13.2 \text{ moles HNO}_3 \times \frac{63.0 \text{ g HNO}_3}{1 \text{ mole HNO}_3} = 832 \text{ g HNO}_3$$

(c) $$\text{Moles H}_2\text{O} = 4.41 \text{ moles TNT} \times \frac{3 \text{ moles H}_2\text{O}}{1 \text{ mole TNT}} = 13.2 \text{ moles H}_2\text{O}$$

$$\text{Grams H}_2\text{O} = 13.2 \text{ moles H}_2\text{O} \times \frac{18.0 \text{ g H}_2\text{O}}{1 \text{ mole H}_2\text{O}} = 238 \text{ g H}_2\text{O}$$

6. (a) $$3\text{Ca(OH)}_2 + 2\text{H}_3\text{PO}_4 \rightarrow \text{Ca}_3(\text{PO}_4)_2 + 6\text{H}_2\text{O}$$
   148g   ?g   ?g   ?g

(b) $$\text{Moles Ca(OH)}_2 = 148 \text{ g} \times \frac{1 \text{ mole}}{74.1 \text{ g}} = 2.00 \text{ moles Ca(OH)}_2$$

$$\text{Moles Ca}_3(\text{PO}_4)_2 = 2.00 \text{ moles Ca(OH)}_2 \times \frac{1 \text{ mole Ca}_3(\text{PO}_4)_2}{3 \text{ moles Ca(OH)}_2}$$

$$= 0.667 \text{ mole Ca}_3(\text{PO}_4)_2$$

$$\text{Grams Ca}_3(\text{PO}_4)_2 = 0.667 \text{ mole} \times \frac{310.3 \text{ g}}{\text{mole}} = 207 \text{ g Ca}_3(\text{PO}_4)_2$$

(c) $$\text{Moles H}_3\text{PO}_4 = 2.00 \text{ moles Ca(OH)}_2 \times \frac{2 \text{ moles H}_3\text{PO}_4}{3 \text{ moles Ca(OH)}_2}$$

$$= 1.33 \text{ moles H}_3\text{PO}_4$$

$$\text{Grams H}_3\text{PO}_4 = 1.33 \text{ moles} \times \frac{98.0 \text{ g}}{\text{mole}} = 130 \text{ g H}_3\text{PO}_4$$

$$\text{Moles H}_2\text{O} = 2.00 \text{ moles Ca(OH)}_2 \times \frac{6 \text{ moles H}_2\text{O}}{3 \text{ moles Ca(OH)}_2} = 4.00 \text{ moles H}_2\text{O}$$

$$\text{Grams H}_2\text{O} = 4.00 \text{ moles} \times \frac{18.0 \text{ g}}{\text{mole}} = 72.0 \text{ g H}_2\text{O}$$

7. (a) $$2\text{NH}_4\text{Cl} + \text{H}_2\text{SO}_4 \rightarrow (\text{NH}_4)_2\text{SO}_4 + 2\text{HCl}$$
   15.9g   ?g   ?g   ?g

(b) $$\text{Moles NH}_4\text{Cl} = 15.9 \text{ g NH}_4\text{Cl} \times \frac{1 \text{ mole NH}_4\text{Cl}}{53.5 \text{ g NH}_4\text{Cl}} = 0.297 \text{ mole NH}_4\text{Cl}$$

$$\text{Moles } H_2SO_4 = 0.297 \text{ mole NH}_4\text{Cl} \times \frac{1 \text{ mole } H_2SO_4}{2 \text{ moles NH}_4\text{Cl}} = 0.149 \text{ mole } H_2SO_4$$

$$\text{Grams } H_2SO_4 = 0.149 \text{ mole } H_2SO_4 \times \frac{98.1 \text{ g } H_2SO_4}{1 \text{ mole } H_2SO_4} = 14.6 \text{ g } H_2SO_4$$

(c) $\text{Moles } (NH_4)_2SO_4 = 0.297 \text{ mole NH}_4\text{Cl} \times \dfrac{1 \text{ mole } (NH_4)_2SO_4}{2 \text{ moles NH}_4\text{Cl}}$

$$= 0.149 \text{ mole } (NH_4)_2SO_4$$

$\text{Grams } (NH_4)_2SO_4 = 0.149 \text{ mole } (NH_4)_2SO_4 \times \dfrac{132.1 \text{ g } (NH_4)_2SO_4}{1 \text{ mole } (NH_4)_2SO_4}$

$$= 19.7 \text{ g } (NH_4)_2SO_4$$

$$\text{Moles HCl} = 0.297 \text{ mole NH}_4\text{Cl} \times \frac{2 \text{ moles HCl}}{2 \text{ moles NH}_4\text{Cl}} = 0.297 \text{ mole HCl}$$

$$\text{Grams HCl} = 0.297 \text{ mole HCl} \times \frac{36.5 \text{ g HCl}}{1 \text{ mole HCl}} = 10.8$$

8. (a) $3BaCl_2 + 2K_3PO_4 \rightarrow Ba_3(PO_4)_2 + 2KCl$
        0.208g   ?g   ?g   ?g

(b) $\text{Moles BaCl}_2 = 0.208 \text{ g} \times \dfrac{1 \text{ mole}}{208.3 \text{ g}} = 0.000999 \text{ mole BaCl}_2$

$$\text{Moles KCl} = 0.000999 \text{ mole BaCl}_2 \times \frac{2 \text{ moles KCl}}{3 \text{ mole BaCl}_2} = 0.000666 \text{ mole KCl}$$

$$\text{Grams KCl} = 0.000666 \text{ mole} \times \frac{74.6 \text{ g}}{\text{mole}} = 0.497 \text{ g KCl}$$

(c) $\text{Moles K}_3PO_4 = 0.000999 \text{ mole BaCl}_2 \times \dfrac{2 \text{ moles K}_3PO_4}{3 \text{ moles BaCl}_2}$

$$= 0.000666 \text{ mole K}_3PO_4$$

$$\text{Grams K}_3PO_4 = 0.000666 \text{ mole} \times \frac{212.3 \text{ g}}{\text{mole}} = 0.141 \text{ g K}_3PO_4$$

$$\text{Moles Ba}_3(PO_4)_2 = 0.000999 \text{ mole BaCl}_2 \times \frac{1 \text{ mole Ba}_3(PO_4)_2}{3 \text{ moles BaCl}_2}$$

$$= 0.000333 \text{ mole } Ba_3(PO_4)_2$$

$$\text{Grams } Ba_3(PO_4)_2 = 0.000333 \cancel{\text{ mole }} \times \frac{601.9 \text{ g}}{\cancel{\text{mole}}} = 0.200 \text{ g } Ba_3(PO_4)_2$$

9. Grams of sample before heating = 5.00 g
    Grams of sample after heating = 4.00 g
    Grams of O_2 evolved = 1.00 g

$$2KClO_3 \rightarrow 2KCl + 3O_2$$
$$?g 1.00g$$

$$\text{Moles } O_2 = 1.00 \cancel{\text{ g } O_2} \times \frac{1 \text{ mole } O_2}{32.0 \cancel{\text{ g } O_2}} = 0.0313 \text{ mole } O_2$$

$$\text{Moles } KClO_3 = 0.0313 \cancel{\text{ mole } O_2} \times \frac{2 \text{ moles } KClO_3}{3 \cancel{\text{ moles } O_2}} = 0.0209 \text{ mole } KClO_3$$

$$\text{Grams } KClO_3 = 0.0209 \cancel{\text{ mole } KClO_3} \times \frac{122.6 \text{ g } KClO_3}{1 \cancel{\text{ mole } KClO_3}} = 2.56 \text{ g } KClO_3$$

$$\text{Percent } KClO_3 = \frac{2.56 \cancel{\text{ g }} KClO_3}{5.00 \cancel{\text{ g }} \text{ sample}} \times 100 = 51.2\%$$

10. Grams of sample before heating   = 10.00 g
    Grams of sample after heating   = 8.00 g
    Grams of oxygen lost   = 2.00 g

$$2NaClO_3 \rightarrow 2NaCl + 3O_2$$
$$?g 2.00g$$

$$\text{Moles } O_2 = 2.0 \cancel{\text{ g } O_2} \times \frac{1 \text{ mole}}{32.0 \cancel{\text{ g } O_2}} = 0.0625 \text{ mole } O_2$$

$$\text{Moles } NaClO_3 = 0.0625 \cancel{\text{ mole } O_2} \times \frac{2 \text{ moles } NaClO_3}{3 \cancel{\text{ moles } O_2}} = 0.0417 \text{ mole } NaClO_3$$

$$\text{Grams } NaClO_3 = 0.0417 \cancel{\text{ mole }} \times \frac{106.5 \text{ g}}{\cancel{\text{mole}}} = 4.44 \text{ g } NaClO_3$$

$$\text{Percent NaClO}_3 = \frac{4.44 \text{ g}}{10.00 \text{ g sample}} \times 100 = 44.4\%$$

11. (a) $3\text{BaO}_2 + 2\text{H}_3\text{PO}_4 \rightarrow 3\text{H}_2\text{O}_2 + \text{Ba}_3(\text{PO}_4)_2$

      338g   ?grams   ?grams   ?grams

(b) $\text{Moles BaO}_2 = 338 \text{ g BaO}_2 \times \dfrac{1 \text{ mole BaO}_2}{169.3 \text{ g BaO}_2} = 2.00 \text{ moles BaO}_2$

$\text{Moles H}_2\text{O}_2 = 2.00 \text{ moles BaO}_2 \times \dfrac{3 \text{ moles H}_2\text{O}_2}{3 \text{ moles BaO}_2} = 2.00 \text{ moles H}_2\text{O}_2$

$\text{Grams H}_2\text{O}_2 = 2.00 \text{ moles H}_2\text{O}_2 \times \dfrac{34.0 \text{ g H}_2\text{O}_2}{1 \text{ mole H}_2\text{O}_2} = 68.0 \text{ g H}_2\text{O}_2$

(c) $\text{Moles H}_3\text{PO}_4 = 2.00 \text{ moles BaO}_2 \times \dfrac{2 \text{ moles H}_3\text{PO}_4}{3 \text{ moles BaO}_2} = 1.33 \text{ moles H}_3\text{PO}_4$

$\text{Grams H}_3\text{PO}_4 = 1.33 \text{ moles H}_3\text{PO}_4 \times \dfrac{98.0 \text{ g H}_3\text{PO}_4}{1 \text{ mole H}_3\text{PO}_4} = 13\overline{0} \text{ g H}_3\text{PO}_4$

12. (a) $\text{Pb} + \text{I}_2 \rightarrow \text{PbI}_2$

      ?g ?g 1.38g

(b) $\text{Moles PbI}_2 = 1.38 \text{ g} \times \dfrac{1 \text{ mole}}{461.0 \text{ g}} = 0.00299 \text{ mole PbI}_2$

$\text{Moles Pb} = 0.00299 \text{ mole PbI}_2 \times \dfrac{1 \text{ mole Pb}}{1 \text{ mole PbI}_2} = 0.00299 \text{ mole Pb}$

$\text{Grams Pb} = 0.00299 \text{ mole} \times \dfrac{207.2 \text{ g}}{\text{mole}} = 0.620 \text{ g Pb}$

$\text{Moles I}_2 = 0.00299 \text{ mole PbI}_2 \times \dfrac{1 \text{ mole I}_2}{1 \text{ mole PbI}_2} = 0.00299 \text{ mole I}_2$

$\text{Grams I}_2 = 0.00299 \text{ mole} \times \dfrac{253.8 \text{ g}}{\text{mole}} = 0.759 \text{ g I}_2$

13. $\text{Mg} + \text{H}_2\text{SO}_4 \rightarrow \text{MgSO}_4 + \text{H}_2$

Grams Mg used = $2\overline{0}0$ g at start – 56 g left = 144 g Mg

Moles Mg used = 144 $\cancel{\text{g Mg}}$ × $\dfrac{1 \text{ mole Mg}}{24.3 \cancel{\text{ g Mg}}}$ = 5.93 moles Mg

Moles H_2 produced = 5.93 $\cancel{\text{moles Mg}}$ × $\dfrac{1 \text{ mole } H_2}{1 \cancel{\text{ mole Mg}}}$ = 5.93 moles H_2

Grams H_2 produced = 5.93 $\cancel{\text{moles } H_2}$ × $\dfrac{2.0 \text{ g } H_2}{1 \cancel{\text{ mole } H_2}}$ = 11.9 g H_2

14. $Mg + 2HCl \rightarrow MgCl_2 + H_2$

Start of reaction   = 216.8 g HCl and 100.0 g Mg
After reaction   = 28.00 g Mg remain
Grams of Mg used   = 72.0 g Mg

Moles Mg = 72.0 $\cancel{\text{g}}$ × $\dfrac{1 \text{ mole}}{24.3 \cancel{\text{ g}}}$ = 2.96 moles Mg

Moles H_2 = 2.96 $\cancel{\text{moles Mg}}$ × $\dfrac{1 \text{ mole } H_2}{1 \cancel{\text{ mole Mg}}}$ = 2.96 moles H_2

Grams H_2 = 2.96 $\cancel{\text{moles}}$ × $\dfrac{2.0 \text{ g}}{\cancel{\text{mole}}}$ = 5.92 g H_2 produced

15. $2C_2H_6 + 7O_2 \rightarrow 4CO_2 + 6H_2O$
        90.0 g   ?grams

Moles C_2H_6 = 90.0 $\cancel{\text{g } C_2H_6}$ × $\dfrac{1 \text{ mole } C_2H_6}{30.0 \cancel{\text{ g } C_2H_6}}$ = 3.00 moles C_2H_6

Moles O_2 = 3.00 $\cancel{\text{moles } C_2H_6}$ × $\dfrac{7 \text{ moles } O_2}{2 \cancel{\text{ moles } C_2H_6}}$ = 10.5 moles O_2

Grams O_2 = 10.5 $\cancel{\text{moles } O_2}$ × $\dfrac{32.0 \text{ g } O_2}{1 \cancel{\text{ mole } O_2}}$ = 336 g O_2

Grams air = 336 $\cancel{\text{g } O_2}$ × $\dfrac{1 \text{ g air}}{0.230 \cancel{\text{ g } O_2}}$ = 1,460 g

16. $CH_4 + 2O_2 \rightarrow CO_2 + 2H_2O$

Moles CH_4 = 64.0 $\cancel{\text{g}}$ × $\dfrac{1 \text{ mole}}{16.0 \cancel{\text{ g}}}$ = 4.00 moles CH_4

$$\text{Moles } O_2 = 4.00 \text{ moles CH}_4 \times \frac{2 \text{ moles } O_2}{1 \text{ mole CH}_4} = 8.00 \text{ moles } O_2$$

$$\text{Grams } O_2 = 8.00 \text{ moles} \times \frac{32.0 \text{ g}}{\text{mole}} = 256 \text{ g } O_2$$

$$\text{Grams air} = 256 \text{ g } O_2 \times \frac{100 \text{ g air}}{23.0 \text{ g } O_2} = \begin{array}{l} 1{,}113 \text{ g air or } 1{,}\overline{1}00 \text{ g air to 3 significant} \\ \text{figures} \end{array}$$

17. (a) $2C_4H_{10} + 13O_2 \rightarrow 8CO_2 + 10H_2O$
     23.2g   ?grams   ?grams ?grams

    (b) $\text{Moles C}_4H_{10} = 23.2 \text{ g C}_4H_{10} \times \dfrac{1 \text{ mole C}_4H_{10}}{58.0 \text{ g C}_4H_{10}} = 0.400 \text{ mole C}_4H_{10}$

    $$\text{Moles } O_2 = 0.400 \text{ moles C}_4H_{10} \times \frac{13 \text{ moles } O_2}{2 \text{ moles C}_4H_{10}} = 2.60 \text{ moles } O_2$$

    $$\text{Grams } O_2 = 2.60 \text{ moles } O_2 \times \frac{32.0 \text{ g } O_2}{1 \text{ mole } O_2} = 83.2 \text{ g } O_2$$

    (c) $\text{Moles CO}_2 = 0.400 \text{ mole C}_4H_{10} \times \dfrac{8 \text{ moles CO}_2}{2 \text{ moles C}_4H_{10}} = 1.60 \text{ moles CO}_2$

    $$\text{Grams CO}_2 = 1.60 \text{ moles CO}_2 \times \frac{44.0 \text{ g CO}_2}{1 \text{ mole CO}_2} = 70.4 \text{ g CO}_2$$

    $$\text{Moles H}_2O = 0.400 \text{ mole C}_4H_{10} \times \frac{10 \text{ moles H}_2O}{2 \text{ moles C}_4H_{10}} = 2.00 \text{ moles H}_2O$$

    $$\text{Grams H}_2O = 2.00 \text{ moles H}_2O \times \frac{18.0 \text{ g H}_2O}{1 \text{ mole H}_2O} = 36.0 \text{ g H}_2O$$

18. (a) $2C_2H_6 + 7O_2 \rightarrow 4CO_2 + 6H_2O$
     $18\overline{0}$g   ?g   ?g   ?g

    (b) $\text{Moles C}_2H_6 = 18\overline{0} \text{ g} \times \dfrac{1 \text{ mole}}{30.0 \text{ g}} = 6.00 \text{ moles C}_2H_6$

    $$\text{Moles } O_2 = 6.00 \text{ moles C}_2H_6 \times \frac{7 \text{ moles } O_2}{2 \text{ moles C}_2H_6} = 21.0 \text{ moles } O_2$$

$$\text{Grams O}_2 = 21.0 \text{ moles} \times \frac{32.0 \text{ g}}{\text{mole}} = 672 \text{ g O}_2$$

(c) $$\text{Moles CO}_2 = 6.00 \text{ moles C}_2\text{H}_6 \times \frac{2 \text{ moles CO}_2}{1 \text{ mole C}_2\text{H}_6} = 12.0 \text{ moles CO}_2$$

$$\text{Grams CO}_2 = 12.0 \text{ moles} \times \frac{44.0 \text{ g}}{\text{mole}} = 528 \text{ g CO}_2$$

$$\text{Moles H}_2\text{O} = 6.00 \text{ moles C}_2\text{H}_6 \times \frac{3 \text{ moles H}_2\text{O}}{1 \text{ mole C}_2\text{H}_6} = 18.0 \text{ moles H}_2\text{O}$$

$$\text{Grams H}_2\text{O} = 18.0 \text{ moles} \times \frac{18.0 \text{ g}}{\text{mole}} = 324 \text{ g H}_2\text{O}$$

19. $3\text{O}_2 \rightarrow 2\text{O}_3$
       64.0g   ?g

$$\text{Moles O}_2 = 64.0 \text{ g O}_2 \times \frac{1 \text{ mole O}_2}{32.0 \text{ g O}_2} = 2.00 \text{ moles O}_2$$

$$\text{Moles O}_3 = 2.00 \text{ moles O}_2 \times \frac{2 \text{ moles O}_3}{3 \text{ moles O}_2} = 1.33 \text{ moles O}_3$$

$$\text{Grams O}_3 = 1.33 \text{ moles O}_3 \times \frac{48.0 \text{ g O}_3}{1 \text{ mole O}_3} = 64.0 \text{ g O}_3$$

20. $3\text{O}_2 \rightarrow 2\text{O}_3$
        ?g   0.048g

$$\text{Moles O}_3 = 0.048 \text{ g} \times \frac{1 \text{ mole}}{48.0 \text{ g}} = 0.0010 \text{ mole O}_3$$

$$\text{Moles O}_2 = 0.0010 \text{ mole O}_3 \times \frac{3 \text{ moles O}_2}{2 \text{ moles O}_3} = 0.0015 \text{ mole O}_2$$

$$\text{Grams O}_2 = 0.0015 \text{ mole} \times \frac{32.0 \text{ g}}{1 \text{ mole}} = 0.048 \text{ g O}_2$$

21.   (a) $2\text{Al(OH)}_3 + 3\text{H}_2\text{SO}_4 \rightarrow \text{Al}_2(\text{SO}_4)_3 + 6\text{H}_2\text{O}$
              ?grams   ?grams   500g   ? grams

$$\text{Moles Al}_2(\text{SO}_4)_3 \;=\; 5\overline{0}0 \text{ g } \cancel{\text{Al}_2(\text{SO}_4)_3} \times \frac{1 \text{ mole Al}_2(\text{SO}_4)_3}{342.3 \text{ g } \cancel{\text{Al}_2(\text{SO}_4)_3}}$$

$$= 1.46 \text{ moles Al}_2(\text{SO}_4)_3$$

$$\text{Moles Al(OH)}_3 \;=\; 1.46 \cancel{\text{ moles Al}_2(\text{SO}_4)_3} \times \frac{2 \text{ moles Al(OH)}_3}{1 \cancel{\text{ mole Al}_2(\text{SO}_4)_3}}$$

$$= 2.92 \text{ moles Al(OH)}_3$$

$$\text{Grams Al(OH)}_3 \;=\; 2.92 \cancel{\text{ moles Al(OH)}_3} \times \frac{78.0 \text{ g Al(OH)}_3}{1 \cancel{\text{ mole Al(OH)}_3}}$$

$$= 228 \text{ g Al(OH)}_3$$

(b) $$\text{Moles H}_2\text{SO}_4 \;=\; 1.46 \cancel{\text{ moles Al}_2(\text{SO}_4)_3} \times \frac{3 \text{ moles H}_2\text{SO}_4}{1 \cancel{\text{ mole Al}_2(\text{SO}_4)_3}}$$

$$= 4.38 \text{ moles H}_2\text{SO}_4$$

$$\text{Grams H}_2\text{SO}_4 \;=\; 4.38 \cancel{\text{ moles H}_2\text{SO}_4} \times \frac{98.1 \text{ g H}_2\text{SO}_4}{1 \cancel{\text{ mole H}_2\text{SO}_4}}$$

$$= 430 \text{ g H}_2\text{SO}_4$$

(c) $$\text{Moles H}_2\text{O} \;=\; 1.46 \cancel{\text{ moles Al}_2(\text{SO}_4)_3} \times \frac{6 \text{ moles H}_2\text{O}}{1 \cancel{\text{ mole Al}_2(\text{SO}_4)_3}}$$

$$= 8.76 \text{ moles H}_2\text{O}$$

$$\text{Grams H}_2\text{O} = 8.76 \cancel{\text{ moles H}_2\text{O}} \times \frac{18.0 \text{ g H}_2\text{O}}{1 \cancel{\text{ mole H}_2\text{O}}} = 158 \text{ g H}_2\text{O}$$

22. (a) $\text{Zn} + \text{S} \rightarrow \text{ZnS}$
    ?g ?g 2.44g

(b) $$\text{Moles ZnS} = 2.44 \text{ g} \times \frac{1 \text{ mole}}{97.5 \text{ g}} = 0.0250 \text{ mole ZnS}$$

$$\text{Moles Zn} = 0.0250 \cancel{\text{ mole ZnS}} \times \frac{1 \text{ mole Zn}}{1 \cancel{\text{ mole ZnS}}} = 0.0250 \text{ mole Zn}$$

$$\text{Grams Zn} = 0.0250 \cancel{\text{ mole}} \times \frac{65.4 \text{ g}}{\cancel{\text{mole}}} = 1.64 \text{ g Zn}$$

$$\text{Moles S} = 0.0250 \; \cancel{\text{mole ZnS}} \times \frac{1 \text{ mole S}}{1 \; \cancel{\text{mole ZnS}}} = 0.0250 \text{ mole S}$$

$$\text{Grams S} = 0.0250 \; \cancel{\text{mole}} \times \frac{32.1 \text{ g}}{\cancel{\text{mole}}} = 0.803 \text{ g S}$$

23. (a) $Fe_2O_3 + 3CO \rightarrow 2Fe + 3CO_2$

        ?g   ?g   454.0g   ?g

    (b) $$\text{Moles Fe} = 454.0 \; \cancel{\text{g Fe}} \times \frac{1 \text{ mole Fe}}{55.8 \; \cancel{\text{g Fe}}} = 8.14 \text{ moles Fe}$$

    $$\text{Moles Fe}_2\text{O}_3 = 8.14 \; \cancel{\text{moles Fe}} \times \frac{1 \text{ mole Fe}_2\text{O}_3}{2 \; \cancel{\text{moles Fe}}} = 4.07 \text{ moles Fe}_2\text{O}_3$$

    $$\text{Grams Fe}_2\text{O}_3 = 4.07 \; \cancel{\text{moles Fe}_2\text{O}_3} \times \frac{159.6 \text{ g Fe}_2\text{O}_3}{1 \; \cancel{\text{mole Fe}_2\text{O}_3}} = 65\bar{0} \text{ g Fe}_2\text{O}_3$$

    (c) $$\text{Moles CO} = 8.14 \; \cancel{\text{moles Fe}} \times \frac{3 \text{ moles CO}}{2 \; \cancel{\text{moles Fe}}} = 12.2 \text{ moles CO}$$

    $$\text{Grams CO} = 12.2 \; \cancel{\text{moles CO}} \times \frac{28.0 \text{ g CO}}{1 \; \cancel{\text{mole CO}}} = 342 \text{ g CO}$$

    $$\text{Moles CO}_2 = 8.14 \; \cancel{\text{moles Fe}} \times \frac{3 \text{ moles CO}_2}{2 \; \cancel{\text{moles Fe}}} = 12.2 \text{ moles CO}_2$$

    $$\text{Grams CO}_2 = 12.2 \; \cancel{\text{moles CO}_2} \times \frac{44.0 \text{ g CO}_2}{1 \; \cancel{\text{mole CO}_2}} = 536 \text{ g CO}_2$$

24. (a) $Cu + 2AgNO_3 \rightarrow Cu(NO_3)_2 + 2Ag$

        ?g   1.70g   ?g   ?g

    (b) $$\text{Moles AgNO}_3 = 1.70 \; \cancel{\text{g}} \times \frac{1 \text{ mole}}{169.9 \; \cancel{\text{g}}} = 0.0100 \text{ mole AgNO}_3$$

    $$\text{Moles Cu} = 0.0100 \; \cancel{\text{mole AgNO}_3} \times \frac{1 \text{ mole Cu}}{2 \; \cancel{\text{moles AgNO}_3}} = 0.00500 \text{ mole Cu}$$

    $$\text{Grams Cu} = 0.00500 \; \cancel{\text{mole}} \times \frac{63.5 \text{ g}}{\cancel{\text{mole}}} = 0.318 \text{ g Cu}$$

(c)   Moles Cu(NO$_3$)$_2$ = 0.0100 ~~mole AgNO$_3$~~ × $\dfrac{\text{1 mole Cu(NO}_3)_2}{\text{2 ~~moles AgNO$_3$~~}}$

= 0.00500 mole Cu(NO$_3$)$_2$

Grams Cu(NO$_3$)$_2$ = 0.00500 ~~mole~~ × $\dfrac{187.5 \text{ g}}{\text{~~mole~~}}$ = 0.938 g Cu(NO$_3$)$_2$

Moles Ag = 0.0100 ~~mole AgNO$_3$~~ × $\dfrac{\text{2 mole Ag}}{\text{2 ~~mole AgNO$_3$~~}}$ = 0.0100 mole Ag

Grams Ag = 0.0100 ~~mole~~ × $\dfrac{107.9 \text{ g}}{\text{~~mole~~}}$ = 1.08 g Ag

25. (a) $4NH_3$ + $5O_2$ $\xrightarrow{\text{Pt}}$ $4NO$ + $6H_2O$
         425 g   ? grams   ? grams   ? grams

(b)   Moles NH$_3$ = 425 ~~g NH$_3$~~ × $\dfrac{\text{1 mole NH}_3}{\text{17.0 g NH}_3}$ = 25.0 moles NH$_3$

Moles O$_2$ = 25.0 ~~moles NH$_3$~~ × $\dfrac{\text{5 moles O}_2}{\text{4 ~~moles NH$_3$~~}}$ = 31.3 moles O$_2$

Grams O$_2$ = 31.3 ~~moles O$_2$~~ × $\dfrac{32.0 \text{ g O}_2}{\text{1 ~~mole O$_2$~~}}$ = $1,\overline{0}00$ g O$_2$

(c)   Moles NO = 25.0 ~~moles NH$_3$~~ × $\dfrac{\text{4 moles NO}}{\text{4 ~~moles NH$_3$~~}}$ = 25.0 moles NO

Grams NO = 25.0 ~~moles NO~~ × $\dfrac{30.0 \text{ g NO}}{\text{1 ~~mole NO~~}}$ – = $75\overline{0}$ g NO

Moles H$_2$O = 25.0 ~~moles NH$_3$~~ × $\dfrac{\text{6 moles H}_2\text{O}}{\text{4 ~~moles NH$_3$~~}}$ = 37.5 moles H$_2$O

Grams H$_2$O = 37.5 ~~moles H$_2$O~~ × $\dfrac{18.0 \text{ g H}_2\text{O}}{\text{1 ~~mole H$_2$O~~}}$ = 675 g H$_2$O

26. (a) $C_6H_{12}O_6$ + $6O_2$ → $6CO_2$ + $6H_2O$
        ?g   3.20g   ?g   ?g

(b)   Moles O$_2$ = 3.20 ~~g~~ × $\dfrac{\text{1 mole}}{\text{32.0 ~~g~~}}$ = 0.100 mole O$_2$

$$\text{Moles } C_6H_{12}O_6 = 0.100 \text{ mole } O_2 \times \frac{1 \text{ mole } C_6H_{12}O_6}{6 \text{ moles } O_2}$$

$$= 0.0167 \text{ mole } C_6H_{12}O_6$$

$$\text{Grams } C_6H_{12}O_6 = 0.0167 \text{ mole } \times \frac{180.0 \text{ g}}{\text{mole}} = 3.01 \text{ g } C_6H_{12}O_6$$

(c) $$\text{Moles } CO_2 = 0.100 \text{ mole } O_2 \times \frac{1 \text{ mole } CO_2}{1 \text{ mole } O_2} = 0.100 \text{ mole } CO_2$$

$$\text{Grams } CO_2 = 0.100 \text{ mole } \times \frac{44.0 \text{ g}}{\text{mole}} = 4.40 \text{ g } CO_2$$

$$\text{Moles } H_2O = 0.100 \text{ mole } O_2 \times \frac{1 \text{ mole } H_2O}{1 \text{ mole } O_2} = 0.100 \text{ mole } H_2O$$

$$\text{Grams } H_2O = 0.100 \text{ mole } \times \frac{18.0 \text{ g}}{\text{mole}} = 1.80 \text{ g } H_2O$$

27. $$Zn + Cu(NO_3)_2 \rightarrow Zn(NO_3) + Cu$$
173 g   5$\overline{0}$0 g   ? g_2

$$\text{Grams Zn reacted} = 3\overline{0}0 \text{ g added} - 127 \text{ g left} = 173 \text{ g Zn}$$

$$\text{Moles Zn reacted} = 173 \text{ g Zn} \times \frac{1 \text{ mole Zn}}{65.4 \text{ g Zn}} = 2.65 \text{ moles Zn}$$

$$\text{Moles } Zn(NO_3)_2 = 2.65 \text{ moles Zn} \times \frac{1 \text{ mole } Zn(NO_3)_2}{1 \text{ mole Zn}} = 2.65 \text{ moles } Zn(NO_3)_2$$

$$\text{Grams } Zn(NO_3)_2 = 2.65 \text{ moles } Zn(NO_3)_2 \times \frac{189.4 \text{ g } Zn(NO_3)_2}{1 \text{ mole } Zn(NO_3)_2} = 502 \text{ g } Zn(NO_3)_2$$

28. (a) $$H_2 + I_2 \rightarrow 2HI$$
?g   ?g   320g

(b) $$\text{Moles HI} = 32\overline{0} \text{ g} \times \frac{1 \text{ mole}}{127.9 \text{ g}} = 2.50 \text{ moles HI}$$

$$\text{Moles } H_2 = 2.50 \text{ moles HI} \times \frac{1 \text{ mole } H_2}{2 \text{ moles HI}} = 1.25 \text{ moles } H_2$$

$$\text{Grams H}_2 = 1.25 \text{ moles} \times \frac{2.00 \text{ g}}{\text{mole}} = 2.50 \text{ g H}_2$$

$$\text{Moles I}_2 = 2.50 \text{ moles HI} \times \frac{1 \text{ mole I}_2}{2 \text{ moles HI}} = 1.25 \text{ moles I}_2$$

$$\text{Grams I}_2 = 1.25 \text{ moles} \times \frac{253.8 \text{ g}}{\text{mole}} = 317.3 \text{ g I}_2 \quad (317 \text{ g to three sig. figures})$$

29. (a) $\quad \text{C}_a\text{C}_2 + 2\text{H}_2\text{O} \rightarrow \text{Ca(OH)}_2 + \text{C}_2\text{H}_2$

        128g   144g   ?grams   ?grams

(b) $\quad \text{Moles CaC}_2 = 128 \text{ g CaC}_2 \times \dfrac{1 \text{ mole CaC}_2}{64.0 \text{ g CaC}_2} = 2.00 \text{ moles CaC}_2$

$$\text{Moles H}_2\text{O} = 144 \text{ g H}_2\text{O} \times \frac{1 \text{ mole H}_2\text{O}}{18.0 \text{ g H}_2\text{O}} = 8.00 \text{ moles H}_2\text{O}$$

$$\text{Moles H}_2\text{O used} = 2.00 \text{ moles CaC}_2 \times \frac{2 \text{ moles H}_2\text{O}}{1 \text{ mole CaC}_2} = 4.00 \text{ moles H}_2\text{O}$$

H_2O is in excess and CaC_2 is the limiting reagent.

$$\text{Moles Ca(OH)}_2 = 2.00 \text{ moles CaC}_2 \times \frac{1 \text{ mole Ca(OH)}_2}{1 \text{ mole CaC}_2}$$

$$= 2.00 \text{ moles Ca(OH)}_2$$

$$\text{Grams Ca(OH)}_2 = 2.00 \text{ moles Ca(OH)}_2 \times \frac{74.1 \text{ g Ca(OH)}_2}{1 \text{ mole Ca(OH)}_2}$$

$$= 148 \text{ g Ca(OH)}_2$$

$$\text{Moles C}_2\text{H}_2 = 2.00 \text{ moles C}_2\text{H}_2 \times \frac{1 \text{ mole Ca(OH)}_2}{1 \text{ mole C}_2\text{H}_2} = 2.00 \text{ moles C}_2\text{H}_2$$

$$\text{Grams C}_2\text{H}_2 = 2.00 \text{ moles C}_2\text{H}_2 \times \frac{26.0 \text{ g C}_2\text{H}_2}{1 \text{ mole C}_2\text{H}_2} = 52.0 \text{ g C}_2\text{H}_2$$

30. (a) $\quad 4\text{NH}_3 + 5\text{O}_2 \rightarrow 4\text{NO} + 6\text{H}_2\text{O}$

        102.0g   320.0g   ?g   ?g

(b) Moles NH_3 = (102.0 g)$\left(\dfrac{1 \text{ mole}}{17.0 \text{ g}}\right)$ = 6.00 moles

Moles O_2 = (320.0 g)$\left(\dfrac{1 \text{ mole}}{32.0 \text{ g}}\right)$ = 10.00 moles

The moles of NH_3 are limiting. Therefore, use the moles of NH_3 to calculate the moles of NO and H_2O that form.

Moles NO = (6.00 moles NH_3)$\left(\dfrac{4 \text{ moles NO}}{4 \text{ moles } NH_3}\right)$ = 6.00 moles NO

Grams NO = (6.00 moles)$\left(\dfrac{30.0 \text{ g}}{1 \text{ mole}}\right)$ = 18$\bar{0}$ g

Moles H_2O = (6.00 moles NH_3)$\left(\dfrac{6 \text{ moles } H_2O}{4 \text{ moles } NH_3}\right)$ = 9.00 moles H_2O

Grams H_2O = (9.00 moles)$\left(\dfrac{18.0 \text{ g}}{1 \text{ mole}}\right)$ = 162 g

31. (a) $Fe_2O_3 + 3CO \rightarrow 2Fe + 3CO_2$
399.8g   168.0g   ?g   ?g

(b) Moles Fe_2O_3 = (399.8 g)$\left(\dfrac{1 \text{ mole}}{159.6 \text{ g}}\right)$ = 2.505 moles

Moles CO = (168.0 g)$\left(\dfrac{1 \text{ mole}}{28.0 \text{ g}}\right)$ = 6.00 moles

The moles of CO are limiting. Therefore, use the moles of CO to calculate the moles of Fe and CO_2 that form.

Moles Fe = (6.00 moles CO)$\left(\dfrac{2 \text{ moles Fe}}{3 \text{ moles CO}}\right)$ = 4.00 moles Fe

Grams Fe = (4.00 moles)$\left(\dfrac{55.8 \text{ g}}{1 \text{ mole}}\right)$ = 223 g

Moles CO_2 = (6.00 moles CO)$\left(\dfrac{3 \text{ moles } CO_2}{3 \text{ moles CO}}\right)$ = 6.00 moles CO_2

Grams CO_2 = (6.00 moles CO_2)$\left(\dfrac{44.0 \text{ g}}{1 \text{ mole}}\right)$ = 264 g

32. (a) $N_2 + 3H_2 \rightarrow 2NH_3$
         0.014 g   0.020g   ?g

$$\text{Moles } N_2 = 0.014 \text{ g} \times \frac{1 \text{ mole}}{28 \text{ g}} = 0.00050 \text{ mole } N_2$$

$$\text{Moles } H_2 = 0.020 \text{ g} \times \frac{1 \text{ mole}}{2.0 \text{ g}} = 0.010 \text{ mole } H_2$$

The N_2 is limiting. Therefore, we use the moles of N_2 to caclulate the moles of NH_3 that form.

$$\text{Moles } NH_3 = 0.00050 \text{ mole } N_2 \times \frac{2 \text{ moles } NH_3}{1 \text{ mole } N_2} = 0.0010 \text{ mole } NH_3$$

$$\text{Grams } NH_3 = 0.0010 \text{ mole} \times \frac{17.0 \text{ g}}{\text{mole}} = 0.017 \text{ g } NH_3$$

33. (a) $2H_2 + O_2 \rightarrow 2H_2O$
         $10\overline{\text{g}}$ 64g   ?grams

(b) $\text{Moles } H_2 = 10\overline{\text{g}} \, H_2 \times \dfrac{1 \text{ mole } H_2}{2.0 \text{ g } H_2} = 5.0 \text{ moles } H_2$

$$\text{Moles } O_2 = 64 \text{ g } O_2 \times \frac{1 \text{ mole } O_2}{32.0 \text{ g } O_2} = 2.0 \text{ moles } O_2$$

Find the limiting reactant. Assume that all H_2 is used.

$$\text{Moles } O_2 \text{ needed} = 5.0 \text{ moles } H_2 \times \frac{1 \text{ mole } O_2}{2 \text{ moles } H_2} = 2.5 \text{ moles } O_2$$

Since 2.5 moles O_2 would be needed and we have just 2.0 moles O_2, the O_2 is the limiting reactant.

$$\text{Moles } H_2O \text{ formed} = 2.0 \text{ moles } O_2 \times \frac{2 \text{ moles } H_2O}{1 \text{ mole } O_2} = 4.0 \text{ moles } H_2O$$

$$\text{Grams } H_2O = 4.0 \text{ moles } H_2O \times \frac{18.0 \text{ g } H_2O}{1 \text{ mole } H_2O} = 72 \text{ g } H_2O$$

34. $C_3H_8 + 5O_2 \rightarrow 3CO_2 + 4H_2O$
    11.0g   32g   ?g   ?g

Moles $C_3H_8 = 11.0 \text{ g} \times \dfrac{1 \text{ mole}}{44.0 \text{ g}} = 0.250$ mole C_3H_8

Moles $O_2 = 32 \text{ g} \times \dfrac{1 \text{ mole}}{32.0 \text{ g}} = 1.0$ mole O_2

The limiting reactant is oxygen. Therefore, we use the moles of oxygen to calculate the moles of CO_2 and H_2O that form.

Moles $CO_2 = 1.0 \text{ mole } O_2 \times \dfrac{3 \text{ moles } CO_2}{5 \text{ moles } O_2} = 0.60$ mole CO_2

Grams $CO_2 = 0.60 \text{ mole} \times \dfrac{44.0 \text{ g}}{\text{mole}} = 26.4$ g CO_2 or 26 g to two sig. figures

Moles $H_2O = 1.0 \text{ mole } O_2 \times \dfrac{4 \text{ moles } H_2O}{5 \text{ moles } O_2} = 0.80$ mole H_2O

Grams $H_2O = 0.80 \text{ mole} \times \dfrac{18.0 \text{ g}}{\text{mole}} = 14.4$ g H_2O or 14 g to two sig. figures

35. (a) $Ca_3P_2 + 6H_2O \rightarrow 2PH_3 + 3Ca(OH)_2$
           515g   216g   ?grams   ?grams

(b)   Moles $Ca_3P_2 = 515 \text{ g } Ca_3P_2 \times \dfrac{1 \text{ mole } Ca_3P_2}{182.3 \text{ g } Ca_3P_2} = 2.83$ moles Ca_3P_2

Moles $H_2O = 216 \text{ g } H_2O \times \dfrac{1 \text{ mole } H_2O}{18.0 \text{ g } H_2O} = 12.0$ moles H_2O

Find the limiting reactant. Assume that all Ca_3P_2 is used.

Moles H_2O needed $= 2.83 \text{ moles } Ca_3P_2 \times \dfrac{6 \text{ moles } H_2O}{1 \text{ mole } Ca_3P_2}$

$= 17.0$ moles H_2O

Since 17.0 moles would be needed and we have just 12.0 moles H_2O, the H_2O is the limiting reactant.

$$\text{Moles PH}_3 \text{ produced} = 12.0 \text{ moles } H_2O \times \frac{2 \text{ moles PH}_3}{6 \text{ moles } H_2O} = 4.00 \text{ moles PH}_3$$

$$\text{Grams PH}_3 = 4.00 \text{ moles PH}_3 \times \frac{34.0 \text{ g PH}_3}{1 \text{ mole PH}_3} = 136 \text{ g PH}_3$$

(c) $$\text{Moles Ca(OH)}_2 \text{ produced} = 12.0 \text{ moles } H_2O \times \frac{3 \text{ moles Ca(OH)}_2}{6 \text{ moles } H_2O}$$

$$= 6.00 \text{ moles Ca(OH)}_2$$

$$\text{Grams Ca(OH)}_2 = 6.00 \text{ moles Ca(OH)}_2 \times \frac{74.1 \text{ g Ca(OH)}_2}{1 \text{ mole Ca(OH)}_2} = 445 \text{ g Ca(OH)}_2$$

36.   (a) $2Al + Fe_2O_3 \rightarrow Al_2O_3 + 2Fe$
      135g $80\overline{0}$g   ?g   ?g

(b) $$\text{Moles Al} = 135 \text{ g} \times \frac{1 \text{ mole}}{27.0 \text{ g}} = 5.00 \text{ moles Al}$$

$$\text{Moles Fe}_2O_3 \text{ is } 8\overline{0}0 \text{ g} \times \frac{1 \text{ mole}}{159.6 \text{ g}} = 5.01 \text{ moles Fe}_2O_3$$

The Al is limiting. Therefore, we use the moles of Al to calculate the moles of Al_2O_3 and Fe that form.

$$\text{Moles Al}_2O_3 = 5.01 \text{ moles Al} \times \frac{1 \text{ mole Al}_2O_3}{2 \text{ moles Al}} = 2.51 \text{ moles Al}_2O_3$$

$$\text{Grams Al}_2O_3 = 2.51 \text{ moles} \times \frac{102.0 \text{ g}}{\text{mole}} = 256 \text{ g Al}_2O_3$$

$$\text{Moles Fe} = 5.01 \text{ moles Al} \times \frac{1 \text{ mole Fe}}{1 \text{ mole Al}} = 5.01 \text{ moles Fe}$$

$$\text{Grams Fe} = 5.01 \text{ moles} \times \frac{55.8 \text{ g}}{\text{mole}} = 28\overline{0} \text{ g Fe}$$

37. (a) $Ca_3(PO_4)_2 + 3SiO_2 + 5C \rightarrow 3CaSiO_3 + 5CO_2 + P_2$

     8.0 moles $2\bar{0}$ moles   45 moles   ? moles   ? moles   ? moles

Find the limiting reactant. Assume that all SiO_2 is used.

$$\text{Moles } Ca_3(PO_4)_2 \text{ needed} = 2\bar{0} \text{ moles } SiO_2 \times \frac{1 \text{ mole } Ca_3(PO_4)_2}{3 \text{ moles } SiO_2}$$

$$= 6.7 \text{ moles } Ca_3(PO_4)_2$$

Since the SiO_2 would be used up, leaving some $Ca_3(PO_4)_2$ and C, our assumption was correct and SiO_2 is the limiting reactant.

$$\text{Moles } CaSiO_3 \text{ formed} = 2\bar{0} \text{ moles } SiO_2 \times \frac{3 \text{ moles } CaSiO_3}{3 \text{ moles } SiO_2}$$

$$= 2\bar{0} \text{ moles } CaSiO_3$$

$$\text{Moles CO formed} = 2\bar{0} \text{ moles } SiO_2 \times \frac{5 \text{ moles CO}}{3 \text{ moles } SiO_2} = 33 \text{ moles CO}$$

$$\text{Moles } P_2 \text{ formed} = 2\bar{0} \text{ moles } SiO_2 \times \frac{1 \text{ mole } P_2}{3 \text{ moles } SiO_2} = 6.7 \text{ moles } P_2$$

38. (a) $2Ba + O_2 \rightarrow 2BaO$

     $10\bar{0}$ g $10\bar{0}$ g   ? g

(b) $$\text{Moles Ba} = 10\bar{0} \text{ g} \times \frac{1 \text{ mole}}{137.3 \text{ g}} = 0.728 \text{ mole Ba}$$

$$\text{Moles } O_2 = 10\bar{0} \text{ g} \times \frac{1 \text{ mole}}{32.0 \text{ g}} = 3.13 \text{ moles } O_2$$

The barium is limiting. Therefore, we use the moles of barium to calculate the moles of barium oxide that form.

$$\text{Moles BaO} = 0.728 \text{ mole Ba} \times \frac{1 \text{ mole BaO}}{1 \text{ mole Ba}} = 0.728 \text{ mole BaO}$$

$$\text{Grams BaO} = 0.728 \text{ mole} \times \frac{153.3 \text{ g}}{\text{mole}} \quad 111.6 \text{ g BaO or 112 g}$$
                                                     (3 significant figures)

39. (a) $3Fe + 4H_2O \rightarrow Fe_3O_4 + 4H_2$
            225g   225g   ?g   ?g

$$\text{Moles Fe} = 225 \text{ g Fe} \times \frac{1 \text{ mole Fe}}{55.8 \text{ g Fe}} = 4.03 \text{ moles Fe}$$

$$\text{Moles H}_2\text{O} = 225 \text{ g H}_2\text{O} \times \frac{1 \text{ mole H}_2\text{O}}{18.0 \text{ g H}_2\text{O}} = 12.5 \text{ moles H}_2\text{O}$$

(b) Find the limiting reactant. Assume that all Fe is used.

$$\text{Moles H}_2\text{O needed} = 4.03 \text{ moles Fe} \times \frac{4 \text{ moles H}_2\text{O}}{3 \text{ moles Fe}} = 5.37 \text{ moles H}_2\text{O}$$

Since only 5.37 moles H_2O are reacted, the limiting reactant is Fe.

$$\text{Moles H}_2 \text{ prepared} = 4.03 \text{ moles Fe} \times \frac{4 \text{ moles H}_2}{3 \text{ moles Fe}} = 5.37 \text{ moles H}_2$$

$$\text{Grams H}_2 = 5.37 \text{ moles H}_2 \times \frac{2.00 \text{ g H}_2}{1 \text{ mole H}_2} = 10.7 \text{ g H}_2$$

(c) $\text{Moles Fe}_3\text{O}_4 = 4.03 \text{ moles Fe} \times \dfrac{1 \text{ mole Fe}_3\text{O}_4}{3 \text{ moles Fe}} = 1.34 \text{ moles Fe}_3\text{O}_4$

$$\text{Grams Fe}_3\text{O}_4 = 1.34 \text{ moles Fe}_3\text{O}_4 \times \frac{231.4 \text{ g Fe}_3\text{O}_4}{1 \text{ mole Fe}_3\text{O}_4} = 31\overline{0} \text{ g Fe}_3\text{O}_4$$

40. (a) $S + O_2 \rightarrow SO_2$
            100.0g 200.0g   ?g

(b) $\text{Moles S} = 100.0 \text{ g} \times \dfrac{1 \text{ mole}}{32.1 \text{ g}} = 3.12 \text{ moles S}$

$$\text{Moles O}_2 = 200.0 \text{ g} \times \frac{1 \text{ mole}}{32.0 \text{ g}} = 6.25 \text{ moles O}_2$$

The S is limiting. Therefore, we use the moles of S to calculate the moles of SO_2 that form.

$$\text{Moles SO}_2 = 3.12 \text{ moles S} \times \frac{1 \text{ mole SO}_2}{1 \text{ mole S}} = 3.12 \text{ moles SO}_2$$

$$\text{Grams SO}_2 = 3.12 \text{ moles} \times \frac{64.1 \text{ g}}{\text{mole}} = 2\overline{0}0 \text{ g SO}_2$$

EXTRA EXERCISES

41. (a) $2K + Cl_2 \rightarrow 2KCl$

   10.0g ?moles ?grams

$$\text{Moles K} = 10.0 \text{ g K} \times \frac{1 \text{ mole K}}{39.1 \text{ g K}} = 0.256 \text{ mole K}$$

$$\text{Moles Cl}_2 = 0.256 \text{ moles K} \times \frac{1 \text{ mole Cl}_2}{2 \text{ moles K}} = 0.128 \text{ mole Cl}_2$$

(b) $\text{Moles KCl} = 0.256 \text{ mole K} \times \frac{2 \text{ moles KCl}}{2 \text{ moles K}} = 0.256 \text{ mole KCl}$

$$\text{Grams KCl} = 0.256 \text{ mole KCl} \times \frac{74.6 \text{ g KCl}}{1 \text{ mole KCl}} = 19.1 \text{ g KCl}$$

42. (a) $2Cu(NO_3)_2 \rightarrow 2CuO + 4NO_2 + O_2$

(b) $\text{Moles Cu(NO}_3)_2 = 1\overline{0}0 \text{ g Cu(NO}_3)_2 \times \frac{1 \text{ mole Cu(NO}_3)_2}{187.5 \text{ g Cu(NO}_3)_2}$

$$= 0.533 \text{ mole Cu(NO}_3)_2$$

$$\text{Moles O}_2 = 0.533 \text{ mole Cu(NO}_3)_2 \times \frac{1 \text{ mole O}_2}{2 \text{ moles Cu(NO}_3)_2} = 0.267 \text{ mole O}_2$$

$$\text{Grams O}_2 = 0.267 \text{ mole O}_2 \times \frac{32.0 \text{ g O}_2}{1 \text{ mole O}_2} = 8.54 \text{ g O}_2$$

(c) $\text{Moles NO}_2 = 54.0 \text{ g NO}_2 \times \frac{1 \text{ mole NO}_2}{46.0 \text{ g NO}_2} = 1.17 \text{ moles NO}_2$

$$\text{Moles Cu(NO}_3)_2 = 1.17 \text{ moles NO}_2 \times \frac{2 \text{ moles Cu(NO}_3)_2}{4 \text{ moles NO}_2}$$

$$= 0.585 \text{ mole Cu(NO}_3)_2$$

$$\text{Grams Cu(NO}_3)_2 = 0.585 \text{ mole Cu(NO}_3)_2 \times \frac{187.5 \text{ g Cu(NO}_3)_2}{1 \text{ mole Cu(NO}_3)_2}$$

Grams $Cu(NO_3)_2$ $= 11\bar{0}$ g $Cu(NO_3)_2$

43. $C + O_2 \rightarrow CO_2$

Moles C $= 100$ ~~g C~~ $\times \dfrac{1 \text{ mole C atoms}}{12.0 \text{ ~~g C~~}} = 8.33$ moles C

Moles $O_2 = 150$ ~~g O$_2$~~ $\times \dfrac{1 \text{ mole } O_2}{32.0 \text{ ~~g O$_2$~~}} = 4.69$ moles O_2

(a) Since 1 mole of each reactant is needed, 4.69 moles O_2 react with 4.69 moles C, and O_2 is the limiting reactant.

(b) Moles CO_2 formed $= 4.69$ ~~moles O$_2$~~ $\times \dfrac{1 \text{ mole } CO_2}{1 \text{ ~~mole O$_2$~~}} = 4.69$ moles CO_2

Grams CO_2 formed $= 4.69$ ~~moles CO$_2$~~ $\times \dfrac{44.0 \text{ g } CO_2}{1 \text{ ~~mole CO$_2$~~}} = 206$ g CO_2

44. (a) $2H_2 + O_2 \rightarrow 2H_2O$

(b) Moles $H_2 = 8.70$ ~~g H$_2$~~ $\times \dfrac{1 \text{ mole } H_2}{2.0 \text{ ~~g H$_2$~~}} = 4.4$ moles H_2

Moles $O_2 = 64.0$ ~~g O$_2$~~ $\times \dfrac{1 \text{ mole } O_2}{32.0 \text{ ~~g O$_2$~~}} = 2.00$ moles O_2

Since 2.00 moles O_2 react with 4.0 moles H_2, O_2 is the limiting reactant and 0.4 mole of H_2 is unreacted.

Grams H_2 unreacted $= 0.4$ ~~mole H$_2$~~ $\times \dfrac{2.0 \text{ g } H_2}{1 \text{ ~~mole H$_2$~~}} = 0.8$ g H_2

Moles H_2O formed $= 2.00$ ~~moles O$_2$~~ $\times \dfrac{2 \text{ moles } H_2O}{1 \text{ ~~mole O$_2$~~}} = 4.00$ moles H_2O

Grams H_2O formed $= 4.00$ ~~moles H$_2$O~~ $\times \dfrac{18.0 \text{ g } H_2O}{1 \text{ ~~mole H$_2$O~~}} = 72.0$ g H_2O

After the reaction is completed, there are 72.0 g H_2O and 0.8 g H_2.

45. $2KClO_3 \rightarrow 2KCl + 3O_2$

$$\text{Moles KClO}_3 = 1000 \text{ g KClO}_3 \times \frac{1 \text{ mole KClO}_3}{122.6 \text{ g KClO}_3} = 8.16 \text{ moles KClO}_3$$

$$\text{Moles O}_2 = 8.16 \text{ moles KClO}_3 \times \frac{3 \text{ moles O}_2}{2 \text{ moles KClO}_3} = 12.2 \text{ moles O}_2$$

$$\text{Grams O}_2 = 12.2 \text{ moles O}_2 \times \frac{32.0 \text{ g O}_2}{1 \text{ mole O}_2} = 39\overline{0} \text{ g O}_2$$

46. $Zn + H_2SO_4 \rightarrow ZnSO_4 + H_2$

$$\text{Moles H}_2 = 60\overline{0} \text{ g H}_2 \times \frac{1 \text{ mole H}_2}{2.0 \text{ g H}_2} = 30\overline{0} \text{ moles H}_2$$

$$\text{Moles Zn} = 30\overline{0} \text{ moles H}_2 \times \frac{1 \text{ mole Zn}}{1 \text{ mole H}_2} = 30\overline{0} \text{ moles Zn}$$

$$\text{Grams Zn} = 30\overline{0} \text{ moles Zn} \times \frac{65.4 \text{ g Zn}}{1 \text{ mole Zn}} = 19{,}600 \text{ g Zn}$$

(or $20{,}\overline{0}00$ g to two significant figures)

47. (a) $Pb + Cu(NO_3)_2 \rightarrow Pb(NO_3)_2 + Cu$

(b) $$\text{Moles Pb} = 50.0 \text{ g Pb} \times \frac{1 \text{ mole Pb}}{207.2 \text{ g Pb}} = 0.241 \text{ mole Pb}$$

$$\text{Moles Pb(NO}_3)_2 = 0.241 \text{ mole Pb} \times \frac{1 \text{ mole Pb(NO}_3)_2}{1 \text{ mole Pb}}$$

$$= 0.241 \text{ mole Pb(NO}_3)_2$$

$$\text{Moles Cu} = 0.241 \text{ mole Pb} \times \frac{1 \text{ mole Cu}}{1 \text{ mole Pb}} = 0.241 \text{ mole Cu}$$

$$\text{Grams Pb(NO}_3)_2 = 0.241 \text{ mole Pb(NO}_3)_2 \times \frac{331.2 \text{ g Pb(NO}_3)_2}{1 \text{ mole Pb(NO}_3)_2}$$

$$= 79.8 \text{ g Pb(NO}_3)_2$$

$$\text{Grams Cu} = 0.241 \text{ mole Cu} \times \frac{63.5 \text{ g Cu}}{1 \text{ mole Cu}} = 15.3 \text{ g Cu}$$

48. $2Al + 3H_2SO_4 \rightarrow Al_2(SO_4)_3 + 3H_2$

$$\text{Moles Al} = 60.0 \text{ g Al} \times \frac{1 \text{ mole Al}}{27.0 \text{ g Al}} = 2.22 \text{ moles Al}$$

$$\text{Moles } H_2 = 2.22 \; \cancel{\text{moles Al}} \times \frac{3 \text{ moles } H_2}{2 \; \cancel{\text{moles Al}}} = 3.33 \text{ moles } H_2$$

$$\text{Grams } H_2 = 3.33 \; \cancel{\text{moles } H_2} \times \frac{2.0 \text{ g } H_2}{1 \; \cancel{\text{mole } H_2}} = 6.7 \text{ g } H_2$$

49. $HCl + NaOH \rightarrow NaCl + H_2O$

$$\text{Moles } HCl = 36.5 \; \cancel{\text{g } HCl} \times \frac{1 \text{ mole } HCl}{36.5 \; \cancel{\text{g } HCl}} = 1.00 \text{ mole } HCl$$

$$\text{Moles } NaOH = 80.0 \; \cancel{\text{g } NaOH} \times \frac{1 \text{ mole } NaOH}{40.0 \; \cancel{\text{g } NaOH}} = 2.00 \text{ moles } NaOH$$

Since 1.00 mole HCl reacts with 1.00 mole NaOH, 1.00 mole NaOH is unreacted.

$$\text{Moles } NaCl \text{ produced} = 1.00 \; \cancel{\text{mole } HCl} \times \frac{1 \text{ mole } NaCl}{1 \; \cancel{\text{mole } HCl}} = 1.00 \text{ mole } NaCl$$

$$\text{Grams } NaCl = 1.00 \; \cancel{\text{mole } NaCl} \times \frac{58.5 \text{ g } NaCl}{1 \; \cancel{\text{mole } NaCl}} = 58.5 \text{ g } NaCl$$

$$\text{Grams } NaOH \text{ unreacted} = 1.00 \; \cancel{\text{mole } NaOH} \times \frac{40.0 \text{ g } NaOH}{1 \; \cancel{\text{mole } NaOH}} = 40.0 \text{ g } NaOH$$

50. $2C + O_2 \rightarrow 2CO$

$$\text{Moles } C = 48.0 \; \cancel{\text{g } C} \times \frac{1 \text{ mole } C}{12.0 \; \cancel{\text{g } C}} = 4.00 \text{ moles } C$$

$$\text{Moles } O_2 = 64.0 \; \cancel{\text{g } O_2} \times \frac{1 \text{ mole } O_2}{32.0 \; \cancel{\text{g } O_2}} = 2.00 \text{ moles } O_2$$

Since 2.00 moles O_2 react with 4.00 moles C, both reactants are used up.

$$\text{Moles } CO = 2.00 \; \cancel{\text{moles } O_2} \times \frac{2 \text{ moles } CO}{1 \; \cancel{\text{mole } O_2}} = 4.00 \text{ moles } CO$$

$$\text{Grams } CO = 4.00 \; \cancel{\text{moles } CO} \times \frac{28.0 \text{ g } CO}{1 \; \cancel{\text{mole } CO}} = 112 \text{ g } CO$$

12 HEATS OF REACTION: CHEMISTRY AND ENERGY

SELF-TEST EXERCISES

1. The matching terms are as follows: 1. (c), 2. (a), 3. (d), 4. (b)

2. The symbol H stands for the term *enthalpy*.

3. (a) The sum of the heat contents of the products is *more than* the sum of those of the reactants in an endothermic reaction.
   (b) The sum of the heat contents of the products is *less than* the sum of those of the reactants in an exothermic reaction.

4. The change in heat content during a chemical reaction is called the *heat of reaction*.

5. A *calorie* is a measure of heat energy. It is the amount of heat needed to raise the temperature of 1 gram of water 1 degree Celsius. *Specific heat* is the number of calories needed to raise the temperature of 1 gram of a substance by 1 degree Celsius.

6. Standard-state conditions are 25°C and 1 atm pressure. Having standard-state conditions allows us to calculate the heat released or absorbed during a chemical reaction. It gives us a basis for comparison.

7. $? \text{ cal} = (c)(m)(\Delta t)$
    $= (1.\underline{00} \text{ cal/g} - \text{°C})(50.0 \text{ g})(60.0 \text{°C})$
    $= 3,000 \text{ cal or } 3.00 \times 10^3 \text{ cal}$

114

8. $\text{? cal} = (c)(m)(\Delta t)$
    $= (1.00 \text{ cal/g } °C)(500.0 \text{ g})(75.0°C)$
    $= 37,500 \text{ cal or } 37.5 \text{ kcal}$

9. $\text{? cal} = (c)(m)(\Delta t)$
    $= (0.107 \text{ cal/g}°C)(40.0 \text{ g})(2\overline{6}0 \text{ °C})$
    $= 1,110 \text{ cal.}$

10. $\text{? cal} = (c)(m)(\Delta t)$
    $= (0.0920 \text{ cal/g} - °C)(100.0 \text{ g})(35.0°C)$
    $= 322 \text{ cal or } 0.322 \text{ kcal}$

11. $\text{? cal} = (c)(m)(\Delta t)$
    $= (0.581 \text{ cal/g} - °C)(100.0 \text{ mL})(0.800 \text{ g/mL})(45.0°C)$
    $= 2,090 \text{ cal or } 2.09 \text{ kcal}$

12. $M = D \times V = (0.800 \text{ g} - °C)(50.0°C) = 40.0 \text{ g}$
    $\text{? cal} = (c)(m)(\Delta t)$
    $= (0.581 \text{ cal/g} - °C)(40.0 \text{ g})(30.0°C)$
    $= 697 \text{ cal or } 0.697 \text{ kcal}$

13. $308 \text{ cal} = (0.0308 \text{ cal/g} - °C)(1,000 \text{ g})(t_f - 20.0°C)$
    (where t_f is the final temperature)
    $t_f = 30.0°C$

14. $\text{? cal} = (c)(m)(\Delta t)$

$$\Delta t = \frac{\text{cal}}{(c)(m)} = \frac{5,\overline{0}00 \text{ cal}}{\left(0.0308 \dfrac{\text{cal}}{\text{g} - °C}\right) 2,\overline{0}00 \text{ g}} = 81.2°C$$

$\Delta t = t_f - t_i$ 　　　　　　$\Delta t + t_i = t_f$
　　　　　　　　　　　　　　$81.2 + 10.0 = t_f$
　　　　　　　　　　　　　　$91.2°C = t_f$

15. Given: $H_2(g) + \frac{1}{2} O_2(g) \rightarrow H_2O(l)$

Moles of $H_2 = 0.146 \text{ g } H_2 \times \dfrac{1 \text{ mole } H_2}{2.00 \text{ g } H_2} = 0.0730 \text{ mole } H_2$

Heat generated $= (c)(m)(\Delta t)$
　　　　　　　　$= (1.\underline{00} \text{ cal/g} - °C)(5\overline{0}0 \text{ g})(10.0°C)$
　　　　　　　　$= 5,\overline{0}00 \text{ cal or } 5.00 \text{ kcal (for } 0.0730 \text{ mole)}$

$$\Delta H_R = \frac{kcal}{mole} = \frac{-5.00 \text{ kcal}}{0.0730 \text{ mole}} = -68.5 \text{ kcal/mole}$$

16.   ? cal = $(c)(m)(\Delta t)$

   ? cal = $\left(1.00 \dfrac{cal}{g - °C}\right)(1,\overline{0}00 \text{ g})(99.9°C - 32.0°C)$

   = 67,900 cal or 67.9 kcal

17.   (a) $S(s) + 1\frac{1}{2} O_2(g) \rightarrow SO_3(g) + 94.45$ kcal

   (b) $\frac{1}{2} H_2(g) + \frac{1}{2} Br_2(l) \rightarrow HBr(g) + 8.7$ kcal

   (c) $C(s) + 2Cl_2(g) \rightarrow CCl_4(l) + 33.4$ kcal

   (d) $\frac{1}{2} N_2(g) + \frac{1}{2} O_2(g) \rightarrow NO(g) - 21.5$ kcal

18.   (a) $\frac{1}{2} H_2(g) + \frac{1}{2} F_2(g) \rightarrow HF(g) + 64.2$ kcal

   (b) $\frac{1}{2} H_2(g) + \frac{1}{2} Cl_2(g) \rightarrow HCl(g) + 22.1$ kcal

   (c) $\frac{1}{2} H_2(g) + \frac{1}{2} Br_2(g) \rightarrow HBr(g) + 8.7$ kcal

19.   A positive ΔH value in an equation indicates an exothermic reaction; an example is

$$H_2(g) + \frac{1}{2} O_2(g) \rightarrow H_2O(l) + 68.3 \text{ kcal}$$

A negative ΔH value in an equation indicates an endothermic reaction; an example is

$$\frac{1}{2} H_2(g) + \frac{1}{2} I_2(s) \rightarrow HI(g) - 6.2 \text{ kcal}$$

20.   (a)   *Enthalpy* is the heat content of a chemical substance and is represented by the symbol H.
   (b)   Enthalpy is represented by the symbol H, but the change in enthalpy, which is what we measure in a chemical reaction, is ΔH.

21. $H_2(g) + S(s) \rightarrow H_2S(g)$

ΔH_f for $H_2S(g) = 4.8$ kcal/mole

Moles H_2S = 102 g H₂S × $\dfrac{1 \text{ mole } H_2S}{34.1 \text{ g } H_2S}$ = 2.99 moles H_2S

Heat released = −4.8 kcal/mole × 2.99 moles
= −14.4 kcal or −14 kcal (two significant figures)

22. Moles BaO = (15.3 g)$\left(\dfrac{1 \text{ mole}}{153.3 \text{ g}}\right)$ = 0.0998 mole BaO

Heat released = (0.0998 mole)$\left(\dfrac{133 \text{ kcal}}{1 \text{ mole}}\right)$ = 13.3 kcal

23. $H_2(g) + \dfrac{1}{2} O_2(g) \rightarrow H_2O(g) + 57.8$ kcal

For kilograms of steam:

Moles $H_2O(g)$ = 1,$\overline{0}$00 g H₂O × $\dfrac{1 \text{ mole } H_2O}{18.0 \text{ g } H_2O}$ = 55.6 moles $H_2O(g)$

Heat evolved = 57.8 kcal/mole × 55.6 moles = 3,210 kcal

24. $2C_6H_{14}(l) + 19O_2(g) \rightarrow 12CO_2(g) + 14H_2O(l) + 1{,}980$ kcal

The equation shows that 2 moles of hexane produce 1,980 kcal. Therefore 20 moles of hexane would produce 19, 800 kcal.

Grams C_6H_{14} = (20.00 moles)$\left(\dfrac{86.0 \text{ g}}{1 \text{ mole}}\right)$ = 1,720 g C_6H_{14}

25. (a) $2C_2H_2(g) + 5O_2(g) \rightarrow 4CO_2(g) + 2H_2O(l)$

ΔH_R = ΔH_f(products) − ΔH_f(reactants)

ΔH_R = $[4\Delta H_f(CO_2) + 2\Delta H_f(H_2O)] - [2\Delta H_f(C_2H_2) + 5\Delta H_f(O_2)]$

= [4(−94.1 kcal) + 2(−68.3 kcal)] − [2(54.2 kcal) + 0]

= −376.4 kcal − 136.6 kcal − 108.4 kcal

= −621.4 kcal

(b)   Moles C_2H_2 = 5,2$\overline{0}$0 $\text{g }C_2H_2$ $\times \dfrac{1 \text{ mole } C_2H_2}{26.0 \text{ g } C_2H_2}$ = 2$\overline{0}$0 moles C_2H_2

Heat produced $= \dfrac{-621.4 \text{ kcal}}{2 \text{ moles } C_2H_2} \times 2\overline{0}0 \text{ moles } C_2H_2$

$= -62{,}140$ kcal (or $-62{,}100$ kcal for three significant figures)

26. $C(\text{graphite}) + O_2(g) \rightarrow CO_2(g) + 94.1$ kcal

Moles $CO_2 = (88\overline{0} \text{ g}) \left(\dfrac{1 \text{ mole}}{44.0 \text{ g}} \right) = 20.0$ moles CO_2

The equation shows that for each mole of CO_2 produced, 94.1 kcal of heat are produced.

? kcal $= (20.0 \text{ moles}) \left(\dfrac{94.1 \text{ kcal}}{1 \text{ mole}} \right)$

$= 1{,}882$ kcal (or $1{,}880$ kcal for three significant figures)

27.   Given: $BaO_2(s) + 2HCl(g) \rightarrow BaCl_2(s) + H_2O_2(l)$

(a) $\Delta H_R = \Delta H_f(\text{products}) - \Delta H_f(\text{reactants})$

$= [-205.6 \text{ kcal} - 44.8 \text{ kcal}] - [-150.5 \text{ kcal} + 2(-22.1 \text{ kcal})]$

$= -55.7$ kcal

(b)   The molecular mass of $BaO_2 = 169.3$

Grams $BaO_2 = 5\overline{0}0 \text{ kcal} \times \dfrac{1 \text{ mole } BaO_2}{55.7 \text{ kcal}} \times \dfrac{169.3 \text{ g } BaO_2}{1 \text{ mole } BaO_2}$

$= 1{,}520$ g BaO_2

28.   First determine the number of moles of oxygen gas in 640 g O_2.

Moles $O_2 = (640 \text{ g}) \left(\dfrac{1 \text{ mole}}{32.0 \text{ g}} \right) = 20.0$ moles O_2

The thermochemical equation is

$$H_2O(l) \rightarrow H_2(g) + \frac{1}{2}O_2(g) - 68.3 \text{ kcal}$$

The equation tells us that we require 68.3 kcal of energy for each 0.5 mole of O_2 produced. Therefore, to produce 20.0 moles of O_2, we need:

$$? \text{ kcal} = \left(\frac{68.3 \text{ kcal}}{0.500 \text{ mole}}\right)(20.0 \text{ moles}) \quad = 2,732 \text{ kcal or } 2,730 \text{ kcal (three sig. figures)}$$

29. Given: $P_2O_5(s) + 3H_2O(l) \rightarrow 2H_3PO_4(aq) + 228.5 \text{ kcal}$

$$\begin{aligned}\Delta H_R &= -228.5 \text{ kcal} = \Delta H_{f(\text{products})} - \Delta H_{f(\text{reactants})}\\ &= -228.5 \text{ kcal} = [2(-308.2 \text{ kcal})] - [\Delta H_{P_2O_5(s)} + 3(-68.3 \text{ kcal})]\\ &= -228.5 \text{ kcal} = [-616 \text{ kcal}] - [\Delta H_{P_2O_5} + 204.9 \text{ kcal}]\end{aligned}$$

$$\Delta H^0_{P_2O_5} = -183.0 \text{ kcal}$$

30. Moles C $= (1.2 \text{ g})\left(\dfrac{1 \text{ mole}}{12.0 \text{ g}}\right) = 0.10$ mole C

$$? \text{ cal} = (c)(m)(\Delta t) = \left(1.00\,\frac{\text{cal}}{\text{g} - {}^\circ\text{C}}\right)(470.5 \text{ g})(20.0{}^\circ\text{C}) = 9,410 \text{ cal}$$

$$? \frac{\text{kcal}}{\text{mole}} = \frac{9.41 \text{ kcal}}{0.10 \text{ mole}} = 94 \frac{\text{kcal}}{\text{mole}}$$

31. $2S(s) + 3O_2(g) \rightarrow 2SO_3(g)$

Heat evolved $= 1,890 \text{ g} \times \Delta t = 1,890 \times 5.00{}^\circ\text{C} = 9,450 \text{ cal}$

Moles S atoms used $= 3.20 \text{ g} \times \dfrac{1 \text{ mole S atoms}}{32.1 \text{ g}} = 0.0997$ mole S

Moles SO_3 formed $= 0.0997 \text{ mole S} \times \dfrac{2 \text{ moles } SO_3}{2 \text{ moles S}} = 0.0997 \text{ kcal/mole}$

$$\text{kcal/mole} = \frac{9,450 \text{ cal}}{0.0997 \text{ mole}} \times \frac{1 \text{ kcal}}{1,000 \text{ cal}} = -94.8 \text{ kcal/mole}$$

or $\qquad\qquad\qquad \Delta H_f = -94.8 \text{ kcal/mole}$

The value of −94.45 is given in Table 10.2.

32. The ΔH_f^0 of $K_2O(s)$ is –86.4 kcal. The number of moles of K_2O in 188.4 g is

$$\text{Moles } K_2O = (188.4 \text{ g})\left(\frac{1 \text{ mole}}{94.2 \text{ g}}\right) = 2.00 \text{ moles } K_2O$$

Therefore, the heat released is calculated as follows:

$$? \text{ kcal} = (2.00 \text{ moles})\left(\frac{-86.4 \text{ kcal}}{1 \text{ mole}}\right) = -173 \text{ kcal}$$

33. $C_{16}H_{34}(l) + 24\frac{1}{2} O_2(g) \rightarrow 16CO_2(g) + 17H_2O(l) + 2{,}560 \text{ kcal}$

$\Delta H_R = -2{,}560 \text{ kcal} = \Delta H_{f(\text{products})} - \Delta H_{f(\text{reactants})}$
$-2{,}560 \text{ kcal} = [16(-94.1 \text{ kcal})] + [17(-68.3 \text{ kcal})] - [\Delta H_{C_{16}H_{34}}]$
$-2{,}560 \text{ kcal} = -1{,}506 \text{ kcal} - 1{,}161 \text{ kcal} - \Delta H_{C_{16}H_{34}}$
$\Delta H_{C_{16}H_{34}} = -107 \text{ kcal}$

34. $\frac{1}{2} H_2(g) + \frac{1}{2} Cl_2(g) \rightarrow HCl(g) + 22.1 \text{ kcal}$

$$\text{Moles } HCl = (7.30 \text{ g})\left(\frac{1 \text{ mole}}{36.5 \text{ g}}\right) = 0.200 \text{ mole } HCl$$

$$? \text{ kcal} = (0.200 \text{ mole})\left(\frac{22.1 \text{ kcal}}{1 \text{ mole}}\right) = 4.42 \text{ kcal}$$

35. Given: $S(s) + \frac{1}{2} O_2(g) \rightarrow SO_2(g)$

$\Delta H_{SO_2(g)} = -70.96 \text{ kcal/mole}$

$$\text{Heat released} = 70.96 \text{ kcal/mole} \times 12.8 \text{ g } SO_2 \times \frac{1 \text{ mole } SO_2}{64.0 \text{ g } SO_2} = 14.2 \text{ kcal}$$

36. The ΔH_f^0 of $HBr(g)$ is –8.7 kcal. The number of moles of $HBr(g)$ in 1,618 g is

$$\text{Moles } HBr(g) = (1{,}618 \text{ g})\left(\frac{1 \text{ mole}}{80.9 \text{ g}}\right) = 20.0 \text{ moles } HBr(g)$$

Therefore, the heat released is calculated as follows:

$? \text{ kcal} = (20.0 \text{ moles})\left(\dfrac{-8.7 \text{ kcal}}{1 \text{ mole}}\right) = -174 \text{ kcal or } -170 \text{ kcal (two significant figures)}$

37. Given: $H_2(g) + I_2(g) \rightarrow 2HI(g)$

ΔH_f for $HI(g) = +6.2 \text{ kcal/mole}$

Heat absorbed $= 6.2 \text{ kcal/mole} \times 51.2 \text{ g HI} \times \dfrac{1 \text{ mole HI}}{127.9 \text{ g HI}} = 2.5 \text{ kcal}$

38. $C_2H_2 + 2\frac{1}{2} O_2(g) \rightarrow 2CO_2(g) + H_2O(l) + 312.0 \text{ kcal}$

$\Delta H^0_R = \Delta H^0_{f(\text{products})} - \Delta H^0_{f(\text{reactants})}$

$-312.0 \text{ kcal} = [2(-94.1 \text{ kcal}) + 1(-68.3 \text{ kcal})] - [1(\Delta H^0_{f(\text{acetylene})})]$

$\Delta H^0_{f(\text{acetylene})} = 55.5 \text{ kcal/mole}$

39. Given: $2SO_2(g) + O_2(g) = 2SO_3(g)$

$\Delta H_R = \Delta H_{f(\text{products})} - \Delta H_{f(\text{reactants})}$

$= [2(-94.45 \text{ kcal}) - 2(-70.96 \text{ kcal})]$

$= -188.9 \text{ kcal} + 141.9 \text{ kcal}$

$= -47.0 \text{ kcal}$

40. $CaO(s) + H_2O(l) \rightarrow Ca(OH)_2(s) + 15.6 \text{ kcal}$

Find ΔH^0_f of $Ca(OH)_2(s)$. We know that

$\Delta H = \Delta H^0_{f(\text{products})} - \Delta H^0_{f(\text{reactants})}$

$-15.6 = \Delta H^0_{Ca(OH)_2} - (\Delta H^0_{CaO} + \Delta H^0_{H_2O})$

$-15.6 = \Delta H^0_{Ca(OH)_2} - (151.9 - 68.3)$

$-15.6 = \Delta H^0_{Ca(OH)_2} + 220.2$

$-235.8 \text{ kcal} = \Delta H^0_{Ca(OH)_2}$

41.   Given: $2H_2O_2(l) \rightarrow 2H_2O(l) + O_2(g)$

(a) $\Delta H_R = \Delta H_f(\text{products}) - \Delta H_f(\text{reactants})$

$= 2(-68.3 \text{ kcal}) - [2(-44.8 \text{ kcal})]$

$= -47.0 \text{ kcal}$

(b)   From (a) we know that $\Delta H_R = -47.0$ kcal for 2 moles of H_2O_2. For 204 g H_2O_2:

$$\text{Heat produced} = \frac{47.0 \text{ kcal}}{2 \text{ moles } H_2O_2} \times 204 \text{ g } H_2O_2 \times \frac{1 \text{ mole } H_2O_2}{34.0 \text{ g } H_2O_2} = 141 \text{ kcal}$$

42. $\Delta H^0_{f(BaCl_2)} = -205.56 \text{ kcal/mole}$

$$\text{Moles } BaCl_2 = (2,\overline{000} \text{ g})\left(\frac{1 \text{ mole}}{208.3 \text{ g}}\right) = 9.602 \text{ moles } BaCl_2$$

$$\text{Heat released} = (9.60 \text{ mole})\left(\frac{205.56 \text{ kcal}}{1 \text{ mole}}\right) = \quad 1,973 \text{ kcal or } 1,970 \text{ kcal (to three sig. figures)}$$

43.   Given: $2KClO_3(s) \rightarrow 2KCl(s) + 3O_2(g)$

$\Delta H_R = \Delta H_f(\text{products}) - \Delta H_f(\text{reactants})$

$= [2(-104.18 \text{ kcal})] - [2(-93.50 \text{ kcal})]$

$= -208.36 \text{ kcal} + 187.00 \text{ kcal}$

$= -21.36 \text{ kcal}$

44. $Na(s) + \frac{1}{2} Cl_2(g) \rightarrow NaCl(s)$

0.230 g $\downarrow$
$\downarrow \div 23.0$
0.0100 mole   0.0100 mole

? cal $= (c)(m)(\Delta t)$

$\left(1.000 \dfrac{\text{cal}}{\text{g - °C}}\right) (24.55 \text{ g})(40.0°C) = 982 \text{ cal} = 0.982 \text{ kcal}$

Therefore, $\Delta H_f^0 = \dfrac{-0.982 \text{ kcal}}{0.0100 \text{ mole}} = -98.2 \dfrac{\text{kcal}}{\text{mole}}$

45. (a) $PCl_5(s) + 4H_2O(l) \rightarrow H_3PO_4(aq) + 5HCl(aq)$

    (b) $\Delta H_R = \Delta H_{f(\text{products})} - \Delta H_{f(\text{reactants})}$

    $= [-308.2 \text{ kcal} + 5(-40.02 \text{ kcal})] - [-95.35 \text{ kcal} + 4(-68.3 \text{ kcal})]$

    $= -308.2 \text{ kcal} - 200.10 \text{ kcal} + 95.35 \text{ kcal} + 273.2 \text{ kcal}$

    $= -139.8 \text{ kcal}$

    (c) Heat produced $= \dfrac{139.8 \text{ kcal}}{1 \text{ mole}} \times 41.70 \text{ g} \times \dfrac{1 \text{ mole } PCl_5}{208.5 \text{ g}} = 27.96 \text{ kcal}$

46. $C(\text{graphite}) + 2H_2O(g) \rightarrow CO_2(g) + 2H_2(g) - 31.39 \text{ kcal}$

    Heat absorbed $= (5.00 \text{ moles } CO_2)\left(\dfrac{31.39 \text{ kcal}}{\text{mole}}\right) = 157 \text{ kcal}$

47. Given: $3CuO(s) + 2NH_3(g) \rightarrow 3Cu(s) + 3H_2O(l) + N_2(g) + 71.1 \text{ kcal}$

    $\Delta H_R = \Delta H_{f(\text{products})} - \Delta H_{f(\text{reactants})}$

    $-71.1 \text{ kcal} = [3(-68.3 \text{ kcal})] - [3\Delta H_{f(CuO)} + 2(-11.04 \text{ kcal})]$

    $-71.1 \text{ kcal} = -204.9 \text{ kcal} - 3\Delta H_{f(CuO)} + 22.08 \text{ kcal}$

    $\Delta H_{fCuO}^0 = -37.2 \text{ kcal}$

48. $CO(g) + \frac{1}{2} O_2(g) \rightarrow CO_2(g) + 67.64 \text{ kcal}$

    Heat released $= (5.00 \text{ moles})\left(\dfrac{67.64 \text{ kcal}}{\text{mole}}\right) = 338 \text{ kcal}$

EXTRA EXERCISES

49. Heat energy released $= (c)(m)(\Delta t)$

    $= (1.00 \text{ cal/g} - °C)(42\overline{0} \text{ g})(15.0°C)$

    $= 6,3\overline{0}0 \text{ cal}$

50. Given: $CaCO_3(s) \rightarrow CaO(s) + CO_2(g) - 42.5$ kcal

ΔH_R $= 42.5$ kcal $= \Delta H_{f(products)} - \Delta H_{f(reactants)}$

$= 42.5$ kcal $= (-151.9$ kcal $- 94.1$ kcal$) - (\Delta H_{CaCO_3})$

ΔH_{CaCO_3} $= -288.5$ kcal

The value given in Table 12.2 is the same.

51. Compound ΔH_f^0

(a) +54.2, endothermic; heat is absorbed
(b) –22.1, exothermic; heat is released
(c) –68.3, exothermic; heat is released
(d) +6.2, endothermic; heat is absorbed

52. Given: $CH_4(g) + 2O_2(g) \rightarrow CO_2(g) + 2H_2O(g)$

$C_2H_2(g) + \dfrac{5}{2} O_2(g) \rightarrow 2CO_2(g) + H_2O(g)$

For $CH_4(g)$,

$\Delta H_R = [-94.1$ kcal $+ 2(-57.8$ kcal$)] - (-17.9$ kcal$) = -191.8$ kcal

For $C_2H_2(g)$,

$\Delta H_R = [(-94.1$ kcal$) - 57.8$ kcal$] - (54.2$ kcal$) = -300.2$ kcal

$C_2H_2(g)$ releases more energy: 300.2 kcal compared to 191.8 kcal for CH_4.

53. In order for $N_2O_4(g)$ to form $NO_2(g)$, many bonds must be broken. Therefore, we would predict that the reaction would be endothermic.

54. Moles C $= (1.00 \text{ kg})\left(\dfrac{1,000 \text{ g}}{1 \text{ kg}}\right)\left(\dfrac{70.0 \text{ g C}}{100 \text{ g coal}}\right)\left(\dfrac{1 \text{ mole}}{12.0 \text{ g}}\right) = 58.3$ moles

Heat energy $= (94 \text{ kcal/mole})(58.3 \text{ moles}) = 5,500$ kcal

55. $\dfrac{\text{kcal}}{\text{g}}$ (for H_2) $= \left(\dfrac{58 \text{ kcal}}{1 \text{ mole } H_2}\right)\left(\dfrac{1 \text{ mole } H_2}{2.0 \text{ g } H_2}\right) = 29$ kcal/g

$$\frac{kcal}{g} \text{ (for CH}_4\text{)} = \left(\frac{213 \text{ kcal}}{1 \text{ mole CH}_4}\right)\left(\frac{1 \text{ mole CH}_4}{16.0 \text{ g CH}_4}\right) = 13.3 \text{ kcal/g}$$

$$\frac{kcal}{g} \text{ (for C)} = \left(\frac{94 \text{ kcal}}{1 \text{ mole C}}\right)\left(\frac{1 \text{ mole C}}{12.0 \text{ g C}}\right) = 7.8 \text{ kcal/g}$$

56. Exothermic reactions have a negative ΔH because the sum of the heat contents of the products is less than the sum of those of the reactants. Endothermic reactions have a positive ΔH because the sum of the heat contents of the products is greater than the sum of those of the reactants.

57. Given: $CH_4(g) + 2O_2(g) \rightarrow CO_2(g) + 2H_2O(l)$

$$\Delta H_R = 213 \text{ kcal/mole } CH_4$$

For 50.0 moles of CH_4,

$$\Delta H_R = (213 \text{ kcal/mole})(50.0 \text{ moles}) = 10,600 \text{ kcal}$$

58. Given: $H_2O(l) \rightarrow H_2O(g)$

$$\Delta H_{vaporization} = \Delta H_f[\text{for } H_2O(g)] - \Delta H_f[\text{for } H_2O(l)]$$

$$= (-57.8 \text{ kcal}) - (-68.3 \text{ kcal}) = 10.5 \text{ kcal}$$

13

THE GASEOUS STATE: IDEAL BEHAVIOR

SELF-TEST EXERCISES

1. The five basic principles of the kinetic theory are as follows:

    a. Nearly all gases are composed of molecules. (The so-called noble gases are composed of atoms, not molecules. Remember, atoms of noble gases don't combine readily with other atoms.)

    b. The forces of attraction between gas molecules increase as the molecules move closer together. At normal atmospheric pressure and room temperature, distances between gas molecules are large compared to the size of the molecules.

    c. Gas molecules are always in motion. They often collide with other gas molecules or with their container. After collisions occur, the molecules do not stick together; and they do not lose any energy on account of the collisions.

    d. Gas molecules move faster when the temperature rises and slower when the temperature drops.

    e. All gas molecules (heavy as well as light) have the same average kinetic energy—that is, energy of motion—at the same temperature.

2. A gas that behaves exactly as predicted by the kinetic theory under all conditions of temperature and pressure is called an "ideal gas." The molecules of an ideal gas would have no attraction to each other regardless of the temperature and pressure. Molecules of "real gases" do have some attraction to one another, especially at high pressures and low temperatures.

126

3. (a) $? \text{ atm} = 1{,}862 \text{ torr} \times \dfrac{1 \text{ atm}}{760 \text{ torr}} = 2.45 \text{ atm}$

    (b) $? \text{ atm} = 471 \text{ torr} \times \dfrac{1 \text{ atm}}{760 \text{ torr}} = 0.620 \text{ atm}$

    (c) $? \text{ atm} = 6{,}080 \text{ torr} \times \dfrac{1 \text{ atm}}{760 \text{ torr}} = 8.00 \text{ atm}$

    (d) $? \text{ atm} = 125 \text{ torr} \times \dfrac{1 \text{ atm}}{760 \text{ torr}} = 0.164 \text{ atm}$

4. (a) $? \text{ atm} = 35\bar{0} \text{ torr} \times \dfrac{1 \text{ atm}}{760 \text{ torr}} = 0.461 \text{ atm}$

    (b) $? \text{ atm} = 2{,}5\overline{00} \text{ torr} \times \dfrac{1 \text{ atm}}{760 \text{ torr}} = 3.29 \text{ atm}$

    (c) $? \text{ atm} = 1{,}9\bar{6}0 \text{ torr} \times \dfrac{1 \text{ atm}}{760 \text{ torr}} = 2.58 \text{ atm}$

5. (a) $? \text{ torr} = 4.00 \text{ atm} \times \dfrac{76\bar{0} \text{ torr}}{1 \text{ atm}} = 3{,}040 \text{ torr}$

    (b) $? \text{ torr} = 0.400 \text{ atm} \times \dfrac{76\bar{0} \text{ torr}}{1 \text{ atm}} = 304 \text{ torr}$

    (c) $? \text{ torr} = 0.00200 \text{ atm} \times \dfrac{76\bar{0} \text{ torr}}{1 \text{ atm}} = 1.52 \text{ torr}$

    (d) $? \text{ torr} = 5.25 \text{ atm} \times \dfrac{76\bar{0} \text{ torr}}{1 \text{ atm}} = 3{,}990 \text{ torr}$

6. (a) $? \text{ torr} = 2.00 \text{ atm} \times \dfrac{76\bar{0} \text{ torr}}{1 \text{ atm}} = 1{,}520 \text{ torr}$

    (b) $? \text{ torr} = 0.250 \text{ atm} \times \dfrac{76\bar{0} \text{ torr}}{1 \text{ atm}} = 19\bar{0} \text{ torr}$

    (c) $? \text{ torr} = 0.123 \text{ atm} \times \dfrac{76\bar{0} \text{ torr}}{1 \text{ atm}} = 93.5 \text{ torr}$

7. (a) $? \text{ atm} = 76 \text{ torr} \times \dfrac{1 \text{ atm}}{760 \text{ torr}} = 0.10 \text{ atm}$

(b) $? \text{ atm} = 2{,}660 \text{ torr} \times \dfrac{1 \text{ atm}}{760 \text{ torr}} = 3.50 \text{ atm}$

(c) $? \text{ atm} = 3.80 \text{ torr} \times \dfrac{1 \text{ atm}}{760 \text{ torr}} = 0.00500 \text{ atm}$

8. (a) $? \text{ atm} = 152 \text{ torr} \times \dfrac{1 \text{ atm}}{760 \text{ torr}} = 0.200 \text{ atm}$

(b) $? \text{ atm} = 304 \text{ torr} \times \dfrac{1 \text{ atm}}{760 \text{ torr}} = 0.400 \text{ atm}$

(c) $? \text{ atm} = 0.152 \text{ torr} \times \dfrac{1 \text{ atm}}{760 \text{ torr}} = 0.000200 \text{ atm}$

9. (a) $? \text{ torr} = 0.0100 \text{ atm} \times \dfrac{760 \text{ torr}}{1 \text{ atm}} = 7.60 \text{ torr}$

(b) $? \text{ torr} = 12.0 \text{ atm} \times \dfrac{760 \text{ torr}}{1 \text{ atm}} = 9{,}120 \text{ torr}$

(c) $? \text{ torr} = 5.50 \text{ atm} \times \dfrac{760 \text{ torr}}{1 \text{ atm}} = 4{,}180 \text{ torr}$

10. (a) $? \text{ torr} = 0.200 \text{ atm} \times \dfrac{76\bar{0} \text{ torr}}{1 \text{ atm}} = 152 \text{ torr}$

(b) $? \text{ torr} = 15.2 \text{ atm} \times \dfrac{76\bar{0} \text{ torr}}{1 \text{ atm}} = 11{,}600 \text{ torr}$

(c) $? \text{ torr} = 7.6 \text{ atm} \times \dfrac{76\bar{0} \text{ torr}}{1 \text{ atm}} = 5{,}800 \text{ torr}$

11. $P_i = 60.0 \text{ torr}$ $P_f = 20.0 \text{ torr}$

$V_i = 90.0 \text{ mL}$ $V_f = ?$

$\dfrac{P_i}{P_f} = \dfrac{V_f}{V_i}$, $\dfrac{60.0 \text{ torr}}{20.0 \text{ torr}} = \dfrac{V_f}{90.0 \text{ mL}}$, $V_f = 27\bar{0} \text{ mL}$

12. $P_i V_i = P_f V_f$ so $V_f = \dfrac{P_i V_i}{P_f}$

$$V_f = \frac{(0.500 \text{ atm})(40.0 \text{ L})}{0.200 \text{ atm}} = 1\overline{0}0 \text{ L}$$

13. $P_i = 3.00$ atm $\qquad\qquad P_f = 38\overline{0}$ torr $= 0.500$ atm

$V_i = 5\overline{0}0$ mL $\qquad\qquad V_f = ?$

$$\frac{P_i}{P_f} = \frac{V_f}{V_i} , \qquad \frac{3.00 \text{ atm}}{0.500 \text{ atm}} = \frac{V_f}{500 \text{ mL}} , \qquad V_f = 3,\overline{0}00 \text{ mL}$$

14. $P_iV_i = P_fV_f \qquad$ so $\qquad V_f = \dfrac{P_iV_i}{P_f}$

$$V_f = \frac{(2.00 \text{ atm})(25\overline{0} \text{ mL})}{0.526 \text{ atm}} = 951 \text{ mL}$$

15. $P_i = 1,9\overline{0}0$ torr $\qquad\qquad V_i = 25\overline{0}$ mL

$P_f = ?$ $\qquad\qquad V_f = 50.0$ mL

$$\frac{P_i}{P_f} = \frac{V_f}{V_i} , \qquad \frac{1,9\overline{0}0 \text{ torr}}{P_f} = \frac{50.0 \text{ mL}}{250 \text{ mL}} , \qquad P_f = 9,5\overline{0}0 \text{ torr}$$

16. $P_iV_i = P_fV_f \qquad$ so $\qquad P_f = \dfrac{P_iV_i}{V_f}$

$$P_f = \frac{(1,520 \text{ torr})(455 \text{ cm}^3)}{75.0 \text{ cm}^3} = 9,220 \text{ torr}$$

17. $T_i = 127°C + 273 = 4\overline{0}0$ K $\qquad V_i = 0.500$ L

$T_f = ?$ $\qquad\qquad V_f = 2.00$ L

$$\frac{T_i}{T_f} = \frac{V_i}{V_f} , \qquad \frac{4\overline{0}0 \text{ K}}{T_f} = \frac{0.500 \text{ L}}{2.00 \text{ L}} , \qquad T_f = 1,600 \text{ K} \quad \text{or} \quad 1,327°C$$

18. $\dfrac{V_i}{T_i} = \dfrac{V_f}{T_f} , \qquad T_i = 90.0°C + 273 = 363$ K

$$T_f = \frac{V_fT_i}{V_i} = \frac{(5.50 \text{ L})(363 \text{ K})}{(4.00 \text{ L})} = 499 \text{ K}$$

$T_f = 499$ K $- 273 = 226°C$

19. $T_i = -73°C + 273 = 2\overline{0}0$ K $V_i = 8.00$ L

 $T_f = ?$ $V_f = 32.0$ L

 $\dfrac{T_i}{T_f} = \dfrac{V_i}{V_f}$, $\dfrac{2\overline{0}0 \text{ K}}{T_f} = \dfrac{8.00 \text{ L}}{32.0 \text{ L}}$, $T_f = 8\overline{0}0$ K

 $T_f = 8\overline{0}0$ K $- 273 = 527°C$

20. $\dfrac{V_i}{T_i} = \dfrac{V_f}{T_f}$, $T_i = 85°C + 273 = 358$ K

 $T_f = \dfrac{V_f T_i}{V_i} = \dfrac{(4.50 \text{ L})(358 \text{ K})}{(7.50 \text{ L})} = 215$ K

 $°C = 215$ K $- 273 = -58°C$

21. $T_i = 327°C + 273 = 6\overline{0}0$ K $V_i = 2\overline{0}0$ L

 $T_f = -173°C + 273 = 1\overline{0}0$ K $V_f = ?$

 $\dfrac{T_i}{T_f} = \dfrac{V_i}{V_f}$, $\dfrac{6\overline{0}0 \text{ K}}{1\overline{0}0 \text{ K}} = \dfrac{2\overline{0}0 \text{ L}}{V_f}$, $V_f = 33.3$ L

22. $\dfrac{V_i}{T_i} = \dfrac{V_f}{T_f}$ $T_i = 400°C + 273 = 673$ K

 $V_f = \dfrac{V_i T_f}{T_i}$ $T_f = -73°C + 273 = 200$ K

 $V_f = \dfrac{(45\overline{0} \text{ L})(200 \text{ K})}{673 \text{ K}} = 134$ L

23. (a) $? °C = 3\overline{0}0$ K $- 273 = 27°C$

 (b) $? °C = 20$ K $- 273 = -253°C$

24. (a) $? °C = 353$ K $- 273 = 8\overline{0}°C$

 (b) $? °C = 3$ K $- 273 = -27\overline{0}°C$

25. (a) $? K = \overline{1}0\,°C + 273 = 283\ K$

(b) $? K = -\overline{1}0\,°C + 273 = 263\ K$

(c) $? K = -73°C + 273 = \overline{20}0\ K$

26. (a) $? K = °C + 273 = 15°C + 273 = 288\ K$

(b) $? K = -15°C + 273 = 258\ K$

(c) $? K = -50°C + 273 = 223\ K$

27. (a) $? °C = 0\ K - 273 = -273°C$

(b) $? °C = \overline{10}0\ K - 273 = -173°C$

(c) $? °C = \overline{20}0\ K - 273 = -73°C$

(d) $? °C = \overline{30}0\ K - 273 = 27°C$

28. (a) $? °C = 5\ K - 273 = -268°C$

(b) $? °C = 150\ K - 273 = -123°C$

(c) $? °C = 250\ K - 273 = -23°C$

(d) $? °C = 350\ K - 273 = 77°C$

29. (a) $? K = \overline{2}0\,°C + 273 = 293\ K$

(b) $? K = 0°C + 273 = 273\ K$

(c) $? K = -\overline{10}0\,°C + 273 = 173\ K$

(d) $100°C = 212°F$
$? K = 100°C + 273$
$= 373\ K$

30. (a) $? K = 25°C + 273 = 298\ K$

(b) $? K = -5°C + 273 = 268\ K$

(c) $? K = -75°C + 273 = 198\ K$

(d) $? \,°C = \dfrac{424°F - 32}{1.8} = 218°C$ $K = 218°C + 273 = 491 \text{ K}$

31. $P_i = 4.00 \text{ atm}$ $P_f = ?$

$V_i = 8.00 \text{ L}$ $V_f = 24.0 \text{ L}$

$T_i = 27°C + 273 = 300 \text{ K}$ $T_f = 227°C + 273 = 5\overline{0}0 \text{ K}$

$\dfrac{P_i V_i}{T_i} = \dfrac{P_f V_f}{T_f}$, $\dfrac{(4.00 \text{ atm})(8.00 \text{ L})}{300 \text{ K}} = \dfrac{P_f (24.0 \text{ L})}{500 \text{ K}}$, $P_f = 2.22 \text{ atm}$

32. $\dfrac{P_i V_i}{T_i} = \dfrac{P_f V_f}{T_f}$

$P_f = \dfrac{P_i V_i T_i}{T_i V_f} = \dfrac{(0.20 \text{ atm})(8.0 \text{ L})(623 \text{ K})}{(316 \text{ K})(10.0 \text{ L})} = 0.32 \text{ atm}$

33. $P_i = 1{,}520 \text{ torr}$ $P_f = ?$

$T_i = 20.0°C + 273 = 293 \text{ K}$ $T_f = 34.0°C + 273 = 307 \text{ K}$

$\dfrac{P_i}{P_f} = \dfrac{T_i}{T_f}$, $\dfrac{1{,}520 \text{ torr}}{P_f} = \dfrac{293 \text{ K}}{307 \text{ K}}$,

$P_f = 1{,}593 \text{ torr or } 1{,}590 \text{ torr (for three significant figures)}$

34. $\dfrac{P_i}{T_i} = \dfrac{P_f}{T_f}$

$P_f = \dfrac{P_i T_f}{T_i} = \dfrac{(760 \text{ torr})(308 \text{ K})}{(303 \text{ K})} = 773 \text{ torr}$

35. $V_i = 4\overline{0}0 \text{ mL}$ $V_f = ?$

$P_i = 1.00 \text{ atm}$ $P_f = 7\overline{8}0 \text{ torr} = 1.03 \text{ atm}$

$T_i = 25°C + 273 = 298 \text{ K}$ $T_f = 50.0°C + 273 = 323 \text{ K}$

$\dfrac{P_i V_i}{T_i} = \dfrac{P_f V_f}{T_f}$, $\dfrac{(1.00 \text{ atm})(4\overline{0}0 \text{ L})}{298 \text{ K}} = \dfrac{(1.03 \text{ atm})(V_f)}{323 \text{ K}}$,

$V_f = 421 \text{ mL}$

36. $\dfrac{P_iV_i}{T_i} = \dfrac{P_fV_f}{T_f}$

$V_f = \dfrac{P_iV_iT_f}{T_iP_f} = \dfrac{(1.20\ \text{atm})(350.0\ \text{mL})(328\ \text{K})}{(301\ \text{K})(2.00\ \text{atm})} = 229\ \text{mL}$

37. P_{H_2O} at $3\overline{0}\,°C = 31.8$ torr

$P_{gas} = P_{total} - P_{H_2O} = 78\overline{0}$ torr $- 32$ torr $= 748$ torr

$P_i = 748$ torr $\qquad\qquad P_f = 76\overline{0}$ torr

$V_i = 8\overline{0}\overline{0}$ mL $\qquad\qquad V_f = ?$

$T_i = 30.0°C + 273 = 303$ K $\qquad T_f = 273$ K

$\dfrac{P_iV_i}{T_i} = \dfrac{P_fV_f}{T_f}$, $\qquad \dfrac{(748\ \text{torr})(8\overline{0}\overline{0}\ \text{mL})}{303\ \text{K}} = \dfrac{(76\overline{0}\ \text{torr})(V_f)}{273\ \text{K}}$,

$V_f = 709$ mL

38. $\dfrac{P_iV_i}{T_i} = \dfrac{P_fV_f}{T_f}$

$V_f = \dfrac{P_iV_iT_f}{T_iP_f} = \dfrac{(790.0\ \text{torr} - 28.4\ \text{torr})(750.0\ \text{mL})(273\ \text{K})}{(301\ \text{K})(760\ \text{torr})}$,

$V_f = 682$ mL

39. $V_i = 5\overline{0}\overline{0}$ mL $\qquad\qquad V_f = ?$

$T_i = 273$ K $\qquad\qquad T_f = 1\overline{0}\,°C + 273 = 283$ K

$P_i = 1.00$ atm $= 76\overline{0}$ torr $\qquad P_i = 1,\overline{0}\overline{0}\overline{0}$ torr

$\dfrac{P_iV_i}{T_i} = \dfrac{P_fV_f}{T_f}$, $\qquad \dfrac{(76\overline{0}\ \text{torr})(5\overline{0}\overline{0}\ \text{mL})}{273\ \text{K}} = \dfrac{(1,\overline{0}\overline{0}\overline{0}\ \text{torr})(V_f)}{283\ \text{K}}$,

$V_f = 394$ mL

40. $\dfrac{P_iV_i}{T_i} = \dfrac{P_fV_f}{T_f}$

$$V_f = \frac{P_i V_i T_f}{T_i P_f} = \frac{(800 \text{ torr} - 42 \text{ torr})(1.00 \text{ L})(273 \text{ K})}{(308 \text{ K})(760 \text{ torr})},$$

$$V_f = 0.884 \text{ L}$$

41. Assume no change in temperature.

$V_i = V_i$ $\qquad\qquad\qquad V_f = ?$

$P_i = 4.0 \text{ atm}$ $\qquad\qquad\qquad P_f = 1.5 \text{ atm}$

$$\frac{V_i}{V_f} = \frac{P_f}{P_i}, \qquad \frac{V_i}{V_f} = \frac{1.5 \text{ atm}}{4.0 \text{ atm}}, \qquad V_f = \frac{4.0\ V_i}{1.5}, \qquad V_f = 2.7\ V_i$$

The new volume would be about 2.7 times the original volume.

42. Assume no change in temperature.

$V_i = V_i$ $\qquad\qquad\qquad V_f = ?$

$P_i = 2.00 \text{ atm}$ $\qquad\qquad\qquad P_f = 4.50 \text{ atm}$

$$P_i V_i = P_f V_f$$

$$V_f = \frac{P_i V_i}{P_f} = \frac{(2.00 \text{ atm})(V_i)}{4.50 \text{ atm}}, \qquad V_f = 0.444\ V_i$$

The new volume would be about 0.444 that of the original volume.

43. $P_i = 25.0 \text{ atm}$ $\qquad\qquad\qquad P_f = ?$

$T_i = 50.0°C + 273 = 323 \text{ K}$ $\qquad\qquad T_f = \overline{5}00°C + 273 = 773 \text{ K}$

$V_i = V_f$ (that is, volume is constant)

$$\frac{P_i}{P_i} = \frac{T_i}{T_f}, \qquad \frac{0.25 \text{ atm}}{P_f} = \frac{323 \text{ K}}{773 \text{ K}}, \qquad P_f = 59.8 \text{ atm}$$

44. $\dfrac{P_i}{T_i} = \dfrac{P_f}{T_f}$

$$P_f = \frac{P_i T_f}{T_i} = \frac{(15.0 \text{ atm})(323 \text{ K})}{(623 \text{ K})} = 7.78 \text{ atm}$$

45. $V_i = 4\overline{00}$ mL $V_f = ?$

$T_i = 127°C + 273 = 4\overline{00}$ K $T_f = 273$ K

$P_i = 3.00$ atm $P_f = 1.00$ atm

$$\frac{P_iV_i}{T_i} = \frac{P_fV_f}{T_f} \ , \qquad \frac{(3.00 \text{ atm})(4\overline{00} \text{ mL})}{400 \text{ K}} = \frac{(1.00 \text{ atm})(V_f)}{273 \text{ K}} \ ,$$

$V_f = 819$ mL

46. $\dfrac{P_iV_i}{T_i} = \dfrac{P_fV_f}{T_f}$

$$V_f = \frac{P_iV_iT_f}{T_iP_f} = \frac{(2.50 \text{ atm})(40.0 \text{ mL})(273 \text{ K})}{(373 \text{ K})(1.00 \text{ atm})} = 73.2 \text{ mL}$$

47. $V_i = 3\overline{00}$ mL $V_f = ?$

$P_i = P_{\text{total}} - P_{H_2O}$ $P_f = 7\overline{60}$ torr

$\quad = 7\overline{50}$ torr $- 13$ torr $T_f = 273$ K

$\quad = 737$ torr

$T_i = 15.0°C + 273 = 288$ K

$$\frac{P_iV_i}{T_i} = \frac{P_fV_f}{T_f} \ , \qquad \frac{(737 \text{ torr})(3\overline{00} \text{ mL})}{288 \text{ K}} = \frac{(7\overline{60} \text{ torr})(V_f)}{273 \text{ K}} \ ,$$

$V_f = 276$ mL

48. $\dfrac{P_iV_i}{T_i} = \dfrac{P_fV_f}{T_f}$

$$V_f = \frac{P_iV_iT_f}{T_iP_f} = \frac{(815 \text{ torr} - 27 \text{ torr})(250 \text{ mL})(273 \text{ K})}{(300 \text{ K})(760 \text{ torr})} \ ,$$

$V_f = 236$ mL

49.

Data Set	P	V	n	T
1	constant	increase	constant	INCREASE
2	INCREASE	decrease	constant	constant
3	decrease	INCREASE	increase	constant

50.

Data Set	P	V	n	T
1	decrease	INCREASE	constant	constant
2	DECREASE	increase	constant	constant
3	increase	constant	constant	INCREASE

51. Total pressure is the sum of the partial pressures.

$$P_{total} = P_{Ar} + P_{He} + P_{Ne} + P_{Xe}$$

$$= 125 \text{ torr} + 255 \text{ torr} + 152 \text{ torr} + 304 \text{ torr}$$

$$= 836 \text{ torr}$$

52. Total pressure $= 2\overline{0}0 \text{ torr} + 15\overline{0} \text{ torr} + 9\overline{0} \text{ torr} + 15\overline{0} \text{ torr}$

$$= 59\overline{0} \text{ torr}$$

53. 80% N_2 means that N_2 exerts 80% of the total pressure.

$$P_{N_2} = 760 \text{ torr} \times 0.80$$

$$= 608 \text{ torr or } 610 \text{ torr (for two significant figures)}$$

54. $\dfrac{P_i V_i}{T_i} = \dfrac{P_f V_f}{T_f}$

$$V_f = \frac{P_i V_i T_f}{P_f T_i} = \frac{(77\overline{0} \text{ torr} - 19.8 \text{ torr})(75\overline{0} \text{ mL})(273 \text{ K})}{(760 \text{ torr})(295 \text{ K})} = 685 \text{ mL}$$

55. $C_4H_{10} + 13O_2 \rightarrow 8CO_2 + 10H_2O$
$5.00L ?L ?L$

$$\text{L of } H_2O = (5.00 \text{ L } C_4H_{10})\left(\frac{10 \text{ L } H_2O}{2 \text{ L } C_4H_{10}}\right) = 25.0 \text{ L}$$

$$\text{L of } O_2 = (5.00 \text{ L } C_4H_{10})\left(\frac{13 \text{ L } O_2}{2 \text{ L } C_4H_{10}}\right) = 32.5 \text{ L}$$

56. $2C_2H_6(g) + 7O_2(g) \rightarrow 4CO_2(g) + 6H_2O(g)$
    15.0L   ?L

    $$\text{L water vapor} = (15.0 \text{ L ethane})\left(\frac{6 \text{ L water vapor}}{2 \text{ L ethane}}\right)$$

    $$= 45.0 \text{ L water vapor}$$

57. $\text{L O}_2 = (4.00 \text{ moles O}_2)(22.4 \text{ L/mole}) = 89.6 \text{ L O}_2$

58. $\text{L H}_2 \text{ gas} = (3.00 \text{ moles})\left(\frac{22.4 \text{ L}}{1.00 \text{ mole}}\right) = 67.2 \text{ L H}_2 \text{ gas}$

59. $2Na + 2H_2O \rightarrow 2NaOH + H_2$
     ?grams   10.0L

    $$\text{Moles H}_2 = (10.0 \text{ L})\left(\frac{1 \text{ mole H}_2}{22.4 \text{ L}}\right) = 0.446 \text{ mole H}_2$$

    $$\text{Moles Na} = (0.466 \text{ mole H}_2)\left(\frac{2 \text{ moles Na}}{1 \text{ mole H}_2}\right) = 0.892 \text{ mole Na}$$

    $$\text{Grams Na} = (0.893 \text{ mole})\left(\frac{23.0 \text{ g}}{1 \text{ mole}}\right) = 20.5 \text{ g Na}$$

60. $2Li + 2H_2O \rightarrow 2LiOH + H_2$
     ?grams   10.0L at STP
                               $\downarrow \div 22.4$
                               0.446 mole

    $$\text{Moles Li} = (0.446 \text{ mole H}_2)\left(\frac{2 \text{ moles Li}}{1 \text{ mole H}_2}\right) = 0.892 \text{ mole Li}$$

    $$\text{Grams Li} = (0.892 \text{ mole Li})\left(\frac{6.9 \text{ g}}{1 \text{ mole Li}}\right) = 6.2 \text{ g Li}$$

61. $2H_2 + O_2 \rightarrow 2H_2O$
    80mL   80mL

    Assume that 80 mL of H_2 react.

$$\text{mL O}_2 \text{ used} = (80 \text{ mL H}_2)\left(\frac{1 \text{ mL O}_2}{2 \text{ mL H}_2}\right) = 40 \text{ mL O}_2$$

$$\text{mL O}_2 \text{ uncombined} = 80 \text{ mL} - 40 \text{ mL} = 40 \text{ mL O}_2$$

$$\text{mL H}_2\text{O formed} = (80 \text{ mL H}_2)\left(\frac{2 \text{ mL H}_2\text{O}}{2 \text{ mL H}_2}\right) = 80 \text{ mL O}_2$$

62. $$2H_2 \ + \ O_2 \ \rightarrow \ 2H_2O$$

Start	1.00 L	1.00 L	—
Use	1.00 L	0.50 L	
Produce			1.00 L

$$\text{g O}_2 \text{ uncombined} = (0.50 \text{ L})\left(\frac{1 \text{ mole}}{22.4 \text{ L}}\right)\left(\frac{32.0 \text{ g}}{1 \text{ mole}}\right) = 0.71 \text{ g O}_2$$

$$\text{g H}_2\text{O formed} = (1.00 \text{ L})\left(\frac{1 \text{ mole}}{22.4 \text{ L}}\right)\left(\frac{18.0 \text{ g}}{1 \text{ mole}}\right) = 0.804 \text{ g H}_2\text{O}$$

63. (a)   Given: $2SO_2(g) + O_2(g) \rightarrow 2SO_3(g)$

(b) $$\text{L O}_2 = (150 \text{ L SO}_2)\left(\frac{1 \text{ L O}_2}{2 \text{ L SO}_2}\right) = 75.0 \text{ L O}_2$$

(c) $$\text{L SO}_3 = (150 \text{ L SO}_2)\left(\frac{2 \text{ L SO}_3}{2 \text{ L SO}_2}\right) = 150 \text{ L SO}_3$$

64. (a) $$2NO_2 \ + \ O_2 \ \rightarrow \ 2NO_2$$
$$10.0 \text{ L} \quad \ ?L \quad \quad ?L$$

$$2 : 1 : 2$$
$$10 : x : y \qquad \qquad x = 5, \ y = 10$$

(b)   Therefore 5.00 L of O_2 gas are needed.

(c)   And 10.0 L of NO_2 gas are produced.

65. (a)   Given: $2C_4H_{10}(g) + 13O_2(g) \rightarrow 8CO_2(g) + 10H_2O(g)$

(b) $$\text{L O}_2 = (15.0 \text{ L C}_4\text{H}_{10})\left(\frac{13 \text{ L O}_2}{2 \text{ L C}_4\text{H}_{10}}\right) = 97.5 \text{ L O}_2$$

(c) $L\ CO_2 = (15.0\ \cancel{L\ C_4H_{10}})\left(\dfrac{8\ L\ CO_2}{2\ \cancel{L\ C_4H_{10}}}\right) = 60.0\ L\ CO_2$

$L\ H_2O = (15.0\ \cancel{L\ C_4H_{10}})\left(\dfrac{10\ L\ H_2}{2\ \cancel{L\ C_4H_{10}}}\right) = 75.0\ L\ H_2O$

66. $C_3H_8 + 5O_2 \rightarrow 3CO_2 + 4H_2O$
     25.0L   ?L   ?L

(b) $L\ O_2\ needed = (25.0\ \cancel{L\ C_3H_8})\left(\dfrac{5\ L\ O_2}{1\ \cancel{L\ C_3H_8}}\right) = 125\ L\ O_2$

(c) $L\ CO_2\ produced = (25.0\ \cancel{L\ C_3H_8})\left(\dfrac{3\ L\ CO_2}{1\ \cancel{L\ C_3H_8}}\right) = 75.0\ L\ CO_2$

67. Given:

(a) $N_2(g) + 2O_2(g) \rightarrow 2NO_2(g)$

(b) $mL\ N_2\ reacting = (75.0\ \cancel{mL\ O_2})\left(\dfrac{1\ mL\ N_2}{2\ \cancel{mL\ O_2}}\right) = 37.5\ mL\ N_2$

$mL\ N_2\ uncombined = 75.0\ mL\ added - 37.5\ mL\ reacted = 37.5\ mL$

(c) $mL\ NO_2\ formed = (75.0\ \cancel{mL\ O_2})\left(\dfrac{2\ mL\ NO_2}{2\ \cancel{mL\ O_2}}\right) = 75.0\ mL\ NO_2$

68. (a) N_2 + $3H_2$ $\rightarrow$ $2NH_3$

(b)   Start 120.0 mL   120.0 mL   —

     Use   40.0 mL   120.0 mL   —

(c)   Produce   80.0 mL

     Note: 80 mL of N_2 remains.

69. $P = 1{,}520\ torr = 2.00\ atm$ $V = 3.00\ L$

$R = 0.0821\ \dfrac{(L)(atm)}{(K)(mole)}$ $T = 27°C + 273 = \overline{300}\ K$

$$PV = nRT \quad \text{or} \quad n = \frac{PV}{RT} = \frac{(2.00 \text{ atm})(3.00 \text{ L})}{\left(0.0821 \frac{\text{(L)(atm)}}{\text{(K)(mole)}}\right)(3\overline{00} \text{ K})} = 0.244 \text{ mole } N_2 = 6.83 \text{ g } N_2$$

70. $PV = nRT$

$$PV = \frac{gRT}{MM}$$

$$? \text{ grams} = \frac{PVMM}{RT} = \frac{(3.000 \text{ atm})(2.00 \text{ L})(2.0 \text{ g/mole})}{\left(0.0821 \frac{\text{(L)(atm)}}{\text{(K)(mole)}}\right)(4\overline{00} \text{ K})} = 0.37 \text{ g}$$

71. $P = 1.00 \text{ atm}$ $\qquad\qquad\qquad V = 22.4 \text{ L}$

$T = 273 \text{ K}$ $\qquad\qquad\qquad n = 1.00 \text{ mole}$ $\qquad\qquad R = ?$

$$PV = nRT \quad \text{or} \quad R = \frac{PV}{nT} = \frac{(1.00 \text{ atm})(22.4 \text{ L})}{(1 \text{ mole})(273 \text{ K})} = 0.0821 \frac{\text{(L)(atm)}}{\text{(K)(mole)}}$$

72. $PV = nRT$

$$V = \frac{nRT}{P} = \frac{(0.75 \text{ mole})\left(0.0821 \frac{\text{(L)(atm)}}{\text{(K)(mole)}}\right)(273 \text{ K})}{1.00 \text{ atm}} = 17 \text{ L}$$

73. $P = 1.00 \text{ atm}$ $\qquad\qquad V = ?$

$n = 0.500 \text{ mole}$ $\qquad\qquad T = 273 \text{ K}$ $\qquad\qquad R = 0.0820 \frac{\text{(L)(atm)}}{\text{(K)(mole)}}$

$PV = nRT$

$$V = \frac{nRT}{P} = \frac{(0.500 \text{ mole})\left(0.0821 \frac{\text{(L)(atm)}}{\text{(K)(mole)}}\right)(273 \text{ K})}{1 \text{ atm}} = 11.2 \text{ L}$$

74. $PV = nRT$

$$PV = \frac{gRT}{MM}$$

$$? \text{ grams} = \frac{PVMM}{RT} = \frac{(1.50 \text{ atm})(1.5000 \text{ L})(71.0 \text{ g/mole})}{\left(0.0821 \frac{\text{(L)(atm)}}{\text{(K)(mole)}}\right)(423 \text{ K})} = 4.60 \text{ g}$$

75. $P = 3,04\overline{0} \text{ torr} = 4.000 \text{ atm}$ $\qquad\qquad$ $V = 50\overline{0} \text{ mL} = 0.500 \text{ L}$

$$n = \frac{g}{MM} = \frac{g}{46.0} \qquad\qquad\qquad R = 0.0820 \frac{\text{(L)(atm)}}{\text{(K)(mole)}}$$

$T = 227°\text{C} + 273 = 50\overline{0} \text{ K}$

$$PV = nRT = \frac{gRT}{MM} \quad \text{or} \quad g = \frac{PV(MM)}{RT}$$

$$? \text{ grams} = \frac{(4.000 \text{ atm})(0.500 \text{ L})(46.0 \text{ g/mole})}{\left(0.0821 \frac{\text{(L)(atm)}}{\text{(K)(mole)}}\right)(5\overline{0}\overline{0} \text{ K})} = 2.24 \text{ g}$$

76. $PV = nRT$

$$n = \frac{PV}{RT} = \frac{(1.00 \text{ atm})(2.00 \text{ L})}{\left(0.0821 \frac{\text{(L)(atm)}}{\text{(K)(mole)}}\right)(4\overline{0}\overline{0} \text{ K})} = 0.0609 \text{ mole}$$

77. $P = ?$ $\qquad\qquad\qquad\qquad$ $V = 2,\overline{000} \text{ mL} = 2.000 \text{ L}$

$n = 12.20 \text{ moles } H_2$ $\qquad\qquad$ $T = -73°\text{C} + 273 = 20\overline{0} \text{ K}$

$$R = 0.0821 \frac{\text{(L)(atm)}}{\text{(K)(mole)}}$$

$PV = nRT$

$$P = \frac{nRT}{V} = \frac{(12.20 \text{ moles})\left(0.0821 \frac{\text{(L)(atm)}}{\text{(K)(mole)}}\right)(2\overline{0}\overline{0} \text{ K})}{2.00 \text{ L}} = 1\overline{0}\overline{0} \text{ atm}$$

78. $PV = nRT$

$$P = \frac{nRT}{V} = \frac{(4.00 \text{ moles})\left(0.0821 \frac{\text{(L)(atm)}}{\text{(K)(mole)}}\right)(273 \text{ K})}{5.00 \text{ L}} = 17.9 \text{ atm}$$

79. $PV = nRT$

$$T = \frac{PV}{nR}$$

$P = 38\bar{0}$ torr

$$\text{atm} = 38\bar{0} \text{ torr} \times \frac{1 \text{ atm}}{76\bar{0} \text{ torr}} = 0.500 \text{ atm}$$

$V = 5\overline{00} \text{ mL} = 0.500 \text{ L}$

$$? \text{ moles } (n) = 128 \text{ g SO}_2 \times \frac{1 \text{ mole}}{64.1 \text{ g SO}_2} = 2.00 \text{ moles}$$

$$T = \frac{(0.500 \text{ atm})(0.500 \text{ L})}{(2.00 \text{ moles})\left(0.0821 \frac{\text{(L)(atm)}}{\text{(K)(mole)}}\right)} = 1.52 \text{ K}$$

80. $PV = nRT$

$$T = \frac{PV}{nR} = \frac{\left(\frac{77\bar{0} \text{ torr}}{760 \text{ torr/atm}}\right)(0.950 \text{ L})}{\left(\frac{92.0 \text{ g}}{46.0 \text{ g/mole}}\right)\left(0.0821 \frac{\text{(L)(atm)}}{\text{(K)(mole)}}\right)} = 5.87 \text{ K}$$

? °C = 5.87 K – 273 = –267°C

81. $P = 1.0$ atm $V = 0.50$ L

$T = 25°C + 273 = 298$ K $R = 0.0821 \dfrac{\text{(L)(atm)}}{\text{(K)(mole)}}$

? grams = 1.2 g   MM = ?

(a)   Grams C = $1.2 \text{ g gas} \times \dfrac{0.83 \text{ g C}}{1.0 \text{ g gas}} = 1.0 \text{ g C}$

Grams H = $1.2 \text{ g gas} \times \dfrac{0.17 \text{ g H}}{1.0 \text{ g gas}} = 0.20 \text{ g H}$

Moles H atoms = $0.20 \text{ g} \times \dfrac{1 \text{ mole H atoms}}{1.0 \text{ g}} = 0.20 \text{ mole H}$

Moles C atoms = $1.0 \text{ g} \times \dfrac{1 \text{ mole C atoms}}{12.0 \text{ g}} = 0.083 \text{ mole C}$

$C_{0.083}H_{0.020} = CH_{2.5} = C_2H_5$

(b) $PV = nRT$ or $PV = \dfrac{gRT}{MM}$. Therefore,

$MM = \dfrac{gRT}{PV} = \dfrac{(1.2 \text{ g})\left(0.0821 \frac{\text{(L)(atm)}}{\text{(K)(mole)}}\right)(298 \text{ K})}{(1.0 \text{ atm})(0.500 \text{ L})} = 59 \text{ g/mole}$

(c)   The molecular formula is twice the empirical formula; that is, it is C_4H_{10}.

82. $PV = \dfrac{gRT}{MM}$

$MM = \dfrac{gRT}{PV} = \dfrac{(4.00 \text{ g})\left(0.0821 \frac{\text{(L)(atm)}}{\text{(K)(mole)}}\right)(300 \text{ K})}{(2.64 \text{ atm})(0.500 \text{ L})} = 74.6 \text{ g/mole}$

83. $P = 3{,}040 \text{ torr} = 4.00 \text{ atm}$ $V = 400 \text{ mL} = 0.400 \text{ L}$

$MM = ?$ $g = 2.0$ $T = 127°C + 273 = 400 \text{ K}$

$PV = nRT$ or $PV = \dfrac{gRT}{MM}$ $R = 0.0820 \dfrac{\text{(L)(atm)}}{\text{(K)(mole)}}$

Therefore,

$MM = \dfrac{gRT}{PV} = \dfrac{(2.0 \text{ g})\left(0.0820 \frac{\text{(L)(atm)}}{\text{(K)(mole)}}\right)(400 \text{ K})}{(4.00 \text{ atm})(0.400 \text{ L})} = 41 \text{ g/mole}$

84. $PV = \dfrac{gRT}{MM}$

$\dfrac{g}{V} = \dfrac{PMM}{RT}$

$D = \dfrac{PMM}{RT} = \dfrac{(1.00 \text{ atm})(2.00 \text{ g/mole})}{\left(0.0821 \dfrac{(L)(atm)}{(K)(mole)}\right)(273 \text{ K})} = 0.089 \text{ g/L}$

85. $P = 1.0$ atm $V = 22.4$ L

$g = 32$ $R = 0.0821 \dfrac{(L)(atm)}{(K)(mole)}$

$T = 273$ K $D = ?$

$PV = nRT$ or $PV = \dfrac{gRT}{MM}$ or $\dfrac{g}{V} = \dfrac{(P)(MM)}{RT}$ or $D = \dfrac{(P)(MM)}{RT}$

$D = \dfrac{(1.0 \text{ atm})(32 \text{ g/mole})}{\left(0.0821 \dfrac{(L)(atm)}{(K)(mole)}\right)(273 \text{ K})}$

$= 1.43$ g/L   or 1.4 g/L (for two significant figures)

86. $PV = \dfrac{gRT}{MM}$

$MM = \dfrac{gRT}{PV} = \dfrac{(20.0g)\left(0.0821 \dfrac{(L)(atm)}{(K)(mole)}\right)(303 \text{ K})}{(4.00 \text{ atm})(1.500 \text{ L})} = 82.9 \text{ g/mole}$

87. $P = 6.00$ atm $V = 2,5\overline{0}0$ mL $= 2.500$ L $n = \dfrac{g}{MM}$

$g = 14.63$ g $MM = ?$ $T = 27 °C + 273 = 3\overline{0}0$ K

$PV = nRT$ or $PV = \dfrac{gRT}{MM}$

$$MM = \frac{gRT}{PV} = \frac{(14.63 \text{ g})\left(0.0821 \frac{\text{(L)(atm)}}{\text{(K)(mole)}}\right)(3\overline{00} \text{ K})}{(6.00 \text{ atm})(2.500 \text{ L})} = 24.0 \text{ g/mole}$$

88. $PV = \frac{gRT}{MM}$

$$MM = \frac{gRT}{PV} = \frac{(150.0 \text{ g})\left(0.0821 \frac{\text{(L)(atm)}}{\text{(K)(mole)}}\right)(423 \text{ K})}{(2.63 \text{ atm})(5.00 \text{ L})} = 396 \text{ g/mole}$$

89. Given: 69.57% O and 30.43% N

    (a) Take $1\overline{00}$ g of compound:

    $$\text{Moles O} = (69.57 \text{ g})\left(\frac{1 \text{ mole O}}{16.00 \text{ g}}\right) = 4.346 \text{ moles O}$$

    $$\text{Moles N} = (30.43 \text{ g})\left(\frac{1 \text{ mole N}}{14.00 \text{ g}}\right) = 2.172 \text{ moles N}$$

    $N_{2.17}O_{4.35}$ or NO_2 for the empirical formula

    (b) $P = 1.50$ atm $V = 25\overline{0}$ mL $= 0.250$ L

    $g = 1.44$ $T = 20.0°C + 273 = 293$ K

    $R = 0.082 \frac{\text{(L)(atm)}}{\text{(K)(mole)}}$

    $$MM = \frac{gRT}{PV} = \frac{(1.44 \text{ g})\left(0.0820 \frac{\text{(L)(atm)}}{\text{(K)(mole)}}\right)(293 \text{ K})}{(1.50 \text{ atm})(0.250 \text{ L})} = 92.3 \text{ g/mole}$$

    (c) Empirical formula mass is 46.0, which is one-half of the molecular mass. Therefore, the molecular formula is N_2O_4.

90. $PV = \frac{gRT}{MM}$

$$MM = \frac{gRT}{PV} = \frac{(75.0 \text{ g})\left(0.0820 \frac{\text{(L)(atm)}}{\text{(K)(mole)}}\right)(4\overline{0}0 \text{ K})}{(2.05 \text{ atm})(4.50 \text{ L})} = 267 \text{ g/mole}$$

EXTRA EXERCISES

91. Boyle's Law can be explained by the kinetic theory of gases. As the pressure on a gas is increased at constant temperature, the molecules are forced to move closer to each other, resulting in a decrease in volume, and vice versa. Charles's Law can also be explained by the kinetic theory of gases. As the molecules of a gas are heated at constant pressure, the molecules move farther apart from each other, resulting in an increase in volume. Cooling the gas has the reverse effect.

92. $P_i = 10.0$ atm $P_f = 7\overline{6}0$ torr $= 1.00$ atm

    $V_i = 5.00$ L $V_f = ?$

    $\dfrac{P_i}{P_f} = \dfrac{V_f}{V_i}$ $\dfrac{10.00 \text{ atm}}{1.00 \text{ atm}} = \dfrac{V_f}{5.00 \text{ L}}$ $V_f = 50.0$ L

93. $V_i = 50.0$ L $V_f = ?$

    $P_i = 1.00$ atm $P_f = 2\overline{3}0$ torr $= 0.303$ atm

    $T_i = 25°C + 273 = 298$ K $T_f = -50°C + 273 = 223$ K

    $\dfrac{P_i V_i}{T_i} = \dfrac{P_f V_f}{T_f}$ $\dfrac{(1.00 \text{ atm})(50.0 \text{ L})}{298 \text{ K}} = \dfrac{(0.303 \text{ atm})(V_f)}{223 \text{ K}}$

    $V_f = 124$ L

94. $N_2(g) + 3H_2(g) \rightarrow 2NH_3(g)$

    Find the number of liters of N_2 reacting at 30.0°C and $7\overline{5}0$ torr.

    $P = 7\overline{5}0$ torr $= 0.987$ atm $V = ?$

    $n = (1,\overline{0}00 \text{ g})\left(\dfrac{1 \text{ mole } N_2}{28.0 \text{ g}}\right) = 35.7$ moles N_2

$$T = 30.0°C + 273 = 303 \text{ K} \qquad R = 0.0820 \frac{(L)(atm)}{(K)(mole)}$$

$$PV = nRT$$

$$V = \frac{nRT}{P} = \frac{(35.7 \text{ moles})\left(0.0820 \frac{(L)(atm)}{(K)(mole)}\right)(303 \text{ K})}{0.987 \text{ atm}} = 899 \text{ L N}_2$$

$$? \text{ L NH}_3 = (899 \text{ L N}_2)\left(\frac{2 \text{ L NH}_3}{1 \text{ L N}_2}\right) = 1,8\overline{0}0 \text{ L NH}_3$$

95. (a) $4\overline{0}°F = 4°C$ $K = 4°C + 273 = 277 \text{ K}$

    (b) $18\overline{0}°F = 82°C$ $K = 82°C + 273 = 355 \text{ K}$

    (c) $212°F = 1\overline{00}°C$ $K = 1\overline{00}°C + 273 = 373 \text{ K}$

96. Grams $O_2 = (1.00 \text{ mole O}_2)\left(\frac{32.0 \text{ g O}_2}{1 \text{ mole O}_2}\right) = 32.0 \text{ g O}_2$

    Volume $O_2 = (32.0 \text{ g})\left(\frac{1 \text{ L O}_2}{1.429 \text{ g}}\right) = 22.4 \text{ L O}_2$

97. Molecular mass of $CH_4 = 16.0$. One mole of CH_4 (or 16.0 g CH_4) occupies 22.4 L at STP.

    Density $CH_4 = \frac{\text{mass CH}_4}{\text{volume CH}_4} = \frac{16.0 \text{ g}}{22.4 \text{ L}} = 0.714 \text{ g/L}$

99. $P = \text{constant}$

    $V_i = 272 \text{ mL}$ $V_f = ? \text{ mL}$

    $T_i = 27°C + 273 = 300 \text{ K}$ $T_f = 200°C + 273 = 473 \text{ K}$

    $\dfrac{V_i}{T_i} = \dfrac{V_f}{T_f} \qquad V_f = \dfrac{V_i T_f}{T_i} = \dfrac{(272 \text{ mL})(473 \text{ K})}{300 \text{ K}} = 429 \text{ mL}$

100. $P = 1.00$ atm $T = 27°C + 273 = 3\overline{00}$ K

$V = 2.00$ L $g = 2.56$ g

MM = ? $PV = \dfrac{gRT}{MM}$

$$MM = \frac{gRT}{PV} = \frac{(2.56 \text{ g})\left(0.0820 \dfrac{\text{(L)(atm)}}{\text{(K)(mole)}}\right)(3\overline{00} \text{ K})}{(1.00 \text{ atm})(2.00 \text{ L})} = 31.5 \text{ g/mole} \qquad (O_2 \text{ is } 32)$$

14 THE LIQUID AND SOLID STATES

SELF-TEST EXERCISES

1. (a) The boiling point of a liquid increases with increasing atmospheric pressure because a greater vapor pressure is needed for molecules to escape from the liquid. This can happen only at a higher temperature.

2. The molecules of a gas exhibit very little in terms of attractive forces one to another. Therefore, they are free to move about independently. The result is that gases have no definite shape and no definite volume.

3. The boiling point of a liquid is lowered by a decrease in atmospheric pressure.

4. True. Gases are easily compressed.

5. (a) Liquid   (b) Gas   (c) Solid

6. False. Solids and liquids have definite volume, but gas does not.

7. (a) According to the kinetic theory, liquids take the shape of their container because the molecules can move about each other.
   (b) Liquids have a definite volume because the molecules are attracted to one other with enough force to keep them touching one other.
   (c) According to the kinetic theory, liquids tend to be incompressible because the molecules are already as close to each other as they can get.

8. (a) & (b) According to the kinetic theory, solids have a definite shape and volume because of the forces that hold the crystal lattice together.
   (c) Solids are also incompressible because of their fixed shape and volume.

149

9. Once the water is boiling, it doesn't get any hotter. Turning up the heat on the stove doesn't change the temperature of the water and doesn't speed up the cooking of the potatoes.

10. Because of lower air pressure, a longer baking time is needed to get the brownies to rise properly and reach the right consistency.

11. If the mountain is high enough, the water boils at a significantly lower temperature because of the decrease in atmospheric pressure. Because the temperature of the water is lower when it begins to boil, it takes longer to cook a hardboiled egg on the mountain than at sea level.

12. No. The temperature remains constant at the boiling point.

13. Adding salt to water raises the boiling point because the vapor pressure of the resulting solution is decreased by the solute particles. Therefore a higher temperature is required to make the water boil.

14. Rubbing alcohol has a high equilibrium vapor pressure. If you forget to put the cap on the bottle, the alcohol will evaporate.

15. It is the high-energy molecules of liquid that escape from the container. The low-energy ones get left behind. The liquid therefore has less energy—in other words, less heat. The temperature of the liquid drops.

16. A humidifier could be added to the furnace.

17. For a liquid in an open container, an equilibrium vapor pressure will not be reached, because vapor will constantly be able to escape into the atmosphere.

20. Mercury has a fairly high vapor pressure at room temperature.

21. Gasoline evaporates more quickly than water because it has a higher equilibrium vapor pressure than water at any given temperature. In other words, it is more volatile.

22. The jar with the water at 75°C would have the higher vapor pressure. The higher the temperature, the higher the vapor pressure.

23. In order for a pure liquid to freeze, the molecules must be aligned, or "tied down." If a solute is placed in the pure liquid, the solute inhibits the liquid molecules from aligning. Therefore the freezing point of liquid is lowered.

24. No. You would not smell the fumes from the oil because the oil is not volatile.

25. The matching pairs are as follows: 1. (c), 2. (d), 3. (b), 4. (a).

26. Ethyl alcohol has a much lower boiling point than salad oil.

27. *Dynamic equilibrium* is the state achieved by two opposing processes that proceed at equal rates.

28. The boiling point of a liquid decreases with lower atmospheric pressure, as is typically the case with a rainy or stormy weather system.

29. The *boiling point* is the temperature at which the equilibrium vapor pressure of a liquid equals the atmospheric pressure. The *normal boiling point* is the boiling point of the liquid when the atmospheric pressure is 1 atmosphere.

30. The temperature of the water vapor at the boiling point is 100°C.

31. As ice is heated, the H_2O molecules gain energy and begin to vibrate faster and faster and faster. Eventually they overcome the bonds that have held them together, and the solid ice turns into clear liquid water. As the liquid water is heated, the molecules of H_2O pick up still more energy. When they gain enough energy, they overcome all attraction between them and enter the gaseous state.

32. The white vapors are CO_2 gas. The dry ice sublimes as it is warmed by the water, and the CO_2 gas bubbles become noticeable.

33. (a) *Distillation* is the process of separating a solution of two liquids, or a solid and a liquid, by heating the solution until it boils.
    (b) *Fractional distillation* is the repeated distillation of a solution until an essentially pure product is obtained.

34. The isopropyl alcohol has a lower boiling point. Therefore it is collected first, before the water.

35. (a) *Condensation* is the process by which a vapor changes to a liquid.
    (b) A *distillate* is the substance that is obtained in the distilling process. It is what's collected at the end of the condenser.
    (c) A *distilling head* is typically a piece of glassware that fits into the distillation flask considered on one side, and the condenser on the other.
    (d) A *condenser* is a double-jacketed piece of glassware that allows hot vapors passing through it to be evolved so that the vapor changes to a liquid.

36. There is really no difference between distillation and fractional distillation as far as the overall process is concerned. In fractional distillation, the distillate is distilled over and over again until a specific purity is obtained.

37. Amorphous

39. Well-defined (lattice)

40. Two examples of amorphous solids are glass and paraffin.

41. (a) Solids composed of oppositely charged ions are typically hard and brittle, have high melting points, and are nonconductors of electricity.
     (b) Solids composed of atoms come in two varieties. Metallic solids have high melting points, exhibit varying hardness, and are good conductors of electricity. The nonmetallic solids also have high melting points, are hard and brittle, and are nonconductors of electricity.
     (c) Solids composed of molecules have low melting points, are soft, and are nonconductors of electricity.

42. Atomic and ionic solids typically have high melting points, whereas molecular solids typically have low melting points.

43. A molecular solid

44. False. Ionic solids are hard and brittle with high melting points.

45. An ionic solid

46. True. Molecular solids are nonconductors of electricity.

47. (a) Metallic   (b) Ionic

48. Solids that are good conductors of electricity are atomic solids composed of metallic atoms. Solids that are nonconductors are ionic, molecular, and atomic solids composed of nonmetallic atoms. For a solid to be a conductor, electrons must be able to move about the crystal lattice.

49. (a) Atoms   (b) Molecules   (c) Ions

50. Solids that are hard and brittle are ionic and nonmetallic atomic solids.

51. (a) In atomic crystals that are composed of metallic atoms, it is the attraction of opposite charges that holds the crystal together. When the crystals are nonmetallic, they are held together by covalent bonds.
     (b) Molecular solids are held together by intermolecular forces, such as the forces that occur between polar molecules.
     (c) Ionic solids are held together by the attractive forces that exist between the oppositely charged ions.

52. The solid is probably a molecular solid if it does not conduct electricity and has a low melting point. Molecules would occupy the lattice positions.

54. Six types of crystals are cubic, tetragonal, orthorhombic, monoclinic, triclinic, and hexagonal crystals.

55. (a)   A *crystal lattice* is the symmetrical structure formed by the particles throughout a crystal.
    (b)   A *unit cell* is a repetitive unit in a crystal lattice.

56. Sodium chloride exhibits a cubic crystal structure.

57. Rainwater can pick up various substances as it passes through the atmosphere. Therefore, rainwater is not pure H_2O in a chemical sense.

58. $D = \dfrac{m}{V}$ $\qquad\qquad$ $V = \dfrac{m}{d} = \dfrac{18.4 \text{ g}}{0.92 \text{ g/cm}^3} = 20 \text{ cm}^3$

59. When water freezes and turns to ice, it expands. When ice melts and becomes water, it loses volume. Therefore the water in the glass will not overflow when the ice cube melts.

60. $D = \dfrac{m}{V}$ $\qquad\qquad$ $m = D \times V = (1.00 \text{ g/cm}^3)(535 \text{ cm}^3) = 535 \text{ g}$

61. Volume of a cube $= (4.0 \text{ cm})^3 = 64 \text{ cm}^3$

    $D = \dfrac{m}{V}$ $\quad$ or $\quad$ $m = (D)(V) = (0.92 \text{ g/cm}^3)(64 \text{ cm}^3) = 59 \text{ g}$

62. Bodies of water that now only partially freeze in winter, because the floating ice insulates the water underneath, would completely freeze if ice sank. This would occur because the cold air temperature of winter would freeze the ice at the surface. Then the ice would sink, allowing more water to freeze. The body of water would eventually freeze from the bottom up.

63. The dashed line represents the hydrogen bond between two water molecules in the following structure:

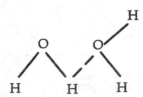

64. The bond angle between hydrogen atoms in a water molecule is 105°.

65. $\text{Volume} = \dfrac{\text{mass}}{\text{density}} = \dfrac{1,\overline{0}00 \text{ g}}{1.00 \text{ g/cm}^3} = 1,\overline{0}00 \text{ cm}^3$

66. A hydrogen bond in water is a bond formed between the hydrogen atom of one water molecule and the oxygen atom of another water molecule.

67. (a) $MgO + H_2O \rightarrow Mg(OH)_2$

    (b) $SO_3 + H_2O \rightarrow H_2SO_4$

    (c) $2Na + 2H_2O \rightarrow 2NaOH + H_2$

68. (a) $CaO + H_2O \rightarrow Ca(OH)_2$

    (b) $SO_2 + H_2O \rightarrow H_2SO_3$

    (c) $2K + 2H_2O \rightarrow 2KOH + H_2$

69. (a) $SrO + H_2O \rightarrow Sr(OH)_2$

    (b) $SO_2 + H_2O \rightarrow H_2SO_3$

    (c) $2Li + 2H_2O \rightarrow 2LiOH + H_2$

70. (a) $Na_2O + H_2O \rightarrow 2NaOH$

    (b) $CO_2 + H_2O \rightarrow H_2CO_3$

    (c) $2Rb + 2H_2O \rightarrow 2RbOH + H_2$

71. $\text{Percent } H_2O = \dfrac{\text{mass of } H_2O}{\text{mass of } CuSO_4 \cdot 5H_2O} \times 100 = \dfrac{(5)(18.0)}{250} \times 100 = 36.0\%$

72. $CaSO_4 \cdot 2H_2O$

    $40.1 + 32.1 + 64.0 + 36.0 = 172.2$

    $\text{Percent } H_2O = \dfrac{36.0}{172.2} \times 100 = 20.9\%$

73. The substance in the cleaning powder that "shakes out white, then turns blue" could be copper(II) sulfate in its anhydrous form.

$$CuSO_4 + 5H_2O \rightarrow CuSO_4 \cdot 5H_2O$$

White   Blue

74. A hydrated salt is one that has its water of hydration. For example, $CuSO_4 \cdot 5H_2O$ is a hydrated salt. An anhydrous salt is one that does not have any water.

75. (a) $\text{Percent } H_2O = \dfrac{\text{mass of } H_2O}{\text{mass of } MgSO_4 \cdot 7H_2O} \times 100 = \dfrac{(7)(18.0)}{246.4} \times 100 = 51.1\%$

     (b) $\text{Percent } H_2O = \dfrac{\text{mass of } H_2O}{\text{mass of } Na_2CO_3 \cdot 10H_2O} \times 100 = \dfrac{(10)(18.0)}{286.0} \times 100 = 62.9\%$

     (c) $\text{Percent } H_2O = \dfrac{\text{mass of } H_2O}{\text{mass of } KAl(SO_4)_2 \cdot 12H_2O} \times 100 = \dfrac{(12)(18.0)}{474.3} \times 100 = 45.5\%$

76. (a) $Ca(ClO_3)_2 \cdot 2H_2O$

          $40 + 71 + 96 + 36 = 243$

          $\text{Percent } H_2O = \dfrac{36.0}{243} \times 100 = 14.8\%$

     (b) $CaCO_3 \cdot 6H_2O$

          $40.1 + 12.0 + 48.0 + 108 = 208.1$

          $\text{Percent } H_2O = \dfrac{108}{208.1} \times 100 = 51.9\%$

     (c) $CaCl_2 \cdot 6H_2O$

          $40.1 + 71.0 + 108 = 219.1$

          $\text{Percent } H_2O = \dfrac{108}{219.1} \times 100 = 49.3\%$

77. (a) $CaSO_4 \cdot 2H_2O \xrightarrow{\text{Heat}} CaSO_4 + 2H_2O$

     (b) $KAl(SO_4)_2 \cdot 12H_2O \xrightarrow{\text{Heat}} KAl(SO_4)_2 + 12H_2O$

78.   (a) $Mg(C_2H_3O_2)_2 \cdot 4H_2O \xrightarrow{\text{Heat}} Mg(C_2H_3O_2)_2 + 4H_2O$

   (b) $MgBr_2 \cdot 6H_2O \xrightarrow{\text{Heat}} MgBr_2 + 6H_2O$

79.   Given: 21.60 g of H_2O

   mass of anhydrous salt = 52.58 g hydrate – 21.60 g H_2O = 30.98 g

   Moles H_2O = $(21.60 \text{ g})\left(\dfrac{1 \text{ mole}}{18.0 \text{ g}}\right)$ = 1.20 moles H_2O

   Moles $CoSO_4$ = $(30.98 \text{ g})\left(\dfrac{1 \text{ mole}}{155.0 \text{ g}}\right)$ = 0.2000 mole $CoSO_4$

   0.2000 mole $CoSO_4$ with 1.20 moles H_2O means the hydrate is in the ratio of 1: 6 or $CoSO_4 \cdot 6H_2O$.

80. $Mg(NO_3)_2 \cdot xH_2O \rightarrow Mg(NO_3)_2 + xH_2O$

   25.64 g   10.80 g

   g anhydrous salt = 25.64 g – 10.80 g = 14.84 g anhydrous salt

   Moles anhydrous salt = $(14.84 \text{ g})\left(\dfrac{1 \text{ mole}}{148.3 \text{ g}}\right)$ = 0.1001 mole anhydrous salt

   Moles H_2O = $(10.80 \text{ g})\left(\dfrac{1 \text{ mole}}{18.0 \text{ g}}\right)$ = 0.600 mole H_2O

   $\dfrac{\text{moles of anhydrous salt}}{\text{moles of water}} = \dfrac{0.1001}{0.600} = \dfrac{1}{6}$

   Therefore the formula of the hydrated salt is $Mg(NO_3)_2 \cdot 6H_2O$

81.   (a)   An *anhydrous salt* contains no water of hydration; an example is $CuSO_4$.
   (b)   A *hygroscopic substance* is one that can absorb water from the atmosphere; an example is $CaCl_2$.
   (c)   A *deliquescent substance* is one that absorbs so much water from the atmosphere that it forms a solution.
   (d)   A *substance that undergoes efflorescence* is one that loses its water of hydration spontaneously when exposed to the atmosphere. For example,

$$Na_2SO_4 \cdot 10H_2O \rightarrow Na_2SO_4 + 10H_2O$$

occurs at room temperature.

82. (a) A salt that has lost its water of hydration is called an *anhydrous* salt.
    (b) A substance that can absorb water from the atmosphere is *hygroscopic*.
    (c) A substance that absorbs enough water from the atmosphere to form a solution is *deliquescent*.
    (d) A salt that can spontaneously lose its water of hydration to the atmosphere is an *efflorescent* salt.

EXTRA EXERCISES

83. The temperature of a pure substance remains constant during a phase change because all the energy absorbed or expended is used to make the change occur.

84. It is a repeating unit.

85. Yes, some substances are already gases at *normal* atmospheric pressure (1.00 atm); an example is CO_2. The *normal boiling point* is defined as the boiling point of a substance at 1 atmosphere of pressure. Therefore many substances do not have normal boiling points.

86. Solids are held in a fixed crystal lattice. Liquid particles are able to move about each other. Gas particles are free to move independently from one another.

87. Steam at 100°C contains more heat than water at 100°C. Therefore the steam causes a more severe burn.

88. Glass is an amorphous solid.

89. Calcium chloride is hygroscopic, which means it can absorb water from the atmosphere. Therefore, when calcium chloride is placed in an enclosed container (a desiccator) with a wet chemical, the calcium chloride will absorb the water from that chemical.

90. Many salts change color when they go from their anhydrous form to their hydrated form. These salts are used on certain novelty weather devices to indicate dry or wet weather.

91.

Type	Melting point	Hardness	Conductivity
Ionic High	Hard and brittle	Nonconductors	
Molecular	Low	Soft	Nonconductors
Atomic			
Metallic	High	Varying hardness	Good conductor
Nonmetallic	High	Hard and brittle	Nonconductors

92. (a) Solid and liquid   (b) Solid   (c) Gas

94. Liquids that evaporate easily have a higher equilibrium vapor pressure than liquids that do not evaporate easily at the same temperature.

95. Water has an unusually high boiling point in relation to its molecular weight. This unusually high boiling point is due to hydrogen bonding between water molecules.

15

THE CHEMISTRY OF SOLUTIONS

SELF-TEST EXERCISES

1. The matching pairs are 1. (c), 2. (a), 3. (d), 4. (b).

2. When a solution is composed of two or more substances in the same state, the substance present in the greater amount is called the solvent.

3. (a) HCl is the solute, water is the solvent.
   (b) CO_2 is the solute, water is the solvent.
   (c) Benzene is the solute, carbon tetrachloride is the solvent.

4. True. This is an example of a solid-solid solution.

5. (a) Silver and gold alloy
   (b) Salt in water
   (c) Hydrogen dissolved in platinum metal
   (d) Alcohol and water

6. (a) The sodium chloride is the solute; the water is the solvent.
   (b) The benzene is the solute; the carbon tetrachloride is the solvent.
   (c) The methyl alcohol is the solute; the ethyl alcohol is the solvent.

7. True. Like dissolves like. This statement refers to the polarity of the molecules.

8. A saturated solution has been produced.

159

9. The point at which no more solute dissolves in a solution is called the *saturation point*.

10. That the two substances are *miscible* means that they will mix together and form a solution. *Immiscible* substances will not mix together to form a solution.

11. (a) A solution that contains less solute than can be dissolved in a given quantity of solvent at a particular temperature is an *unsaturated* solution.
    (b) A solution that contains more solute than is needed for saturation for a given quantity of solvent at a particular temperature is a *supersaturated* solution.

12. (a) 15.0 g of NaCl in 50.0 g of H_2O at 50°C is *unsaturated*.

    (b) 45.5 g of $AgNO_3$ in 50.0 g of water at 50°C is *unsaturated*.

13. An equilibrium between the dissolved and undissolved solute is in progress.

14. You could check for supersaturation by moving the solution, or disturbing it in some manner to make the solute crystallize out. You could also scratch the inside walls of the container with a glass rod to initiate crystallization.

15. (a) Percent magnesium nitrate by mass

$$= \frac{\text{mass of } Mg(NO_3)_2}{\text{mass of solution}} \times 100 = \frac{5.00 \text{ g}}{80.0 \text{ g}} \times 100 = 6.25\%$$

    (b) Percent ethanol by mass

$$= \frac{\text{mass of ethanol}}{\text{mass of solution}} \times 100 = \frac{60.0 \text{ g}}{300.0 \text{ g}} \times 100 = 20.0\%$$

    (c) Percent sodium chloride by mass

$$= \frac{\text{mass of NaCl}}{\text{mass of solution}} \times 100 = \frac{2.00 \text{ g}}{25.0 \text{ g}} \times 100 = 8.00\%$$

16. (a) Percent sodium chloride by mass

$$= \frac{80.0 \text{ g NaCl}}{250 \text{ g solution}} \times 100 = 32.0\%$$

    (b) Percent methyl alcohol by mass

$$= \frac{7.50 \text{ g CH}_3\text{OH}}{400 \text{ g solution}} \times 100 = 1.88\%$$

(c)   Percent potassium nitrate by mass

$$= \frac{50.0 \text{ g KNO}_3}{200 \text{ g solution}} \times 100 = 25.0\%$$

17.   g KOH $= \dfrac{0.10 \text{ g KOH}}{1.0 \text{ g solution}} \times 2\overline{0}0 \text{ g solution} = 2\overline{0} \text{ g KOH}$

18.   g NaOH = (500.0 g NaOH solution)(0.150) = 75.0 g NaOH

19.   (a)   Percent ether by volume $= \dfrac{\text{volume of ether}}{\text{total volume of solution}} \times 100$

$$= \frac{2\overline{0}0 \text{ mL}}{1000 \text{ mL}} \times 100 = 2\overline{0}\%$$

(b)   Percent alcohol by volume

$$= \frac{\text{volume of alcohol}}{\text{total volume of solution}} \times 100 = \frac{5 \text{ mL}}{80 \text{ mL}} \times 100 = 6\%$$

20.   (a)   Percent ether by volume $= \dfrac{300.0 \text{ mL}}{2,000 \text{ mL}} \times 100 = 15.0\%$

(b)   Percent alcohol by volume $= \dfrac{25.0 \text{ mL}}{100.0 \text{ mL}} \times 100 = 25.0\%$

21.   g alcohol $= \dfrac{0.100 \text{ g alcohol}}{1 \text{ g solution}} \times 1\overline{0}0 \text{ g solution} = 10.0 \text{ g alcohol}$

mL alcohol $= \dfrac{1.00 \text{ mL alcohol}}{0.800 \text{ g alcohol}} \times 10.0 \text{ g alcohol} = 12.5 \text{ mL alcohol}$

22.   g alcohol = (250.0 g)(0.100) = 25.0 g alcohol

$$V_{\text{alcohol}} = \frac{m}{D} = \frac{25.0 \text{ g}}{0.800 \text{ g/mL}} = 31.3 \text{ mL}$$

23.   mL chloroform $= \dfrac{0.040 \text{ mL chloroform}}{1.00 \text{ mL solution}} \times 5\overline{0}0 \text{ mL solution} = 2\overline{0} \text{ mL chloroform}$

24. mL CCl$_4$ = (250.0 mL)(0.0500) = 12.5 mL CCl$_4$

25. (a)   Percent NaCl by mass–volume

$$= \frac{\text{mass of NaCl}}{\text{volume of solution}} \times 100 = \frac{5\bar{0} \text{ g NaCl}}{1,500 \text{ mL solution}} \times 100 = 3.3\%$$

(b)   Percent NH$_3$ by mass–volume

$$= \frac{\text{mass of NH}_3}{\text{volume of solution}} \times 100 = \frac{1\bar{0} \text{ g NH}_3}{\bar{2}00 \text{ mL solution}} \times 100 = 5.0\%$$

26. (a)   Percent sodium nitrate by mass–volume $= \dfrac{25.0 \text{ g}}{1,000 \text{ mL}} \times 100 = 2.50\%$

(b)   Percent sodium hydroxide by mass–volume $= \dfrac{15.0 \text{ g}}{100.0 \text{ mL}} \times 100 = 15.0\%$

27. g sugar = 15 g sugar per 100 mL solution in a 15%-by-mass–volume
    sugar–water solution

28. g lactose = (150.0 mL)(0.10) = 15 g lactose

29. Percent sugar by mass $= \dfrac{\text{mass of sugar}}{\text{total mass of solution}} \times 100$

$$\frac{? \text{ g sugar}}{\text{g solution}} = \left(\frac{60 \text{ mg sugar}}{100 \text{ mL solution}}\right)\left(\frac{1 \text{ g sugar}}{1,000 \text{ mg sugar}}\right) \times \left(\frac{1.0 \text{ mL solution}}{1.2 \text{ g solution}}\right)$$

$$= 0.0005 \text{ g sugar/g solution} = 0.05\%$$

30. $M = D \times V = (1.20 \text{ g/mL})(1\bar{0}0 \text{ mL}) = 12\bar{0} \text{ g blood}$

120.0 m g = 0.1200 g

Percent blood sugar by mass $= \dfrac{0.1200 \text{ g}}{12\bar{0} \text{ g}} \times 100 = 0.100\%$

31. (a)   Percent sodium chloride by mass

$$= \frac{\text{mass of NaCl}}{\text{mass of solution}} \times 100 = \frac{25.0 \text{ g NaCl}}{200 \text{ g solution}} \times 100 = 12.5\%$$

(b)   Percent sugar by mass

$$= \frac{\text{mass of sugar}}{\text{mass of solution}} \times 100 = \frac{8.00 \text{ g sugar}}{160 \text{ g solution}} \times 100 = 5.00\%$$

32.   (a)   Percent sodium carbonate by mass $= \dfrac{55.0 \text{ g}}{400.0 \text{ g}} \times 100 = 13.8\%$

(b)   Percent sugar by mass $= \dfrac{14.5 \text{ g}}{290.0 \text{ g}} \times 100 = 5.00\%$

33.   g KCl $= (5\overline{0}0 \text{ g solution})\left(\dfrac{0.060 \text{ g KCl}}{1.0 \text{ g solution}}\right) = 3\overline{0} \text{ g KCl}$

34.   g KNO$_3$ = (750.0 g)(0.0750) = 56.3 g KNO$_3$

35.   (a)   Percent ethyl alcohol by volume

$$= \frac{\text{mL alcohol}}{\text{mL solution}} \times 100 = \frac{1\overline{5}0 \text{ mL alcohol}}{3,000 \text{ mL solution}} \times 100 = 5.0\%$$

(b)   Percent methyl alcohol by volume

$$= \frac{\text{mL alcohol}}{\text{mL solution}} \times 100 = \frac{5\overline{0}0 \text{ mL alcohol}}{60,000 \text{ mL solution}} \times 100 = 0.833\%$$

36.   (a)   Percent isopropyl alcohol by volume $= \dfrac{175 \text{ mL}}{4,000 \text{ mL}} \times 100 = 4.38\%$

(b)   Percent methyl alcohol by volume $= \dfrac{600.0 \text{ mL}}{60,000 \text{ mL}} \times 100 = 1.00\%$

37.   mL ether $= (5\overline{0}0 \text{ g solution})\left(\dfrac{4.0 \text{ g ether}}{100 \text{ g solution}}\right)\left(\dfrac{1.00 \text{ mL ether}}{0.714 \text{ g ether}}\right) = 28 \text{ mL ether}$

38.   g ether = (750.0 g)(0.100) = 75.0 g ether

$$V_{\text{ether}} = \frac{m}{D} = \frac{75.0 \text{ g}}{0.714 \text{ g/cm}^3} = 105 \text{ cm}^3$$

39.   mL ethyl alcohol $= (20\overline{0}0 \text{ mL solution})\left(\dfrac{10.0 \text{ mL alcohol}}{100 \text{ mL solution}}\right)$

$$= 2\overline{0}0 \text{ mL ethyl alcohol}$$

40. mL isopropyl alcohol $= (4,5\overline{0}0 \text{ mL})(0.200) = 9\overline{0}0 \text{ mL isopropyl alcohol}$

41. (a) Percent sodium nitrate by mass–volume

$$= \frac{\text{mass of NaNO}_3}{\text{volume of solution}} \times 100 = \frac{25.0 \text{ g NaNO}_3}{800 \text{ mL solution}} \times 100 = 3.13\%$$

   (b) Percent potassium chloride by mass–volume

$$= \frac{\text{mass of KCl}}{\text{volume of solution}} \times 100 = \frac{0.800 \text{ g KCl}}{16.0 \text{ mL solution}} \times 100 = 5.00\%$$

42. (a) Percent sodium carbonate by mass–volume $= \dfrac{50.0 \text{ g}}{500.0 \text{ mL}} \times 100 = 10.0\%$

   (b) Percent potassium nitrate by mass–volume $= \dfrac{0.160 \text{ g}}{80.0 \text{ mL}} \times 100 = 0.200\%$

43. g NaCl $= (25\overline{0} \text{ mL solution})\left(\dfrac{5.00 \text{ g NaCl}}{100 \text{ mL solution}}\right) = 12.5 \text{ g NaCl}$

44. g NaCl $= (100.0 \text{ mL})(0.0900) = 9.00 \text{ g NaCl}$

45. (a) $M = \dfrac{\text{moles of HCl}}{\text{L of solution}}$ 5.4 g HCl $= 0.15$ mole HCl

   $? M = \dfrac{0.15 \text{ mole}}{0.500 \text{ L}} = 0.30 \ M$ $5\overline{0}0 \text{ mL} = 0.500 \text{ L}$

   (b) 117 g NaCl $= 2.00$ moles

   $? M = \dfrac{\text{moles}}{\text{L}} = \dfrac{2.00 \text{ moles}}{4 \text{ L}} = 0.5 \ M$

46. (a) $? M = \dfrac{0.0323 \text{ mole}}{2.00 \text{ L}} = 0.0162 \ M$ (b) $? M = \dfrac{0.400 \text{ mole}}{5.00 \text{ L}} = 0.0800 \ M$

47. 10.0 percent-by-mass $= 10.0$ g HCl in $1\overline{0}0$ g solution or $1\overline{0}0$ mL solution (if we assume that the density of the solution is 1.00 g/mL)

$$10.0 \text{ g HCl} = 0.274 \text{ mole HCl} \qquad ? M = \frac{0.274 \text{ mole HCl}}{0.100 \text{ L solution}} = 2.74 \ M$$

48. 5.00% HCl solution has 5.00 g HCl per $\overline{100}$ g solution.

$$5.00 \text{ g HCl} = 0.137 \text{ mole} \qquad ? M = \frac{0.137 \text{ mole}}{0.100 \text{ L}} = 1.37 \ M$$

49. $M = \dfrac{\text{moles KOH}}{\text{L solution}}$. Therefore,

Moles KOH = (M)(L solution) = (3.0 M)(0.050 L solution) = 0.15 mole KOH

$$\text{g KOH} = (0.15 \text{ mole KOH})\left(\frac{56.1 \text{ KOH}}{1 \text{ mole KOH}}\right) = 8.4 \text{ g KOH}$$

50. Moles NaOH = (2.00 M)(0.0250 L) = 0.0500 mole NaOH

$$\text{g NaOH} = (0.0500 \text{ mole})\left(40.0 \ \frac{\text{g}}{\text{mole}}\right) = 2.00 \text{ g NaOH}$$

51. $M = \dfrac{\text{moles alcohol}}{\text{L solution}}$. Therefore,

$$\text{Moles alcohol} = (\overline{500} \text{ mg})\left(\frac{1.000 \text{ g}}{1,000 \text{ mg}}\right)\left(\frac{1.0 \text{ mole alcohol}}{46.0 \text{ g solution}}\right) = 0.0109 \text{ mole alcohol}$$

$$? M = \frac{0.0109 \text{ mole alcohol}}{0.100 \text{ L solution}} = 0.109 \ M$$

52. $\overline{400}$ mg $C_2H_5OH = 8.70 \times 10^{-3}$ mole

$$? M = \frac{8.70 \infty 10^{-3} \text{ mole}}{0.100 \text{ L}} = 0.0870 \ M$$

53. 0.85 percent-by-mass-volume salt solution = 0.85 g salt in $\overline{100}$ mL solution.

$$2 M = \frac{\text{moles salt}}{\text{L solution}} = \left(\frac{0.85 \text{ g salt}}{0.10 \text{ L solution}}\right)\left(\frac{1.00 \text{ mole salt}}{58.5 \text{ g salt}}\right) = 0.15 \ M$$

54. Moles NaCl = $(5.85 \text{ g})\left(\dfrac{1 \text{ mole}}{58.5 \text{ g}}\right) = 0.100$ mole NaCl

$$? L = \frac{\text{mole}}{M} = \frac{0.100 \text{ mole}}{2.00 \ M} = 0.0500 \ L = 50.0 \text{ mL}$$

55. (a) $\quad M = \dfrac{\text{moles } H_2SO_4}{\text{L solution}} \qquad 24.5 \text{ g } H_2SO_4 = 0.250 \text{ mole } H_2SO_4$

$$? M = \frac{0.250 \text{ moles } H_2SO_4}{1.50 \text{ L}} = 0.167 \ M$$

(b) $\quad M = \dfrac{\text{moles } KNO_3}{\text{L solution}} \qquad 10.1 \text{ g } KNO_3 = 0.0999 \text{ mole } KNO_3$

$$? M = \frac{0.0999 \text{ mole } KNO_3}{0.500 \text{ L}} = 0.200 \ M$$

56. (a) $\quad$ Moles $H_2SO_4 = (49.0 \text{ g})\left(\dfrac{1 \text{ mole}}{98.1 \text{ g}}\right) = 0.499 \text{ mole } H_2SO_4$

$$? M = \frac{0.499 \text{ mole}}{2.00 \text{ L}} = 0.250 \ M$$

(b) $\quad$ Moles $KNO_3 = (2.02 \text{ g})\left(\dfrac{1 \text{ mole}}{101.1 \text{ g}}\right) = 0.0200 \text{ mole } KNO_3$

$$? M = \frac{0.0200 \text{ mole}}{0.200 \text{ L}} = 0.100 \ M$$

57. $\quad$ 5.00 percent $MgCl_2$ solution $= \dfrac{5.00 \text{ g } MgCl_2}{100 \text{ g solution}}$

$$\text{or} \quad \frac{5.00 \text{ g } MgCl_2}{100 \text{ mL solution}} \quad \text{(for a density of 1.00 g/mL)}$$

$$\frac{5.00 \text{ g } MgCl_2}{100 \text{ mL solution}} = \frac{50.0 \text{ g } MgCl_2}{1.00 \text{ L solution}}$$

$$\text{Moles } MgCl_2 = (50.0 \text{ g } MgCl_2)\left(\frac{1.00 \text{ mole } MgCl_2}{95.3 \text{ g solution}}\right) = 0.525 \text{ mole } MgCl_2$$

$$? M = \frac{0.525 \text{ mole}}{1.00 \text{ L}} = 0.525 \ M$$

58. $\quad$ g $NaNO_3 = (\overline{100} \text{ g})(0.0750) = 7.50 \text{ g } NaNO_3$

There are 7.5 g $NaNO_3$ per $\overline{100}$ g of solution.

$$\text{Moles } NaNO_3 = (7.50 \text{ g})\left(\frac{1 \text{ mole}}{85.0 \text{ g}}\right) = 0.0882 \text{ mole } NaNO_3$$

$$? \, M = \frac{0.0882 \text{ mole}}{0.100 \text{ L}} = 0.882 \, M$$

59. $0.400 \, M \, Na_3PO_4 = \dfrac{0.400 \text{ mole } Na_3PO_4}{1.00 \text{ L solution}}$

g Na_3PO_4

$$= \left(\frac{0.400 \text{ mole}}{1.00 \text{ L solution}}\right)(0.250 \text{ L solution})\left(\frac{164.0 \text{ g } Na_3PO_4}{1.00 \text{ mole}}\right) = 16.4 \text{ g } Na_3PO_4$$

60. Moles $NaC_2H_3O_2 = (0.500 \, M)(0.4000 \text{ L}) = 0.200 \text{ mole } NaC_2H_3O_2$

$$\text{g } NaC_2H_3O_2 = (0.200 \text{ mole})\left(\frac{82.0 \text{ g}}{1 \text{ mole}}\right) = 16.4 \text{ g } NaC_2H_3O_2$$

61. (a) Equivalents of $H_2SO_4 = (4.9 \text{ g})\left(\dfrac{1.0 \text{ equivalent}}{49.1 \text{ g}}\right) = 0.10$ equivalent

(b) Equivalents of $HCl = (7.2 \text{ g})\left(\dfrac{1.0 \text{ equivalent}}{36.5 \text{ g}}\right) = 0.20$ equivalent

(c) Equivalents of $Fe(OH)_3 = (32.1 \text{ g})\left(\dfrac{1.00 \text{ equivalent}}{35.6 \text{ g}}\right) = 0.902$ equivalent

62. (a) Equivalents of $H_2SO_4 = (9.8 \text{ g})\left(\dfrac{1 \text{ equivalent}}{49.1 \text{ g}}\right) = 0.20$ equivalent

(b) Equivalents of $HCl = (3.6 \text{ g})\left(\dfrac{1 \text{ equivalent}}{36.5 \text{ g}}\right) = 0.10$ equivalent

(c) Equivalents of $Fe(OH)_3 = (6.42 \text{ g})\left(\dfrac{1 \text{ equivalent}}{35.6 \text{ g}}\right) = 0.18$ equivalent

63.

Substance	Molecular weight, g/mole	Equivalent weight, g/equivalent
(a) H_2SO_3	82.1	41.1
(b) $Fe(OH)_3$	106.8	35.6
(c) $Fe(OH)_2$	89.8	44.9
(d) H_3BO_3	61.8	20.6

64.

Substance	Molecular weight, g/mole	Equivalent weight, g/equivalent
(a) $HC_2H_3O_2$	60.0	60.0
(b) $NaOH$	40.0	40.0
(c) $Mg(OH)_2$	58.3	29.2
(d) HNO_3	63.0	63.0

65. (a) Equivalents of $H_2SO_3 = (1.23 \text{ g})\left(\dfrac{1 \text{ equivalent}}{41.1 \text{ g}}\right) = 0.0299$ equivalent

(b) Equivalents of $Fe(OH)_3 = (26.7 \text{ g})\left(\dfrac{1 \text{ equivalent}}{35.6 \text{ g}}\right) = 0.750$ equivalent

66. (a) Equivalents of $H_2SO_3 = (246 \text{ g})\left(\dfrac{1 \text{ equivalent}}{41.1 \text{ g}}\right) = 5.99$ equivalents

(b) Equivalents of $NaOH = (4.00 \text{ g})\left(\dfrac{1 \text{ equivalent}}{40.0 \text{ g}}\right) = 0.100$ equivalent

67. (a) g $Fe(OH)_2 = (25.0 \text{ equivalents})\left(\dfrac{44.9 \text{ g}}{1 \text{ equivalent}}\right) = 1{,}120$ g $Fe(OH)_2$

(b) g $H_3BO_3 = (0.450 \text{ equivalent})\left(\dfrac{20.6 \text{ g}}{1 \text{ equivalent}}\right) = 9.27$ g H_3BO_3

68. (a) g $Mg(OH)_2 = (0.250 \text{ equivalent})\left(\dfrac{29.2 \text{ g}}{1 \text{ equivalent}}\right) = 7.30$ g $Mg(OH)_2$

(b) g $HC_2H_3O_2 = (2.00 \text{ equivalent})\left(\dfrac{60.0 \text{ g}}{1 \text{ equivalent}}\right) = 12\bar{0}$ g $HC_2H_3O_2$

69. (a) Equivalents of $H_3PO_4 = (97\bar{0}\text{ g})\left(\dfrac{1\text{ equivalent}}{32.7\text{ g}}\right) = 29.7$ equivalents

$$? N = \dfrac{\text{equivalents}}{L} = \dfrac{29.7\text{ equivalents}}{10.0\text{ L}} = 2.97\ N$$

(b) Equivalents of $Ca(OH)_2 = (3.7\text{ g})\left(\dfrac{1\text{ equivalent}}{37.1\text{ g}}\right) = 0.10$ equivalent

$$? N = \dfrac{0.10\text{ equivalent}}{0.800\text{ L}} = 0.13\ N$$

(c) Moles $H_3PO_4 = (97\bar{0}\text{ g})\left(\dfrac{1\text{ mole}}{98.0\text{ g}}\right) = 9.90$ moles H_3PO_4

$$? M = \dfrac{9.90\text{ moles}}{10.0\text{ L}} = 0.990\ M$$

Moles $Ca(OH)_2 = (3.7\text{ g})\left(\dfrac{1\text{ mole}}{74.1\text{ g}}\right) = 0.050$ mole $Ca(OH)_2$

$$? M = \dfrac{0.050\text{ mole}}{0.800\text{ L}} = 0.063\ M$$

70. (a) Equivalents of $H_3PO_4 = (465\text{ g})\left(\dfrac{1\text{ equivalent}}{32.7\text{ g}}\right) = 14.2$ equivalents

$$? N = \dfrac{14.2\text{ equivalents}}{8.00\text{ L}} = 1.78\ N$$

(b) Equivalents of $Ca(OH)_2 = (740.0\text{ g})\left(\dfrac{1\text{ equivalent}}{37.1\text{ g}}\right) = 19.9$ equivalents

$$? N = \dfrac{19.9\text{ equivalents}}{0.740\text{ L}} = 26.9\ N$$

(c) $M_{H_3PO_4} = \dfrac{1.78\ N}{3} = 0.593\ M;\quad M_{Ca(OH)_2} = \dfrac{26.9\ N}{2} = 13.5\ M$

71. $2.0\ N\ Ca(OH)_2 = \dfrac{2.0\text{ equivalents}}{1.0\text{ L solution}}$

$$\text{g } Ca(OH)_2 = \left(\dfrac{2.0\text{ equivalents}}{1.0\text{ L solution}}\right)(0.800\text{ L})\left(\dfrac{37.1\text{ g}}{1.0\text{ equivalent}}\right) = 59\text{ g } Ca(OH)_2$$

72.   Equivalents of $Mg(OH)_2$ = (3.00 N)(0.750 L) = 2.25 equivalents

   g $Mg(OH)_2$ = (2.25 ~~equivalents~~)$\left(\dfrac{29.2\ g}{1\ equivalent}\right)$ = 65.7 g $Mg(OH)_2$

73.   0.60 N H_3PO_4 = $\dfrac{0.60\ equivalent}{1.0\ L\ solution}$

   ? mL of solution = (4.9 g)$\left(\dfrac{1\ equivalent}{32.7\ g}\right)\left(\dfrac{1.0\ L}{0.60\ equivalent}\right) \times \left(\dfrac{1,000\ mL}{1.000\ L}\right)$

                   = 250 L

74.   Equivalents of H_3PO_4 = (98.0 g)$\left(\dfrac{1\ equivalent}{32.7\ g}\right)$ = 3.00 equivalents

   ? L = $\dfrac{equivalent}{N}$ = $\dfrac{3.00\ equivalents}{0.450\ N}$ = 6.67 L = 6,670 mL

75.   (a) $N = \dfrac{equivalent\ Fe(OH)_2}{L\ solution}$

         11.23 g $Fe(OH)_2$ = 0.125 mole

              $Fe(OH)_2$ = 0.250 equivalent

         ? N = $\dfrac{0.250\ equivalent}{0.250\ L}$ = 1.00 N

   (b)   4.12 g H_3BO_3 = 0.0667 mole H_3BO_3 = 0.200 equivalent

         ? N = $\dfrac{0.200\ equivalent}{0.400\ L}$ = 0.500 N

   (c)   ? M $Fe(OH)_2$ = $\dfrac{0.125\ mole}{0.250\ L}$ = 0.500 M

         ? M H_3BO_3 = $\dfrac{0.0667\ mole}{0.400\ L}$ = 0.167 M

76.   (a)   Equivalents of $Fe(OH)_2$ = (2.246 g)$\left(\dfrac{1\ equivalent}{44.9\ g}\right)$ = 0.0500 equivalent

$$? N = \frac{0.0500 \text{ equivalent}}{0.500 \text{ L}} = 0.100 \text{ N}$$

(b)   Equivalents $H_3BO_3 = (16.48 \text{ g})\left(\frac{1 \text{ equivalent}}{20.6 \text{ g}}\right) = 0.800 \text{ equivalent}$

$$? N = \frac{0.800 \text{ equivalent}}{0.500 \text{ L}} = 1.60 \text{ N}$$

(c) $M_{Fe(OH)_2} = \frac{0.100}{2} = 0.0500 \text{ M}$

$$M_{H_3BO_3} = \frac{1.60}{3} = 0.533 \text{ M}$$

77. $0.500 \text{ N Al(OH)}_3 = \frac{0.500 \text{ equivalent}}{1.00 \text{ L solution}}$

$$\text{g Al(OH)}_3 = \left(\frac{0.500 \text{ equivalent}}{1.00 \text{ L solution}}\right)(0.250 \text{ L})\left(\frac{26.0 \text{ g}}{1.00 \text{ equivalent}}\right) = 3.25 \text{ g Al(OH)}_3$$

78.   Equivalents of $Fe(OH)_3 = (0.250 \text{ N})(0.5000 \text{ L}) = 0.125 \text{ equivalent}$

$$\text{g Fe(OH)}_3 = (0.125 \text{ equivalent})\left(\frac{35.6 \text{ g}}{1 \text{ equivalent}}\right) = 4.45 \text{ g Fe(OH)}_3$$

79. $\text{mL H}_2\text{SO}_4 = (2.94 \text{ g H}_2\text{SO}_4)\left(\frac{1 \text{ equivalent}}{49.1 \text{ g}}\right)\left(\frac{1,\overline{0}00 \text{ mL}}{0.100 \text{ equivalent}}\right) = 599 \text{ mL H}_2\text{SO}_4$

80.   Equivalents of $H_3PO_4 = (29.4 \text{ g})\left(\frac{1 \text{ equivalent}}{32.7 \text{ g}}\right) = 0.899 \text{ equivalent}$

$$? L = \frac{0.899 \text{ equivalent}}{0.200 \text{ N}} = 4.50 \text{ L} = 4,\overline{5}00 \text{ mL}$$

81. $N_c V_c = N_d V_d$ $(16.0)(V_c) = (4.00)(5\overline{0}0 \text{ mL})$

$$V_c = 125 \text{ mL}$$

Take 125 mL of 16.0 N H_2SO_4 and add enough water to make $5\overline{0}0$ mL of solution.

82. $V_c = \dfrac{N_d V_d}{N_c}$ $V_c = \dfrac{(8.00\ N)(250.0\ \text{mL})}{10.0\ N} = 2\overline{00}\ \text{mL}$

Take $2\overline{00}$ mL of 10.0 N H_3PO_4 and add enough water to make 250.0 mL of solution.

83. $N_c V_c = N_d V_d$ $(6)(V_c) = (0.1)(3\ \text{L})$

$V_c = 0.05\ \text{L}$

Take 0.05 L (50 mL) of 6 N NaOH and add enough water to make a total volume of 3 L (3,000 mL).

84. $V_c = \dfrac{(0.20\ N)(4.00\ \text{L})}{2.00\ N} = 0.400\ \text{L} = 4\overline{00}\ \text{mL}$

85. $M_c V_c = M_d V_d$ $(12.0)(V_c) = (5.00)(25\overline{0}\ \text{mL})$

$V_c = 104\ \text{mL}$

Take 104 mL of 12.0 M HCl and add enough water to make $25\overline{0}$ mL of solution.

86. $V_c = \dfrac{(7.50\ M)(450.0\ \text{mL})}{11.0\ M} = 307\ \text{mL}$

Take 307 mL of 11.0 M HNO_3 and add enough water to make 450.0 mL of solution.

87.   3.00 M H_2SO_4 = 6.00 N H_2SO_4 $N_c V_c = N_d V_d$

$(6.00)(V_c) = (0.050)(5.00\ \text{L})$ $V_c = 0.042\ \text{L} = 42\ \text{mL}$

Take 42 mL of 6.00 N H_2SO_4 (3.00 M H_2SO_4) and add enough water to make 5.00 L of solution.

88. $V_c = \dfrac{(0.0200\ N)(4.00\ \text{L})}{2.00\ N} = 0.0400\ \text{L} = 40.0\ \text{mL}$

Take 40.0 mL of 2.00 N $HC_2H_3O_2$ and add enough water to make 5.00 L of solution.

89. *Ions* are atoms that have gained or lost electrons and therefore have a positive or negative charge. *Ionization* is the formation of ions.

90. (a) True   (b) False

91. Solutions that have ions are electrolytic, whereas solutions that do not have ions are nonelectrolytic.

92. Yes, the resulting solution will conduct electricity.

93. An *electrolytic solution* conducts electric current. An example of an electrolytic solution is sodium chloride in water. A *nonelectrolytic solution* does not conduct electric current. An example of a nonelectrolytic solution is sucrose (sugar) in water.

94. A glass of salt water will conduct electricity.

95. *Molality* is the moles of solute per kilogram of solvent. To solve a molality problem, you need to know the grams of solute and the kilograms of solvent.

96. Molality is the moles of solute per kilogram of *solvent*. Molarity is the moles of solute per liter of *solution*.

97. From Problem 53, 0.015 mole NaCl in $\overline{100}$ g H_2O.

$$? \text{ molality} = m = \frac{\text{moles NaCl}}{\text{kg solvent}} = \frac{0.015 \text{ mole NaCl}}{0.100 \text{ kg } H_2O} = 0.15 \text{ } m$$

98. $$\text{molality} = \frac{\text{moles of solute}}{1.000 \text{ kg solvent}}$$

$$? \text{ molality} = \frac{(0.373 \text{ g KCl}/74.6 \text{ g mole})}{0.100 \text{ kg water}} = 0.050 \text{ } m$$

99. (a) $$m = \frac{\text{moles } CH_3OH}{\text{kg } H_2O}$$ 6.4 g CH_3OH = 0.20 mole

$$? \text{ } m = \frac{0.20 \text{ mole } CH_3OH}{0.250 \text{ kg } H_2O} = 0.80 \text{ } m$$

(b) $$m = \frac{\text{moles } C_2H_{12}O_6}{\text{kg } H_2O}$$ 90.0 g $C_6H_{12}O_6$ = 0.500 moles

$$? \text{ } m = \frac{0.500 \text{ mole } C_6H_{12}O_6}{1.500 \text{ kg } H_2O} = 0.333 \text{ } m$$

100. (a) $? \text{ molality} = \dfrac{(0.128 \text{ g}/32.0 \text{ g/mole})}{0.500 \text{ kg water}} = 0.00800 \text{ } m$

    (b) $? \text{ molality} = \dfrac{(45\overline{0} \text{ g}/180.0 \text{ g/mole})}{2.000 \text{ kg water}} = 1.25 \text{ } m$

101. A solute will lower the freezing point of a solution and raise its boiling point.

102. Without antifreeze the water in the radiator would freeze during cold weather. As the water turns to ice, it expands. This in turn would damage the engine and connecting hoses.

103. (a) K_f is the symbol for the freezing-point depression constant for a particular solvent.
    (b) K_b is the symbol for the boiling-point elevation constant for a particular solvent.

104. The freezing-point depression constant for water (K_f) is –1.86°C/molal. The boiling-point elevation constant for water (K_b) is 0.52°C/molal.

105. $\text{Moles C}_2\text{H}_6\text{O}_2 = (1.00 \text{ gal})\left(\dfrac{4.00 \text{ qt}}{1.00 \text{ gal}}\right)\left(\dfrac{1.00 \text{ L}}{1.06 \text{ qt}}\right)\left(\dfrac{1,000 \text{ mL}}{1.00 \text{ L}}\right)$

$$\times \left(\dfrac{1.10 \text{ g}}{1.00 \text{ mL}}\right)\left(\dfrac{1.00 \text{ mole}}{62.0 \text{ g}}\right)$$

$$= 67.0 \text{ moles C}_2\text{H}_6\text{O}_2$$

$\text{kg H}_2\text{O} = (1.00 \text{ gal})\left(\dfrac{4.00 \text{ qt}}{1.00 \text{ gal}}\right)\left(\dfrac{1.00 \text{ L}}{1.06 \text{ qt}}\right)\left(\dfrac{1.00 \text{ kg}}{1.00 \text{ L}}\right) = 3.77 \text{ kg H}_2\text{O}$

$? \text{ } m = \dfrac{\text{moles C}_2\text{H}_6\text{O}_2}{\text{kg H}_2\text{O}} = \dfrac{67.0 \text{ moles}}{3.77 \text{ kg}} = 17.8 \text{ } m$

$\Delta t_f = K_f m = (1.86°\text{C/molal})(17.8 \text{ molal}) = 33.1°\text{C}$

The new freezing-point temperature is –33.1°C.

106. $? \text{ molality} = \dfrac{(5.40 \text{ g}/180.0 \text{ g/mole})}{0.500 \text{ kg}} = 0.0600 \text{ } m$

$\Delta t_b = K_b m = (0.520°\text{C/molal})(0.0600 \text{ molal}) = 0.0312°\text{C}$

Therefore the boiling point is 100.0312°C.

107. $\Delta t_b = K_b m = (0.520°C/\text{molal})(17.8 \text{ molal}) = 9.26°C$

New boiling-point temperature is

$$100.00°C + 9.26°C = 109.26°C.$$

108. ? molality $= \dfrac{(0.184 \text{ g}/92.0 \text{ g}/\text{mole})}{1.000 \text{ kg}} = 0.00200 \text{ molal}$

$\Delta t_b = K_b m = (0.520°C/\text{molal})(0.00200 \text{ molal}) = 0.00104°C$

Therefore the boiling point is 100.00104°C.

109. 27.0 g $C_6H_{12}O_6 = 0.150$ mole $\qquad$? $m = \dfrac{0.150 \text{ mole}}{0.100 \text{ kg}} = 1.50 \text{ } m$

$\Delta t_b = K_b m = (0.52°C/\text{molal})(1.50 \text{ molal}) = 0.78°C$

$\Delta t_f = K_f m = (1.86°C/\text{molal})(1.50 \text{ molal}) = 2.79°C$

The new boiling point = 100.78°C;
The new freezing point = –2.79°C.

110. ? molality $= \dfrac{(0.184 \text{ g}/92.0 \text{ g}/\text{mole})}{1.000 \text{ kg}} = 0.00200 \text{ molal}$

$\Delta t_f = K_f m = (1.86°C/\text{molal})(0.00200 \text{ molal}) = 0.00372°C$

Therefore the new freezing point is –0.00372°C.

111. (a) The passage of water through a semipermeable membrane is the process of *osmosis*.
   (b) The movement of a solute from an area of high solute concentration to an area of low solute concentration is the process of *diffusion*.

112. The mass of the potato will be *lower* because the potato cells act as an osmotic membrane. Therefore, water will leave the potato and enter the saturated NaCl solution in an attempt to dilute it.

113.   The water moves from the 5% KCl solution to the 20% KCl solution. Remember, in osmosis, only water passes through the semipermeable membrane.

114.   The water moves out of the cell, causing the cell to undergo a process known as crenation.

EXTRA EXERCISES

115.   A solute lowers the vapor pressure of the solution below what it would be for the pure solvent alone. Therefore, the temperature required for boiling is higher. In order for a pure liquid to freeze, the molecules must be aligned or "tied down." If a solute is placed in the pure solvent, the solute inhibits the liquid molecules from aligning. Therefore, the freezing point of the liquid is lowered.

116. H^+ concentration in moles/L = 1×10^{-2} M

117. H^+ concentration in moles/L = 1×10^{-2} M

$$\text{Concentration of } H_2SO_4 = (1 \times 10^{-2} \, M \, H^+)\left(\frac{1 \, \text{mole } H_2SO_4}{2 \, \text{moles } H^+}\right)$$

$$= 5 \times 10^{-3} \, M = 1 \times 10^{-2} \, N$$

118. $$\text{g } H_2SO_4 = \left(\frac{5.00 \, g}{100 \, \text{g solution}}\right)\left(\frac{1.00 \, \text{g solution}}{1.00 \, \text{mL solution}}\right) \times \left(\frac{1000 \, \text{mL}}{1.00 \, \text{L}}\right)(10.0 \, \text{L})$$

$$= 5\overline{00} \, \text{g } H_2SO_4$$

119. $$M_{H_2SO_4} = \frac{\text{moles}}{L} \qquad \frac{50.0 \, \text{g } H_2SO_4}{1.00 \, \text{L solution}} = \frac{0.510 \, \text{mole}}{1.00 \, \text{L}}$$

Therefore, $M = 0.510$ and $N = 1.02$.

120.   A solution is homogeneous, whereas a mixture may be heterogeneous.

121.   Placing sodium chloride on ice-covered roads works well until temperatures fall below $-17.8°C$ ($0°F$). Temperatures during Minnesota winters fall well below this, so adding salt to the ice does not have any effect.

122. $1\overline{00}$ g ethanol has the greatest number of moles, giving the largest Δt_f.

123. ? M of concentrated HCl

$$= \left(\frac{1,190 \text{ g solution}}{1.000 \text{ L solution}}\right)\left(\frac{37.00 \text{ g}}{100 \text{ g solution}}\right)\left(\frac{1 \text{ mole}}{36.5 \text{ g}}\right) = 12.1 \text{ } M$$

$$M_c V_c = M_d V_d \qquad\qquad (12.1)(V_c) = (0.500)(\overline{1000} \text{ mL})$$

$$V_c = 41.3 \text{ mL}$$

124. $\Delta t_f = K_f m \quad m = \dfrac{\Delta t_f}{K_f}$ $? m = \dfrac{1.86°\text{C}}{1.86°\text{C}/\text{molal}} = 1.00 \text{ molal}$

$$\text{molal} = \frac{\text{moles solute}}{\text{kg solvent}} = \frac{\text{g solute}/\text{MW solute}}{\text{kg solvent}} \qquad \text{or}$$

$$\text{MM} = \frac{\text{g solute}}{(\text{molal})(\text{kg solvent})} = \frac{15.0 \text{ g}}{(1.00 \text{ molal})(0.100 \text{ kg } H_2O)} = 15\overline{0}$$

125. This would be a 2.00 molal solution, because the 2.00 moles of solute are added to 1.00 L (1.00 kg) of water, not to 1.00 L of *solution* (solute plus solvent).

126. $\Delta t_f = K_f m \quad m = \dfrac{\Delta t_f}{K_f}$ $? m = \dfrac{5.00°\text{C}}{1.86°\text{C}/\text{molal}} = 2.69 \text{ } m$

$$m = \frac{\text{g solute}/\text{mm solute}}{\text{kg solvent}} \qquad \text{or}$$

$$\text{MM} = \frac{\text{g solute}}{(\text{molal})(\text{kg solvent})} = \frac{10.00 \text{ g}}{(2.69m)(1.000 \text{ kg})} = 3.72$$

127. $m = \dfrac{\text{moles NaCl}}{\text{kg } H_2O}$

5.85 g NaCl = 0.100 mole NaCl = 0.200 mole particles (ions)

$$? m = \frac{0.200 \text{ mole ions}}{1.000 \text{ kg } H_2O} = 0.200 \text{ } m$$

$$\Delta t_b = K_b m = (0.520°\text{C}/\text{molal})(0.200 \text{ molal}) = 0.104°\text{C}$$

The boiling point of the solution is 100.104°C.

128. (a)   Equivalents of HCl = (73.0 g)$\left(\dfrac{1 \text{ equivalent}}{36.5 \text{ g}}\right)$ = 2.00 equivalents

(b)   Equivalents of H_2SO_4 = (98.1 g)$\left(\dfrac{1 \text{ equivalent}}{49.1 \text{ g}}\right)$ = 2.00 equivalents

129. (a)   1.00 mole HCl = 1.00 equivalent HCl

(b)   1.00 mole H_2SO_4 = 2.00 equivalents H_2SO_4

16 ACIDS, BASES, AND SALTS

SELF-TEST EXERCISES

1. (a) An Arrhenius *acid* is a substance that releases hydrogen ions in solution.
    (b) An Arrhenius base is a substance that releases hydroxide ions in solution.

2. The matching pairs are 1. (d), 2. (c), 3. (e), 4. (a), 5. (b).

3. Phosphoric acid is used as a "flavor carrying agent" in soda pop. Also, carbonic acid forms from the reaction between water and carbon dioxide.

4. The Arrhenius definition of an acid and base is limited to substances containing hydrogen ions (for acids) and hydroxide ions (for bases).

5. (a) An acid is a proton donor.
    (b) A base is a proton acceptor.

6. Water can act as either a proton donor or a proton acceptor, so it can be a Brønsted-Lowry acid or base.

7. $NH_3 + H_2O \Leftrightarrow NH_4^{1+} + OH^{1-}$

8. (a) $HSO_4^{1-} \rightarrow H^{1+} + SO_4^{2-}$

    (b) $Cl^{1-} + H^{1+} \rightarrow HCl$

9. Acids taste sour and turn blue litmus red. Bases taste bitter, feel slippery, and turn red litmus blue. Salts in aqueous solutions contain ions. Salts are bonded ionically.

10. An indicator.

11. Hydrogen chloride gas is composed of covalently bonded molecules of HCl. When this gas is added to water, it dissociates into hydrogen ions (H^{1+}) and chloride ions (Cl^{1-}), forming hydrochloric acid.

12. A hydronium ion has the formula H_3O^{1+}. Think of it as H_2O that has formed a coordinate covalent bond with a hydrogen ion.

13. Acids can react with some metals and dissolve them. Therefore, acids are usually stored in nonmetal containers.

14. A substance that dissolves in water to produce hydroxide ions is a *base*.

15. The two types of acids are mineral acids and *organic* acids.

16. A substance that dissolves in water to produce hydrogen ions is an *acid*.

17. (a) *Blue* litmus paper turns *red* in acid.
    (b) *Red* litmus paper turns *blue* in a base.

18. False. It is a base that feels soapy or slippery.

19. $HBr + H_2O \rightarrow H_3O^{1+} + Br^{1-}$

20. $HNO_3 + H_2O \rightarrow H_3O^{1+} + NO_3^{1-}$

21. $Ca(OH)_2 \xrightarrow{\text{Water}} Ca^{2+} + 2OH^{1-}$

22. $Mg(OH)_2 \xrightarrow{\text{H}_2\text{O}} Mg^{2+} + 2OH^{1-}$

23. (a) $K_2O + H_2O \rightarrow 2KOH$ (b) $MgO + H_2O \rightarrow Mg(OH)_2$

24. (a) $Li_2O + H_2O \rightarrow 2LiOH$ (b) $CaO + H_2O \rightarrow Ca(OH)_2$

25. (a) $SO_2 + H_2O \rightarrow H_2SO_3$ (b) $CO_2 + H_2O \rightarrow H_2CO_3$

26. (a) $N_2O_5 + H_2O \rightarrow 2HNO_3$ (b) $P_2O_5 + 3H_2O \rightarrow 2H_3PO_4$

27. (a) $2H_3PO_4 + 3Mg(OH)_2 \rightarrow Mg_3(PO_4)_2 + 6H_2O$

(b) $P_2O_5 + 3H_2O \rightarrow 2H_3PO_4$

(c) $K_2O + H_2O \rightarrow 2KOH$

(d) $Mg(OH)_2 + CO_2 \rightarrow MgCO_3 + H_2O$

(e) $3Zn + 2H_3PO_4 \rightarrow Zn_3(PO_4)_2 + 3H_2$

28. (a) $2HC_2H_3O_2 + Ca(OH)_2 \rightarrow Ca(C_2H_3O_2)_2 + 2H_2O$

(b) $Na_2O + H_2O \rightarrow 2NaOH$

(c) $Mg + 2HCl \rightarrow MgCl_2 + H_2$

(d) $Sr(OH)_2 + CO_2 \rightarrow SrCO_3 + H_2O$

(e) $N_2O_5 + H_2O \rightarrow 2HNO_3$

29. If you spill sodium hydroxide on your clothes you might try neutralizing the base with vinegar. The acetic acid in the vinegar will react with the sodium hydroxide.

30. Drinking vinegar or lemon juice might be the best way to neutralize the sodium hydroxide.

31. Vinegar contains acetic acid, and lye contains sodium hydroxide. Therefore, these two substances will react:

$$HC_2H_3O_2 + NaOH \rightarrow NaC_2H_3O_2 + H_2O$$

32. The formation of acid rain can be represented by the following equations:

$$2SO_2 + O_2 \rightarrow 2SO_3$$

$$SO_3 + H_2O \rightarrow H_2SO_4$$

$$SO_2 + H_2O \rightarrow H_2SO_3$$

The sulfuric and sulfurous acids produce acid rain.

33. The SO_2 reacts with moisture in the atmosphere to produce sulfurous and sulfuric acid, ingredients of acid rain. Acid rain can damage the metal machinery at the paper mill.

34. (a) $Mg + 2HCl \rightarrow MgCl_2 + H_2$

(b) $H_2SO_4 + 2NaOH \rightarrow Na_2SO_4 + 2H_2O$

(c) $Mg + H_2SO_4 \rightarrow MgSO_4 + H_2$

(d) $2H_3PO_4 + 3Zn(OH)_2 \rightarrow Zn_3(PO_4)_2 + 6H_2O$

35. (a) $Zn + H_2SO_4 \rightarrow ZnSO_4 + H_2$

(b) $HCl + LiOH \rightarrow LiCl + H_2O$

(c) $Ca + H_2SO_4 \rightarrow CaSO_4 + H_2$

(d) $3Ca(OH)_2 + 2H_3PO_4 \rightarrow Ca_3(PO_4)_2 + 6H_2O$

36. (a) $3Zn + 2H_3PO_4 \rightarrow Zn_3(PO_4)_2 + 3H_2$

(b) $Zn + 2HCl \rightarrow ZnCl_2 + H_2$

(c) $Zn + H_2SO_4 \rightarrow ZnSO_4 + H_2$

37. (a) $Zn + 2HCl \rightarrow ZnCl_2 + H_2$

(b) $2HCl + Ca(OH)_2 \rightarrow CaCl_2 + 2H_2O$

(c) $Mg(OH)_2 + CO_2 \rightarrow MgCO_3 + H_2O$

38. All of the reactions in Exercise 36 may be classified as *single-replacement* reactions.

39. (a) A strong acid is one that ionizes almost completely; an example is HCl.
    (b) A strong base is one that ionizes almost completely; an example is NaOH.

40. A strong acid releases H^{1+} ions in solution. A strong base releases OH^{1-} ions in solution.

41. (a) HNO_3 (b) HF (c) HI

42. (a) H_3PO_4 (b) H_2SO_4 (c) H_3BO_3

43. (a) Sodium hydroxide   (b) Calcium hydroxide
    (c) Iron(II) hydroxide   (d) Aluminum hydroxide

44. (a) Magnesium hydroxide   (b) Zinc hydroxide
    (c) Potassium hydroxide   (d) Lithium hydroxide

45. (a) Nitric acid   (b) Phosphoric acid
    (c) Hydroiodic acid   (d) Sulfuric acid

46. (a) Hydrochloric acid   (b) Sulfurous acid
    (c) Carbonic acid   (d) Acetic acid

47. (a) LiOH   (b) $Ba(OH)_2$ (c) $Fe(OH)_2$ (d) $Fe(OH)_3$

48. (a) KOH   (b) NaOH   (c) $Zn(OH)_2$ (d) $Ca(OH)_2$

49. (a) A weak acid is one that does not dissociate completely; an example is
         $HC_2H_3O_2$.
    (b) A weak base is one that does not dissociate completely; an example is NH_3.

50. False. A weak acid or weak base only partially ionizes.

51. Dynamic equilibrium is the state achieved by two opposing processes that proceed
    at equal rates.

52. The equilibrium for carbon dioxide, water, and carbonic acid can be represented as
    follows:

    $$H_2O + CO_2 \Leftrightarrow H_2CO_3$$

53. $H_2O + H-OH \rightarrow H_3O^{1+} + OH^{1-}$

54. Water has a pH equal to 7. Therefore the $[H^+]$ and the $[OH^-]$ are both 10^{-7}
    moles/L. Two liters of water would have 2×10^{-7} moles of H^+ and 2×10^{-7} moles
    of OH^-.

55. (a) Moderately acidic
    (b) Slightly basic
    (c) Almost neutral (slightly on the basic side)
    (d) Neutral

56. (a) Moderately acidic   (b) Slightly acidic
    (c) Moderately acidic   (d) Slightly acidic

57. The pH of swimming pool water is usually between 7.2 and 7.6. Because of the
    addition of other pool chemicals, the pH will change if it is not actively
    maintained. For example, chlorine will lower the pH due to the formation of
    hypochlorous acid. Therefore the pH must be adjusted daily to help it remain in
    the proper range.

58. Most fish like water that has a neutral pH. Wide variations of pH will kill the fish in the tank.

59. (a)   A difference of two pH units is equivalent to a 10×10 or 100-fold difference in acidity.
    (b)   A difference of five pH units means a 10^5 difference in acidity.

60. A substance whose pH is 3 is 10^4 more acidic than a substance whose pH is 7.

61. The technical definition of pH is pH = $-\log [H^+]$.

62. Shampoo that is "pH-balanced" has a pH equal to that of normal hair.

63. (a)   pH = 3   (b)   pH = 4   (c)   pH = 2
    (d)   pH = 11   (e)   pH = 10   (f)   pH = 5

64. (a)   pH = 5   (b)   pH = 10   (c)   pH = 8
    (d)   pH = 9   (e)   pH = 4   (f)   pH = 6

65. (a) $[H^+] = 10^{-5}$ M, $[OH^-] = 10^{-9}$ M

    (b) $[H^+] = 10^{-9}$ M, $[OH^-] = 10^{-5}$ M

    (c) $[H^+] = 10^{-2}$ M, $[OH^-] = 10^{-12}$ M

    (d) $[H^+] = 10^{-12}$ M, $[OH^-] = 10^{-2}$ M

66. (a) $[H^{1+}] = 10^{-4}$ M, $[OH^{1-}] = 10^{-10}$ M

    (b) $[H^{1+}] = 10^{-7}$ M, $[OH^{1-}] = 10^{-7}$ M

    (c) $[H^{1+}] = 10^{-1}$ M, $[OH^{1-}] = 10^{-13}$ M

    (d) $[H^{1+}] = 10^{-3}$ M, $[OH^{1-}] = 10^{-11}$ M

67. (a) $[H^+] = 10^{-9}$ M, pH = 9   (b) $[H^+] = 10^{-6}$ M, pH = 6

    (c) $[H^+] = 10^{-4}$ M, pH = 4   (d) $[H^+] = 10^{-12}$ M, pH = 12

68. (a) $[H^+] = 10^{-10}$ M, pH = 10   (b) $[H^+] = 10^{-3}$ M, pH = 3

    (c) $[H^+] = 10^{-5}$ M, pH = 5   (d) $[H^+] = 10^{-11}$ M, pH = 11

69. (a) $[OH^-] = 10^{-11} M$ (b) $[OH^-] = 10^{-10} M$

(c) $[OH^-] = 10^{-6} M$ (d) $[OH^-] = 10^{-5} M$

(e) $[OH^-] = 10^{-8} M$ (f) $[OH^-] = 10^{-12} M$

70. (a) $[OH^{1-}] = 10^{-12} M$ (b) $[OH^{1-}] = 10^{-5} M$

(c) $[OH^{1-}] = 10^{-9} M$ (d) $[OH^{1-}] = 10^{-11} M$

(e) $[OH^{1-}] = 10^{-10} M$ (f) $[OH^{1-}] = 10^{-7} M$

71. (a) Sodium sulfide   (b) Potassium bromide
    (c) Sodium sulfate   (d) Potassium nitrate
    (e) Calcium carbonate   (f) Barium iodide

72. (a) Sodium carbonate   (b) Potassium chloride
    (c) Barium chloride   (d) Sodium nitrate
    (e) Calcium nitrate   (f) Calcium iodide

73. (a) $AgNO_3$ (b) $CoCl_2$ (c) Cu_2SO_3 (d) $Hg_3(PO_4)_2$

74. (a) $AgCl$ (b) $Fe(NO_3)_3$ (c) $Fe(NO_3)_2$ (d) $CuCl$

75. Salts are ionic substances. Their aqueous solutions contain ions.

76. Salts are bonded ionically.

77. Salts can be prepared by acid-base reactions, by direct combination of the elements, or by a single-replacement reaction between a metal and an acid.

78. Silver nitrate may be prepared by the following reactions:

$$HNO_3 + AgOH \rightarrow AgNO_3 + H_2O \quad \text{or} \quad 2HNO_3 + Ag_2O \rightarrow 2AgNO_3 + H_2O$$

79. $2LiOH + H_2SO_4 \rightarrow Li_2SO_4 + 2H_2O$

80. $LiOH + HNO_3 \rightarrow LiNO_3 + H_2O$

81. $Zn + 2HBr \rightarrow ZnBr_2 + H_2$

82. $Zn + 2HCl \rightarrow ZnCl_2 + H_2$

83. (a) $Mg + 2HCl \rightarrow MgCl_2 + H_2$

(b) $Zn + H_2SO_4 \rightarrow ZnSO_4 + H_2$

84. (a) $Mg + 2HBr \rightarrow MgBr_2 + H_2$

(b) $Cu + Ag_2SO_4 \rightarrow CuSO_4 + 2Ag$

85. (a) $3KOH + H_3PO_4 \rightarrow K_3PO_4 + 3H_2O$

(b) $Ca(OH)_2 + 2HNO_3 \rightarrow Ca(NO_3)_2 + 2H_2O$

86. (a) $3LiOH + H_3PO_4 \rightarrow Li_3PO_4 + 3H_2O$

(b) $Ca(OH)_2 + 2HCl \rightarrow CaCl_2 + 2H_2O$

87. (a) $2K + Cl_2 \rightarrow 2KCl$ (b) $Ca + Br_2 \rightarrow CaBr_2$

88. (a) $2K + I_2 \rightarrow 2KI$ (b) $Ca + Cl_2 \rightarrow CaCl_2$

89. $N_a = ?$ $N_b = 0.25$

$V_a = 30.0$ mL $V_b = 75.0$ mL

$N_a V_a = N_b V_b$ $N_a = \dfrac{N_b V_b}{V_a}$

$? \, N_a = \dfrac{(0.25\ N)(75.0\ \text{mL})}{30.0\ \text{mL}} = 0.63\ N$

90. $N_a = ?$ $N_b = 1.5$

$V_a = 125$ mL $V_b = 25.0$ mL

$N_a V_a = N_b V_b$ $N_a = \dfrac{N_b V_b}{V_a}$

$? \, N_a = \dfrac{(1.5\ N)(25.0\ \text{mL})}{125\ \text{mL}} = 0.30\ N$

Because hydrochloric acid is a monoprotic acid, 0.30 N HCl is the same as 0.30 M HCl.

91. $N_a = ?$ $N_b = 0.2500$

$V_a = 45.00$ mL $V_b = 50.00$ mL

$N_a V_a = N_b V_b$ $N_a = \dfrac{N_b V_b}{V_a}$

$? \, N_a = \dfrac{(0.2500 \, N)(50.00 \, \text{mL})}{45.00 \, \text{mL}} = 0.2778 \, N$

Because acetic acid is a monoprotic acid, 0.2778 N $HC_2H_3O_2$ is the same as 0.2778 N $HC_2H_3O_2$.

92. $N_a = 0.150 \, N$ $N_b = ?$

$V_a = 75.00$ mL $V_b = 35.0$ mL

$N_a V_a = N_b V_b$ $N_b = \dfrac{N_a V_a}{V_b}$

$? \, N_b = \dfrac{(0.150 \, N)(75.00 \, \text{mL})}{35.00 \, \text{mL}} = 0.321 \, N$

93. $N_a = ?$ $N_b = 0.150$

$V_a = 25.00$ mL $V_b = 30.00$ mL

$N_a V_a = N_b V_b$ $N_a = \dfrac{N_b V_b}{V_a}$

$? \, N_a = \dfrac{(0.150 \, N)(30.00 \, \text{mL})}{25.00 \, \text{mL}} = 0.180 \, N$

Because acetic acid is a monoprotic acid, 0.180 N $HC_2H_3O_2$ is the same as 0.180 N $HC_2H_3O_2$.

94. $N_a = 1.000 \, N$ $N_b = ?$

$V_a = 25.00$ mL $V_b = 35.00$ mL

$N_a V_a = N_b V_b$ $N_b = \dfrac{N_a V_a}{V_b}$

$? \, N_b = \dfrac{(1.000 \, N)(25.00 \, \text{mL})}{35.00 \, \text{mL}} = 0.7143 \, N$

95. $N_a = 1.00\ N$ $N_b = ?$

$V_a = 50.00\ mL$ $V_b = 75.00\ mL$

$N_a V_a = N_b V_b$ $N_b = \dfrac{N_a V_a}{V_b}$

$?\ N_b = \dfrac{(1.00\ N)(50.00\ \cancel{mL})}{75.00\ \cancel{mL}} = 0.667\ N$

Because calcium hydroxide is a dihydroxy base, 0.667 N Ca(OH)$_2$ solution is the same as 0.667/2 or 0.334 M Ca(OH)$_2$ solution.

96. $N_a = 0.150\ N$ $N_b = ?$

$V_a = 25.0\ mL$ $V_b = 30.0\ mL$

$N_a V_a = N_b V_b$ $N_b = \dfrac{N_a V_a}{V_b}$

$?\ N_b = \dfrac{(0.150\ N)(25.0\ \cancel{mL})}{30.0\ \cancel{mL}} = 0.125\ N$

Because sodium hydroxide acts as a monohydroxy base, 0.125 N NaOH is the same as 0.125 M NaOH.

EXTRA EXERCISES

97. (a)   PH$_3$ is a Brø nsted-Lowry acid.

  (b)   NaH is a Brø nsted-Lowry base.

98. (a)   NH$_3$ is a Brø nsted-Lowry base.

  (b)   HCl is a Brø nsted-Lowry acid.

99. (a)   (HSO$_4$)$^{1-}$ is a Brø nsted-Lowry base.

  (b)   (H$_3$O)$^{1+}$ is a Brø nsted-Lowry acid.

100. $[OH^{1-}] = 1 \times 10^{-3}\ M$, pH = 11

101. (a) $HCl + NaOH \rightarrow NaCl + H_2O$

   (b) $BaO + 2HCl \rightarrow BaCl_2 + H_2O$

   (c) $Zn + H_2SO_4 \rightarrow ZnSO_4 + H_2$

102. (a) $OH^{1-} + H_2O \rightarrow H-OH + OH^{1-}$

   (b) $NH_3 + H_2O \rightarrow NH_4^{1+} + OH^{1-}$

   (c) $HSO_4^{1-} + H_2O \rightarrow H_2SO_4 + OH^{1-}$

103. (a) $H_2O + H-OH \rightarrow H_3O^{1+} + OH^{1-}$

   (b) $HCO_3^{1-} + H_2O \rightarrow H_3O^{1+} + CO_3^{2-}$

   (c) . $HNO_3 + H_2O \rightarrow H_3O^{1+} + NO_3^{1-}$

104. Acid rain is the reason why the pH in many New England lakes is decreasing. The formation of acid rain may be represented by the following reaction:

   $$SO_3 \quad + H_2O \ \emptyset \quad H_2SO_4$$

   Sulfur   Sulfuric
   trioxide   acid

105. If in a reaction the PCl_3 accepted a proton, it would be a Brø nsted-Lowry base.

   $$H^{1+} + :PCl_3 \rightarrow \left[H \leftarrow \overset{\overset{\textstyle Cl}{|}}{\underset{\underset{\textstyle Cl}{|}}{P}} - Cl \right]^{1+}$$

106. (a) $2NaOH + H_2SO_4 \rightarrow Na_2SO_4 + 2H_2O$

   (b) $Zn + 2HCl \rightarrow ZnCl_2 + H_2$

   (c) $KOH + HCl \rightarrow KCl + H_2O$

   (d) $SO_2 + H_2O \rightarrow H_2SO_3$

APPENDIX BASIC MATHEMATICS FOR CHEMISTRY

A

SELF-TEST EXERCISES

1. (a) $5 + 12 = 17$

   (b) $-5 - 10 = -15$

   (c) $5 + 10 = 15$

   (d) $-5 + 10 = 5$

2. (a) $3 - (+2) = 1$

   (b) $3 - (-2) = 5$

   (c) $-3 - (+2) = -5$

   (d) $-3 - (-2) = -1$

3. (a) $8 + 25 = 33$

   (b) $8 - 25 = -17$

   (c) $-8 + 25 = 17$

   (d) $-8 - 25 = -33$

4. (a) $55 - (44) = 11$

   (b) $55 - (-44) = 99$

   (c) $-55 - (44) = -99$

   (d) $-55 - (-44) = -11$

5. (a) $\dfrac{1}{8} \times \dfrac{1}{2} = \dfrac{1}{16}$

   (b) $\dfrac{1}{8} \div \dfrac{1}{2} = \dfrac{1}{8} \times 2 = \dfrac{1}{4}$

   (c) $(8)^3 = 8 \times 8 \times 8 = 512$

   (d) $(2)^{-5} = \dfrac{1}{(2)^5} = \dfrac{1}{32}$

6. (a) $\dfrac{3}{5} \times \dfrac{2}{7} = \dfrac{6}{35}$

   (b) $\dfrac{20}{50} \times \dfrac{9}{5} = \dfrac{18}{25}$

190

(c) $\dfrac{5}{6} \div \dfrac{10}{3} = \dfrac{5}{6} \times \dfrac{3}{10} = \dfrac{1}{4}$

(d) $\dfrac{25}{35} \div \dfrac{7}{5} = \dfrac{25}{35} \times \dfrac{5}{7} = \dfrac{25}{49}$

7. (a) $(4)^{-2}(4)^{-5} = (4)^{-7}$

(b) $(4)^2(4)^3 = (4)^5$

(c) $(6)^4(6)^{-2} = (6)^2$

(d) $(5)^{-8}(5)^9 = (5)^1$

8. (a) $\dfrac{(4)^5}{(4)^2} = (4)^3$

(b) $\dfrac{(4)^5}{(4)^{-3}} = (4)^8$

(c) $\dfrac{(a)^3(a)^2}{(a)^4} = (a)^1$

(d) $\dfrac{(b)^6(b)^4}{(b)^3(b)^5} = (b)^2$

9. (a) $(25)^2 = 625$ (b) $(10)^3 = 1{,}000$ (c) $(99)^1 = 99$

(d) $(8)^{-3} = \dfrac{1}{(8)^3} = \dfrac{1}{512}$

(e) $\dfrac{1}{(4)^{-2}} = (4)^2 = 16$

10. (a) $(5)^2(5)^3 = (5)^5$

(b) $(12)^3(12)^9 = (12)^{12}$

(c) $(10)^2(10)^{-2} = 10^0 = 1$

(d) $(4)^{-8}(4)^{-2} = (4)^{-10}$

$\text{or } \dfrac{1}{(4)^{10}}$

11. (a) $\dfrac{(4)^5}{(4)^3} = (4)^2$

(b) $\dfrac{(12)^3}{(12)^{-2}} = (12)^5$

(c) $\dfrac{(20)^{-4}}{(20)^3} = (20)^{-7} \text{ or } \dfrac{1}{(20)^7}$

(d) $\dfrac{(20)^{-4}}{(20)^{-3}} = (20)^{-1} \text{ or } \dfrac{1}{20}$

12. (a) $(4)^4(4)^3(4)^2 = (4)^9$

(b) $(x)^2(x)^3(x)^{-4} = (x)^1$

(c) $\dfrac{(y)^2(y)^8}{(y)^2} = (y)^7$

(d) $\dfrac{(p)^2(p)^{-9}}{(p)^{-8}} = (p)^1$

(e) $\dfrac{(10)^{-3}(10)^5(10)^7}{(10)^{-8}(10)^9} = \dfrac{(10)^9}{10} = (10)^8$

13. (a) $(2)^6 = 64$

(b) $(3)^{-4} = \dfrac{1}{(3)^4} = \dfrac{1}{81}$

(c) $\dfrac{1}{(4)^3} = \dfrac{1}{64}$

(d) $\dfrac{1}{(4)^{-3}} = (4)^3 = 64$

14. (a) $(10)^5(10)^{-2} = (10)^3$

(b) $(2)^{-3}(2)^{-2} = (2)^{-5}$ or $\dfrac{1}{(2)^5}$

(c) $(3)^{-5}(3)^2 = (3)^{-3}$ or $\dfrac{1}{(3)^3}$

(d) $(6)^{-8}(6)^{10} = (6)^2$

15. (a) $\dfrac{(3)^7}{(3)^5} = (3)^2$

(b) $\dfrac{(2)^4(2)^{-6}}{(2)^7(2)^{-12}} = \dfrac{(2)^{-2}}{(2)^{-5}} = (2)^3$

(c) $\dfrac{(a)^{12}(a)^{-10}}{(a)^{-7}(a)^{-6}} = \dfrac{(a)^2}{(a)^{-13}} = (a)^{15}$

(d) $\dfrac{(b)^{-20}(b)^{-10}}{(b)^{-9}(b)^{-8}} = \dfrac{(b)^{-30}}{(b)^{-17}} = (b)^{-13}$ or $\dfrac{1}{(b)^{13}}$

16. $(4 \text{ ft})\left(\dfrac{12 \text{ in.}}{1 \text{ ft}}\right) = 48 \text{ in.}$

17. $A = l \times w, \quad w = \dfrac{A}{l}$

18. $? \text{ yd} = (18 \text{ ft})\left(\dfrac{1 \text{ yd}}{3 \text{ ft}}\right) = 6 \text{ yd}$

19. $? \text{ eggs} = (4 \text{ doz})\left(\dfrac{12 \text{ eggs}}{1 \text{ doz}}\right) = 48 \text{ eggs}$

20. (a) $? \text{ h} = (360 \text{ min})\left(\dfrac{1 \text{ h}}{60 \text{ min}}\right) = 6 \text{ h}$

(b) $? \text{ h} = (7{,}200 \text{ s})\left(\dfrac{1 \text{ min}}{60 \text{ s}}\right)\left(\dfrac{1 \text{ h}}{60 \text{ min}}\right) = 2 \text{ h}$

21. $? \text{ pints} = (8 \text{ quarts})\left(\dfrac{2 \text{ pints}}{1 \text{ quart}}\right) = 16 \text{ pints}$

22. $\dfrac{?\ \text{ft}}{\text{s}} = \left(\dfrac{1\ \text{mi}}{1\ \text{h}}\right)\left(\dfrac{5{,}280\ \text{ft}}{1\ \text{mi}}\right)\left(\dfrac{1\ \text{h}}{3{,}600\ \text{s}}\right) = \dfrac{1.47\ \text{ft}}{1\ \text{s}}$ or $1.47\ \text{ft/s}$

23. $?\ \text{ft} = (72\ \text{in})\left(\dfrac{1\ \text{ft}}{12\ \text{in.}}\right) = 6\ \text{ft}$

24. $?\ \text{in.} = (15\ \text{ft})\left(\dfrac{12\ \text{in.}}{1\ \text{ft}}\right) = 180\ \text{in.}$

25. $?\ \text{ft} = (100\ \text{yd})\left(\dfrac{3\ \text{ft}}{1\ \text{yd}}\right) = 300\ \text{ft}$

26. $?\ \text{in.} = (5\ \text{yd})\left(\dfrac{36\ \text{in.}}{1\ \text{yd}}\right) = 180\ \text{in.}$

27. $?\ \text{doz} = (288\ \text{eggs})\left(\dfrac{1\ \text{doz}}{12\ \text{eggs}}\right) = 24\ \text{doz}$

28. $?\ \text{min} = (24\ \text{h})\left(\dfrac{60\ \text{min}}{1\ \text{h}}\right) = 1{,}440\ \text{min}$

    $?\ \text{s} = (24\ \text{h})\left(\dfrac{3{,}600\ \text{s}}{1\ \text{h}}\right) = 86{,}400\ \text{s}$

29. $?\ \text{gal} = (40\ \text{qt})\left(\dfrac{1\ \text{gal}}{4\ \text{qt}}\right) = 10\ \text{gal}$

30. $\dfrac{?\ \text{mi}}{\text{h}} = \left(\dfrac{22{,}000\ \text{ft}}{1\ \text{s}}\right)\left(\dfrac{1\ \text{mi}}{5{,}280\ \text{ft}}\right)\left(\dfrac{3{,}600\ \text{s}}{1\ \text{h}}\right) = 15{,}000\ \text{mi/h}$

31. (a) $15.4 + 117.33 + 16.909 + 0.044 = 149.683$

    (b) $171.82 - 30.41 = 141.41$

32. (a) $25.431 + 0.761 + 0.325 + 0.008 = 26.525$

    (b) $123.25 - 19.54 = 103.71$

    (c) $98.77 - 38.25 + 45.62 = 106.14$

    (d) $254.37 - 68.26 - 38.33 = 147.78$

33. (a) $(7.33)(4) = 29.32$ (b) $(9.01)(4.28) = 38.5628$

(c)　$(3.111)(8.7) = 27.0657$

34. (a) $\dfrac{6.324}{3.1} = 2.04$

    (b) $\dfrac{25.30}{5.06} = 5$

35. (a) $(9.54)(3.27) = 31.2$

    (b) $(6.5)(7.1) = 46.15$

    (c) $\dfrac{80.4}{2.02} = 39.8$

    (d) $\dfrac{640.75}{8.5} = 75.38$

36. (a) $25a = 100$

    $a = \dfrac{100}{25} = 4$

    (b) $40y + 13 = 26$

    $40y = 13$

    $y = \dfrac{13}{40} = 0.325$

    (c) $12z - 12 = 24$

    $12z = 36$

    $z = \dfrac{36}{12} = 3$

37. (a) $\dfrac{6x}{3} = \dfrac{36}{12}$

    $6x = \dfrac{3 \times 36}{12} = 9$

    $x = \dfrac{9}{6} = \dfrac{3}{2}$

    (b) $12y + 6 = 6y + 12$

    $6y = 6$

    $y = 1$

38. Given: $PV = nRT$

    (a) $P = \dfrac{nRT}{V}$　　(b) $n = \dfrac{PV}{RT}$　　(c) $T = \dfrac{PV}{nR}$　　(d) $\dfrac{n}{v} = \dfrac{P}{RT}$

39. (a) $4t = 64$
    $t = 16$

    (b) $6y + 3 = 45$
    $6y = 42$
    $y = 7$

    (c) $2x - 7 = 33 - 3x$
    $5x = 40$
    $x = 8$

(d) $40k + 8 = 96 + 51k$
$11k = -88$
$k = -8$

40. (a) $A = bcd$

$b = \dfrac{A}{cd}$

(b) $A = bcd$

$c = \dfrac{A}{bd}$

(c) $A = bcd$

$\dfrac{A}{b} = cd$

41. (a) $\dfrac{x}{25} = \dfrac{4}{5}$

$x = 20$

(b) $\dfrac{3}{y} = \dfrac{7}{63}$

$y = 27$

(c) $\dfrac{4t}{12} = \dfrac{2}{3}$

$t = 2$

(d) $\dfrac{2}{5k} = \dfrac{5}{50}$

$k = 4$

42. (a) $\dfrac{k}{5} = \dfrac{9}{45}$

$k = 1$

(b) $\dfrac{2}{7} = \dfrac{h}{28}$

$h = 8$

(c) $\dfrac{72}{f} = \dfrac{9}{2}$

$f = 16$

(d) $\dfrac{18}{6} = \dfrac{12}{y}$

$y = 4$

43. (a) $2 : 5 : 9$
$x : 20 : y$
$x = 8, y = 36$

(b) $7 : 9$
$h : 54$
$h = 42$

(c) $2 : 3 : 5 : 7$
$1 : a : b : c$
$a = 1.5, b = 2.5$
$c = 3.5$

(d) $2 : 5 = 5 : d$
$\dfrac{2}{5} = \dfrac{5}{d}$
$d = 12.5$

44. (a) $m = DV$

(b) $V = \dfrac{m}{D}$

45. $d = \dfrac{m}{V} = \dfrac{25 \text{ g}}{5 \text{ mL}} = 5 \text{ g/mL}$

46. (a) Percent liberal arts $= \dfrac{200}{600} \times 100 = 33.3\%$

(b) Percent laboratory technology $= \dfrac{100}{600} \times 100 = 16.7\%$

(c) Percent health science technology $= \dfrac{300}{600} \times 100 = 50.0\%$

47. To Europe = 2,000 people × 0.40 = 800 people

    To Asia = 2,000 people × 0.30 = 600 people

    To Alaska = 2,000 people × 0.10 = 200 people

    To Miami = 2,000 people × 0.20 = 400 people

48. (a) $11 \times 6 = 66$ (b) $11 + 6 = 17$ (c) $30 \div 5 = 6$

    (d) $30 - 5 = 25$

49. (a) $(12 \times 5) + 5 = 60 + 5 = 65$

    (b) $(20 \div 4) - 2 = 5 - 2 = 3$

    (c) $(10 + 20) \div (5 \times 6) = 30 \div 30 = 1$

    (d) $(100 \times 50) \div (10 \times 40) = 5,000 \div 400 = 12.5$

50. (a) $(50 \times 6) \div 12 = 300 \div 12 = 25$

    (b) $(100 \div 50) \div (15 \times 0.01) = 150 \div 0.15 = 1,000$

    (c) $(0.05 \times 0.30) \div 4 = 0.015 \div 4 = 0.00375$

    (d) $(10,000 \times 5) \div 4,000 = 50,000 \div 4,000 = 12.5$

Solutions to Cumulative Reviews Chapters 1–3

1. True. 2. False. 3. False. Sugar is organic.

4. True. 5. False. They never accomplished this.

6. True 7. False. They never accomplished this.

8. True 9. True. 10. True

11. $A = l \times w$

$A = 12.5 \text{ m} \times 10.2 \text{ m} = 128 \text{ m}^2$ (3 significant figures)

12. $V = l \times w \times h$

$V = 15.25 \text{ cm} \times 12.00 \text{ cm} \times 24.85 \text{ cm}$

$= 4,548 \text{ cm}^3$ (4 significant figures)

13. $V = \pi r^2 h$

$V = (3.14)(14.50 \text{ cm})^2(25.05 \text{ cm}) = 16,540 \text{ cm}^3$ (4 significant figures)

14. 0.28 kg to g, dg, mg

(a) $? \text{ g} = 0.28 \text{ kg} \times \dfrac{1{,}000 \text{ g}}{1 \text{ kg}} = 280 \text{ g}$

(b) $? \text{ dg} = 0.28 \text{ kg} \times \dfrac{10{,}000 \text{ dg}}{1 \text{ kg}} = 2{,}800 \text{ dg}$

(c) $? \text{ mg} = 0.28 \text{ kg} \times \dfrac{100{,}000 \text{ mg}}{1 \text{ kg}} = 280{,}000 \text{ mg}$

15. (a) $? \text{ dm} = 6.8 \text{ m} \times \dfrac{10 \text{ dm}}{1 \text{ m}} = 68 \text{ dm}$

(b) $? \text{ cm} = 6.8 \text{ m} \times \dfrac{100 \text{ cm}}{1 \text{ m}} = 680 \text{ cm}$

(c) $? \text{ mm} = 6.8 \text{ m} \times \dfrac{1{,}000 \text{ mm}}{1 \text{ m}} = 6{,}800 \text{ mm}$

16. (a) $? \text{ cm} = 125 \text{ mm} \times \dfrac{1 \text{ cm}}{10 \text{ mm}} = 12.5 \text{ cm}$

(b) $? \text{ m} = 125 \text{ mm} \times \dfrac{1 \text{ m}}{1{,}000 \text{ mm}} = 0.125 \text{ m}$

(c) $? \text{ km} = 125 \text{ mm} \times \dfrac{1 \text{ km}}{1{,}000{,}000 \text{ mm}} = 0.000125 \text{ km}$

17. (a) $? \text{ L} = 25{,}595 \text{ mL} \times \dfrac{1 \text{ L}}{1{,}000 \text{ mL}} = 25.595 \text{ L}$

(b) $? \text{ dL} = 25{,}595 \text{ mL} \times \dfrac{1 \text{ dL}}{100 \text{ mL}} = 255.95 \text{ dL}$

18. (a) $? \text{ ft} = 50.0 \text{ m} \times \dfrac{3.28 \text{ ft}}{\text{m}} = 164 \text{ ft}$

(b) $? \text{ in.} = 164 \text{ ft} \times \dfrac{12 \text{ in.}}{\text{ft}} = 1{,}970 \text{ in.}$

19. (a) $? \text{ lb} = 25.55 \text{ g} \times \dfrac{0.00220 \text{ lb}}{1 \text{ g}} = 0.0562 \text{ lb}$

(b) $? \text{ oz} = 0.05621 \text{ lb} \times \dfrac{16 \text{ oz}}{1 \text{ lb}} = 0.899 \text{ oz}$

20. 2.54 cm = 1 in. Therefore,

$$(2.54 \text{ cm})^3 = (x \text{ in.})^3$$

$$x = \frac{16.4 \text{ cm}^3}{\text{in.}^3}$$

21. $? \text{ lb} = 165.00 \text{ g} \times \dfrac{0.00220 \text{ lb}}{1 \text{ g}} = 0.363 \text{ lb}$

22. (a) $? \text{ L} = 12.0 \text{ gal} \times \dfrac{0.946 \text{ L}}{1 \text{ qt}} \times \dfrac{4 \text{ qt}}{1 \text{ gal}}$

$$= 45.4 \text{ L} \quad \text{or} \quad 45,400 \text{ mL}$$

(b) $? \text{ ft oz} = 45,300 \text{ mL} \times \dfrac{0.0340 \text{ fl oz}}{1 \text{ mL}} = 1,540 \text{ fl oz}$

23. $D = \dfrac{m}{V}$ $m = 500.0 \text{ g}$ and $V = s^3$ $V = (12.0 \text{ cm})^3$

$$V = (12.0 \text{ cm})^3 = 1,730 \text{ cm}^3$$

$$D = \frac{500.0 \text{ g}}{1,730 \text{ cm}^3} = 0.289 \text{ g/cm}^3$$

24. $D = \dfrac{m}{V}$ $m = 20.0 \text{ g}$ $V = 113.0 \text{ mL}$

$$D = \frac{20.0 \text{ g}}{113.0 \text{ mL}} = 0.177 \text{ g/mL}$$

From Problem 67 in Chapter 2, we learned that the density of air is 1.18×10^{-3} g/mL, so this gas is heavier than air and will not float.

25. $D = \dfrac{m}{V}$ $m = 90.0 \text{ g}$

$V_i = 15.0 \text{ mL}$ $V_f = 30.0 \text{ mL}$ $V_f - V_i = V$

$30.0 \text{ mL} - 15.0 \text{ mL} = 15.0 \text{ mL}$

$$D = \frac{90.0 \text{ g}}{15.0 \text{ mL}} = 6.00 \text{ g/mL}$$

26. $D = 3.50 \text{ g/cm}^3 \qquad m = 937.83 \text{ g}$

$$V = \frac{m}{D} = \frac{937.83 \text{ g}}{3.50 \text{ g/cm}^3} = 268 \text{ cm}^3$$

$$= \frac{4}{3} \pi r^3$$

$$r^3 = \frac{3V}{4\pi} = \frac{(3)(268 \text{ cm}^3)}{(4)(3.14)}$$

$$r = \sqrt[3]{64} = 4.00 \text{ cm}$$

27. (a) $28.64 + 3.2 = 31.84 = 31.8$

    (b) $125.4 \div 13.5 = 9.288 = 9.29$

    (c) $6.55 \times 12.1 = 79.255 = 79.3$

    (d) $98.4 - 0.12 = 98.28 = 98.3$

28. (a) 5×10^3 (b) 5×10^{-4} (c) 6.023×10^8 (d) 3.5000×10^7

29. (a) 5 (b) 4 (c) 5 (d) 4

30. $? \, °C = \frac{\infty F - 32}{1.8}$

    (a) $? \, °C = \frac{45.0 - 32}{1.8} = \frac{13}{1.8} = 7.22 °C$

    (b) $? \, °C = \frac{-10.0 - 32}{1.8} = \frac{-42}{1.8} = -23.3 °C$

    (c) $? \, °C = \frac{450 - 32}{1.8} = \frac{418}{1.8} = 230 °C$

(d) $? °C = \dfrac{-100.0 - 32}{1.8} = \dfrac{-132.0}{1.8} = -73.33°C$

Note: The number of significant figures in the answer is the same as the number of significant figures in the given temperature in °F.

31. $?°F = (1.8 \times °C) + 32$

(a) $?°F = (88.0 \times 1.8) + 32 = 158.4 + 32 = 19\bar{0} °F$

(b) $? °F = (-12.5 \times 1.8) + 32 = -22.5 + 32 = 9.5°F$

(c) $? °F = (65.6 \times 1.8) + 32 = 118.1 + 32 = 15\bar{0} °F$

(d) $? °F = (40\bar{0} \times 1.8) + 32 = 72\bar{0} + 32 = 752°F$

32. Amorphous solids have no definite internal structure or form. Crystalline solids have a fixed, regularly repeating, symmetrical inner structure.

33. (a) Chemical   (b) Physical   (c) Chemical   (d) Physical

34. Heterogeneous matter is made up of different parts with different properties. Homogeneous matter has the same properties throughout.

35. (a) 1 zinc atom, 4 carbon atoms, 6 hydrogen atoms, 4 oxygen atoms
     (b) 2 nitrogen atoms, 8 hydrogen atoms, 1 chromium atom, 4 oxygen atoms

36. Molecular mass is used for compounds composed of molecules. Formula mass is used for compounds composed of ions.

37. Mercury would have a mass of 5 amu.

38. (a) 173.0   (b) 210.0   (c) 31.0   (d) 107.9

39. (a) 232.8   (b) 132.1   (c) 180.0   (d) 251.1

40. The formula of $Al_2(SO_4)_3$ means that this formula unit contains 2 aluminum atoms, 3 sulfur atoms, and 12 oxygen atoms.

41. (a) Mixture   (b) Element   (c) Compound   (d) Compound
     (e) Element   (f) Mixture   (g) Mixture

42. (a) Heterogeneous   (b) Homogeneous   (c) Heterogeneous
     (d) Homogeneous

43. Actinium (Ac), aluminum (Al), americium (Am), argon (Ar), arsenic (As), astatine (At), gold (Au), and silver (Ag)

44. Helium (He), carbon (C), nitrogen (N), oxygen (O), fluorine (F), neon (Ne), phosphorous (P), sulfur (S), chlorine (Cl), argon (Ar), selenium (Se), bromine (Br), krypton (Kr), iodine (I), xenon (Xe), and radon (Rn)

45. (a) Potassium and sulfur
    (b) Silver, chromium, and oxygen
    (c) Potassium, manganese, and oxygen
    (d) Mercury, phosphorus, and oxygen

46. (a) N_2O (b) K_2CrO_4 (c) NH_3 (d) $SrSO_4$

47. (a) Chemical   (b) Physical   (c) Chemical   (d) Physical

48. No is the element nobelium, and NO is the compound nitrogen monoxide.

49. No! During the burning process some of the atoms that compose paper react with oxygen in the air and form gaseous compounds.

50. Add water to the mixture and shake. The salt dissolves and the sand settles to the bottom of the container. Filter the sand and collect the salt water (filtrate). To retrieve the pure salt, evaporate the water.

Solutions to Cumulative Reviews Chapters 4–6

1. Protons and neutrons are found in the nucleus, and electrons are found surrounding the nucleus.

2. Cathode rays came from the cathode.

3. A magnet would deflect particles, not waves. An electric field would easily deflect particles.

4. Ultraviolet light is directed onto a metal and makes it emit electrons.

5. An atom is a sphere of positive electricity in which electrons are embedded. The positive particles balance the negative electrons.

6. Rutherford found that one alpha particle in 20,000 ricocheted. This led him to believe that an atom has a small but dense center of positive charge.

7. New evidence disproved Thomson's theory.

8. Neutrons add mass but no charge.

9. Isotopes are atoms of the same element with different atomic masses. This existence proves that atoms of an element need *not* be identical in size, mass, and shape.

10. **(a)** The number of protons in an atom of an element is called the atomic number of that element. Therefore there are 27 protons in the element cobalt, $_{27}^{59}$Co.

(b) $_{40}^{90}$Zr has 40 protons.

(c) $_{34}^{74}$Se has 34 protons.

11. Use Table 4.2 to determine the percentage natural abundance of each isotope of neon.

(19.992)(0.9092) + (20.994)(0.00257) + (21.991)(0.0882)

    18.18   +   0.0540   +   1.94   = 20.17

12. Use Table 4.2 to determine the percentage natural abundance of ^{15}N. It is 0.37% or 0.0037. Therefore

(0.0037)(100,000 ^{15}N atoms) = 370 N atoms

in the sample.

13. **(a)** $_{17}^{35}$Cl   **(b)** $_{14}^{28}$Si

14. ^{50}Z and ^{52}Z are the two isotopic forms of the hypothetical element Z whose atomic weight is 50.5. Therefore

$50x + 52y = 50.5$

Because the fractions of all isotopes must add up to 1, $x + y = 1$. Next we solve the simultaneous equations:

$$x = y - 1$$
$$50(1-y) + 52y = 50.5$$
$$50 - 50y + 52y = 50.5$$
$$50 + 2y = 50.5$$
$$2y = 0.5$$
$$y = 0.25$$
$$x = 0.75$$

Therefore

Percent $y = 0.25 \times 100 = 25\%$
Percent $x = 0.75 \times 100 = 75\%$

and the percentages are

75% ^{50}Z and 25% ^{52}Z

15. $^{73}_{32}$ Ge has 32 protons, 32 electrons, and 73 – 32, or 41, neutrons.

16. $^{60}_{26}$ Fe has 26 electrons.

17. Looking at Table 4.2, we see that oxygen-16 occurs 99.759% of the time and is the most abundant isotope.

18. Use Table 4.2 to find that ^{7}Li has a 92.58% natural abundance. Therefore

$$(0.9258)(2,\bar{0}00) = 1,900\ ^7\text{Li atoms}$$

would be found in a sample containing $2.0 \times 10^3\ ^7$Li atoms.

19. Looking at Table 4.2, we find that ^{7}Li occurs 92.58% of the time. Therefore

? ^{7}Li atoms $= (1.000 \times 10^6\ ^7\text{Li atoms})(0.9258)$

$= 9.258 \times 10^5$ atoms of ^{7}Li

20. Looking at Table 4.2, we find that ^{29}Si occurs 4.70% of the time. Therefore

? Si Atoms $= \dfrac{470{,}000}{0.0470} = 1.00 \times 10^7$

21. Electrons produce the line spectra of elements.

22. As an electron travels to an energy level farther from the nucleus, the energy of that electron *increases*. The answer is (a).

23. The electron configuration of oxygen is K has 2 and L has 6. Therefore the outermost energy level of an oxygen atom has 6 electrons.

24. (a) K has 1 for $_1$H.
     (b) K has 2 and L has 1 for $_3$Li.

(c) K has 2, L has 8, and M has 1 for $_{11}$Na.

(d) K has 2, L has 8, M has 8, and N has 1 for $_{19}$K.

25. A neutral atom of magnesium has 2 electrons in its outermost energy level because K has 2, L has 8, and M has 2 for $_{12}$Mg.

26. $2 + 8 + 6 = 16$, so the element is $_{16}$S.

27. The chemical properties of an element are determined by the number of electrons in he *outermost energy level*. Therefore the answer is (b).

28. Phosphorus has 5 electrons in its outermost energy level, so it fits into Group VA.

29. $_1$H; K has 1.

$_3$Li; K has 2 and L has 1.

$_{11}$Na; K has 2, L has 8, and M has 1.

$_{19}$K; K has 2, L has 8, M has 8, and N has 1.

30. $_{70}$Yb or any element with a higher atomic number (see Table 5.3 of the text).

31. Raindrops act as prisms when a rainbow is produced naturally.

32. Line spectra are used to analyze the sun and other extraterrestrial bodies.

33. Line spectra of his hair indicated the presence of the element arsenic.

34. Our major source of radiant energy is the sun.

35. Electromagnetic waves travel through the vacuum of space.

36. Both visible and invisible waves are found in the electromagnetic spectrum. Therefore the answer is (c).

37. Heinrich R. Hertz verified the theory of electromagnetic radiation proposed by James Clerk Maxwell by producing electromagnetic waves that were longer than visible light waves.

38. Luminous watch dials absorb light energy and re-emit it when they glow.

39. A sample of an element is heated and it begins to glow.

40. Bundles of energy absorbed or emitted by electrons are called *quanta*.

41. The periodic law states that the chemical properties of elements are periodic functions of their atomic numbers. This means that elements with similar chemical properties recur at regular intervals and are placed accordingly on the periodic table.

42. Moseley was able to determine the nuclear charge or the atomic numbers of the atoms of known elements.

43. Element 107 is a Group VIIB element.

$$1s^2 2s^2 2p^6 3s^2 3p^6 3d^{10} 4s^2 4p^6 4d^{10} 4f^{14}$$

$$5s^2 5p^6 5d^{10} 5f^{14} 6s^2 6p^6 6d^5 7s^2$$

44. Element 106 is a Group VIB element.

$$1s^2 2s^2 2p^6 3s^2 3p^6 3d^{10} 4s^2 4p^6 4d^{10} 4f^{14}$$

$$5s^2 5p^6 5d^{10} 5f^{14} 6s^2 6p^6 6d^4 7s^2$$

45. Elements 18–19, 27–28, 52–53, and 92–93.

46. False. Ionization energy decreases from the top to the bottom of a group.

47. True. Atomic radius generally decreases from left to right across a period of elements.

48. False. A Ca^{2+} ion is a calcium atom that has lost two electrons. The number of protons is not changed.

49. Element 108 should behave like Fe, Ru, and Os.

50. The element is $_{11}Na$.

51. True. The elements on the periodic table show properties that are related to their atomic numbers.

52. False. The element with that configuration is number 10 and belongs in Group VIIIA.

53. Fluorine has the higher ionization potential, because more energy is needed to pull an electron away from an isolated ground-state atom of fluorine than from such an atom of lithium.

54. $1s^2 2s^2 2p^6 3s^2 3p^2$

55. True. The volume of space occupied by an electron is called an orbital.

56. (a) Group IIA forms 2+ ions.
    (b) Group VIA forms 2– ions.

57. (a) Na should have a larger radius than Li because the outermost electron of Na is in energy level three, whereas the outermost electron of Li is in energy level two.
    (b) For the same reason, Ca should have a larger radius than Ca^{2+}.

58. Mg has a lower ionization potential than Cl, because more energy is needed to pull an electron away from an isolated ground-state atom of chlorine than from such an atom of magnesium. Within each period, ionization potential increases from left to right. This results from the decrease in atomic radius moving from left to right in the periodic table.

59. Cs has a larger atomic radius than Li because the number of energy levels increases as we move down through a group in the periodic table.

60. Li should have a larger radius than F. As we move from left to right across a period, the number of protons increases along with the number of electrons. The larger number of protons exert a greater pull on the electrons of the inner energy levels, which causes a shrinking of the atomic radius.

SOLUTIONS TO CUMULATIVE REVIEWS CHAPTERS 7–8

1. (a) $\overset{\bullet}{C}a\bullet$ (b) $[Ca]^{2+}$

2. (a) $\cdot\overset{\bullet\bullet}{\underset{\bullet\bullet}{C}l}:$ (b) $[:\overset{\bullet\bullet}{\underset{\bullet\bullet}{C}l}:]^{1-}$

3. An *ionic bond* is formed by the transfer of electrons from one atom to another. The atoms are always of different elements. A *covalent bond* is formed by the sharing of electrons between two atoms. A *coordinate covalent bond* is a bond in which one element donates the electrons to form the bond.

4.
```
         H   H   H
         ·x  ·x  ·x
   H ˣ C : C : C ẋ H
         x·  ·x  ·x
         H   H   H
```

5. HCl = 0.9; $CaCl_2$ = 2.0; $BaCl_2$ = 2.1; CaF_2 = 3.0

   The values are obtained from Table 7.1 as follows:

H = 2.1	Cl = 3.0	Difference = 0.9
Ca = 1.0	Cl = 3.0	Difference = 2.0

$$
\begin{array}{lll}
Ba = 0.9 & Cl = 3.0 & \text{Difference} = 2.1 \\
Ca = 1.0 & F\ = 4.0 & \text{Difference} = 3.0
\end{array}
$$

6. Using Table 7.1, we determine the electronegativity differences as follows:

$$
\begin{array}{lll}
LiF & = 3.0 & \text{(Li is 1.0, F is 4.0)} \\
NaF & = 3.1 & \text{(Na is 0.9, F is 4.0)} \\
RbF & = 3.2 & \text{(Rb is 0.8, F is 4.0)} \\
CsF & = 3.3 & \text{(Cs is 0.7, F is 4.0)}
\end{array}
$$

Using Table 7.2, we see that an electronegativity difference of 3.3 corresponds to the greatest ionic percentage; therefore, CsF is most ionic.

7. (a) $Cu_2 SO_3$ (b) OsO_4 (c) $(NH_4)_2CO_3$ (d) N_2O

8. (a) $\underline{W}\ Cl_5$.   We know Cl has a charge of 1–. For the compound to be electrically neutral, the tungsten must be 5+.

    (b) $\underline{Sn}\ F_4$.   We know F has a charge of 1–. For the compound to be electrically neutral, the tin must be 4+.

    (c) $\underline{V}\ _2O_5$.   We know O has a charge of 2–. For the compound to be electrically neutral, the vanadium must be 5+.

    (d) $\underline{In}\ I_3$.   We know I has a charge of 1–. For the compound to be electrically neutral, the indium must be 3+.

9. (a) Ammonium iodide   (b) Calcium carbide
    (c) Copper(I) chromate or cuprous chromate

10. X and Y would form the compound X_2Y_3 because X would be X^{3+} and Y would be Y^{2-}.

11. False. The electron dot structure for carbon dioxide is

$$
\overset{xx}{\underset{xx}{O^{x}_{x}}} : C : \overset{xx}{\underset{xx}{{}^{x}_{x}O}} \quad \text{or} \quad \overset{..}{O} = C = \overset{..}{\underset{..}{O}}
$$

12. True.

13. True. All of these electron structures are the same.

14. False. The bonds in a molecule of NH_3 are polar because the difference in electronegativity is 0.9.

15. True.

16. $1s^2 2s^2 2p^4$ is O, and $1s^2 2s^2 2p^6 3s^2$ is Mg. Therefore the compound formed is MgO.

17. Determine the electronegativity differences by using Table 7.1. They are as follows:

    C–H is 0.4   C–Cl is 0.5   C–O is 1.0

    Using Table 7.2 we find that the C–H bond is the most covalent.

18. Na^{1+} and SO_4^{2-} form the compound Na_2SO_4.

19. Atomic number 16 is in group VIA, so it is likely to have an oxidation number of 2–.

20. (a)

$$\left[\begin{array}{c} \overset{xx}{\underset{xx}{\overset{x}{\underset{x}{O}}}} : N \overset{xx}{\underset{\cdot\cdot}{\overset{x}{\underset{x}{O}}}} \\ \overset{xx}{\underset{x}{\overset{x}{O}}} \end{array} \right]^{1-}$$

   (b)

$$\left[\begin{array}{c} H \\ \overset{xx}{H \overset{\cdot}{\underset{x}{N}} \overset{\cdot}{\underset{x}{}} H} \\ \overset{\cdot x}{H} \end{array} \right]$$

21. (a) S is 6+   (b) Mn is 4+
    (c) Mn is 7+   (d) N is 3+

22. (a) Each hydrogen has a partial positive charge, and the oxygen a partial negative charge.
    (b) Hydrogen has a partial positive charge, and iodine a partial negative charge.
    (c) Each chlorine has a partial positive charge, and oxygen a partial negative charge.
    (d) Phosphorus has a partial positive charge, and the chlorines have a partial negative charge.

23. (a) $: \overset{\cdot\cdot}{\underset{\cdot\cdot}{F}} : \overset{\cdot\cdot}{\underset{\cdot\cdot}{F}} :$ (b) $: \overset{\cdot\cdot}{\underset{\cdot\cdot}{Cl}} : \overset{\cdot\cdot}{C} \overset{\cdot\cdot}{\underset{\cdot\cdot}{C}} : \overset{\cdot\cdot}{\underset{\cdot\cdot}{Cl}} :$

(c) 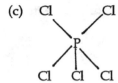   (d)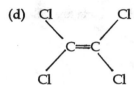

24. (a) 1+   (b) 1–   (c) 2+   (d) 3+

25. (a) $Fe_3(PO_4)_2$ (b) $Hg(CN)_2$ (c) $Zn(HCO_3)_2$

    (d) $Fe_2(Cr_2O_7)_3$

26. (a) In_2S_3 (b) $Mg_3(AsO_4)_2$ (c) Ga_2O_3

    (d) Rb_2Se (e) FeO   (f) $CoCl_2$

    (g) Cu_3N (h) Cu_2O

27. (a) HIO_4 (b) $HClO_3$ (c) HBr   (d) $HClO_2$

28. A coordinate covalent bond is a bond in which one atom donates both electrons to form the bond.

29. Yes. A molecule like carbon tetrachloride has four polar C–Cl bonds, but due to the shape of the molecule, the dipoles cancel out and the center of positive charge in the molecule coincides with the center of negative charge.

30. (a) Group VIA   (b) 6 electrons   (c) 2–

SOLUTIONS TO
CUMULATIVE REVIEWS
CHAPTERS 9–11

1. The molecular mass of $Al_2(SO_4)_3$ is 342.3.

   $$? \text{ moles} = (3.43 \text{ g})\left(\frac{1 \text{ mole}}{342.3 \text{ g}}\right) = 0.0100 \text{ mole}$$

2. The atomic mass of C is 12.0

   $$? \text{ moles} = (4.8 \text{ g})\left(\frac{1 \text{ mole}}{12.0 \text{ g}}\right) = 0.40 \text{ mole}$$

3. (a) $? \text{ g} = 0.750 \text{ mole} \times \dfrac{98.1 \text{ g}}{\text{mole}} = 73.6 \text{ g } H_2SO_4$

   (b) $? \text{ g} = 5.00 \text{ moles} \times \dfrac{18.0 \text{ g}}{\text{mole}} = 90.0 \text{ g } H_2O$

   (c) $? \text{ g} = 0.00700 \text{ mole} \times \dfrac{62.0 \text{ g}}{\text{mole}} = 0.434 \text{ g } H_2CO_3$

   (d) $? \text{ g} = 50.0 \text{ moles} \times \dfrac{60.0 \text{ g}}{\text{mole}} = 3.000 \times 10^3 \text{ g } HC_2H_3O_2$

4. $4.6 \text{ g Na} \times \dfrac{1 \text{ mole}}{23.0 \text{ g}} = 0.20 \text{ mole Na}$

$$? \text{ atoms} = 0.20 \text{ mole Na} \times \frac{6.02 \times 10^{23} \text{atoms}}{1 \text{ mole}} = 1.2 \times 10^{23} \text{ atoms}$$

5. $$? \text{ moles} = 5.328 \text{ g Sn} \times \frac{1 \text{ mole}}{118.7 \text{ g}} = 0.04489 \text{ mole Sn}$$

$$? \text{ moles} = 1.436 \text{ g O} \times \frac{1 \text{ mole}}{16.0 \text{ g}} = 0.08975 \text{ mole O}$$

$$Sn_{\frac{0.4489}{0.4489}} \quad O_{\frac{0.08975}{0.4489}} \qquad \qquad Sn_1O_2 \quad \text{or} \quad SnO_2$$

6. $C_{10}H_{16}O_3$ has a molecular weight of 736.0. The empirical formula weighs

$$\begin{aligned}
10 \times C &= 10 \times 12.0 = 120.0 \\
16 \times H &= 16 \times 1.0 = 16.0 \\
3 \times O &= 3 \times 16.0 = \underline{48.0} \\
& 184.0
\end{aligned}$$

$$(184)x = 736$$

$$x = \frac{736}{184} = 4,$$

so the molecular formula has a mass 4 times the empirical formula mass.

$$(C_{10}H_{16}O_3)_4 = C_{40}H_{64}O_{12}$$

7. CH_2O is the empirical formula and it weighs

$$\begin{aligned}
1 \times C &= 1 \times 12.0 = 12.0 \\
2 \times H &= 2 \times 1.0 = 2.0 \\
1 \times O &= 1 \times 16.0 = \underline{16.0} \\
& 30.0
\end{aligned}$$

$$(30)x = 180$$
$$x = 6,$$

so $(CH_2O)_6 = C_6H_{12}O_6$.

8. $C_9H_8O_4$ weighs 180.0.

(a) $$? \text{ moles} = 36.0 \text{ g} \times \frac{1 \text{ mole}}{180.0 \text{ g}} = 0.200 \text{ mole aspirin}$$

(b)   ? molecules $= 0.200 \text{ mole} \times \dfrac{6.02 \times 10^{23} \text{ molecules}}{\text{mole}} = 1.20 \times 10^{23}$ molecules

(c)   Moles C atoms $= 0.200 \text{ mole aspirin} \times \dfrac{9 \text{ moles C atoms}}{1 \text{ mole aspirin}}$

$$= 1.80 \text{ moles C atoms}$$

(d)   Moles H atoms $= 0.200 \text{ mole aspirin} \times \dfrac{8 \text{ moles H atoms}}{1 \text{ mole aspirin}}$

$$= 1.60 \text{ moles H atoms}$$

(e)   Moles O atoms $= 0.200 \text{ mole aspirin} \times \dfrac{4 \text{ moles H atoms}}{1 \text{ mole aspirin}}$

$$= 0.800 \text{ mole O atoms}$$

9.   6.08 g N + 13.90 g O produce a compound whose molecular mass = 92.0.

$$\text{Moles N} = 6.08 \text{ g N} \times \dfrac{1 \text{ mole}}{14.0 \text{ g}} = 0.434 \text{ mole N}$$

$$\text{Moles O} = 13.90 \text{ g O} \times \dfrac{1 \text{ mole}}{16.0 \text{ g}} = 0.869 \text{ mole O}$$

$N_{\frac{0.434}{0.434}} O_{\frac{0.869}{0.434}} = N_1 O_2 = NO_2$ $(NO_2)x = 92.0$
$(46)x = 92.0$
$x = 2$

Therefore the molecular formula is N_2O_4.

10.   (a) $Ca_3(PO_4)_2$

3 Ca = 120.3
2 P = 62.0
8 O = 128.0
310.3

(b) CH_4

1 C = 12.0
4 H = 4.0
16.0

(c) NO_2

1 N = 14.0
2 O = 32.0
46.0

(d) $Ba(C_2H_3O_2)_2$

1 Ba = 137.3
4 C = 48.0
6 H =   6.0
4 O = 64.0
255.3

11. **(a)** H_2S MM = 34.1

Percent H = $\dfrac{2.0}{34.1}$ × 100 = 5.9%

Percent S = $\dfrac{32.1}{34.1}$ × 100 = 94.1%

(b)   NaCl   MM = 58.5

Percent Na = $\dfrac{23.0}{58.5}$ × 100 = 39.3%

Percent Cl = $\dfrac{35.5}{58.5}$ × 100 = 60.7%

(c) $Fe(C_2H_3O_2)_3$ MM = 232.8

Percent Fe = $\dfrac{55.8}{232.8}$ × 100 = 24.0%

Percent C = $\dfrac{72.0}{232.8}$ × 100 = 30.9%

Percent H = $\dfrac{9.0}{232.8}$ × 100 = 3.9%

Percent O = $\dfrac{96.0}{232.8}$ × 100 = 41.2%

(d) K_2SO_4 MM = 174.3

Percent K = $\dfrac{78.2}{174.3}$ × 100 = 44.9%

Percent S = $\dfrac{32.1}{174.3}$ × 100 = 18.4%

Percent O = $\dfrac{64.0}{174.3}$ × 100 = 36.7%

12.   83.7% C   16.3% H   MM = 86

On the basis of 100.0 g of compound, 83.7 g are C and 16.3 g are H. Therefore, on the basis of moles:

$$\text{Moles C} = (83.7 \text{ g})\left(\frac{1 \text{ mole}}{12.0 \text{ g}}\right) = 6.98 \text{ moles C} \quad (\text{round to } 7)$$

$$\text{Moles H} = (16.3 \text{ g})\left(\frac{1 \text{ mole}}{1.00 \text{ g}}\right) = 16.3 \text{ moles of H}$$

Therefore, the empirical formula is

$$\frac{C_7}{7} \frac{H_{16.3}}{7} = CH_{2.3} = C_3H_7$$

The molecular formula is

$$\left(C_3H_7\right)x = 86$$
$$(43)x = 86$$
$$x = 2$$

The molecular formula is C_6H_{14}.

13. C_5H_7N MM = 162

The empirical formula has a weight of 81, so $(81)x = 162$.

$$(81)x = 162$$

$$x = \frac{162}{81} = 2$$

Therefore the molecular formula is $(C_5H_7N)_2$ or $C_{10}H_{14}N_2$.

C = 120
H = 14
N = 28
‾‾‾‾‾
   162

$$\text{Percent C} = \frac{120}{162} \times 100 = 74.1\%$$

$$\text{Percent H} = \frac{14}{162} \times 100 = 8.6\%$$

$$\text{Percent N} = \frac{28}{162} \times 100 = 17.3\%$$

14. Moles $H_2O = 0.720 \text{ g} \times \dfrac{1 \text{ mole}}{18.0 \text{ g}} = 0.0400$ mole H_2O

Molecules $H_2O \quad = 0.0400 \ \cancel{\text{mole}} \times \dfrac{6.02 \times 10^{23} \text{ molecules}}{\cancel{\text{mole}}}$

$= 2.41 \times 10^{22}$ molecules H_2O

15. $CaCO_3$

$$
\begin{array}{rl}
Ca = & 40.08 \\
3O = & 48.00 \\
C = & \underline{12.01} \\
& 100.09
\end{array}
$$

Every $\overline{100}$ g of $CaCO_3$ contain $4\overline{0}$ g Ca. Also, $1,\overline{000}$ mg of Ca = 1.000 g of Ca.

$$\text{g } CaCO_3 = (1.000 \ \cancel{\text{g Ca}})\left(\dfrac{100.1 \text{ g } CaCO_3}{40.1 \ \cancel{\text{g Ca}}}\right) = 2.50 \text{ g } CaCO_3$$

16. $CaBr_2 + H_2SO_4 \rightarrow 2HBr + CaSO_4$

17. $2Mg + O_2 \rightarrow 2MgO$

18. $NH_3(g) + HCl(g) \rightarrow NH_4Cl(s)$

19. (a) Sugar decomposes in this reaction.
    (b) Hydrogen and bromine combine to form hydrogen bromide in this reaction.
    (c) Chlorine replaces bromine in this single-replacement reaction.
    (d) Both compounds exchange ions in this double-replacement reaction.

20. (a) $H_2 + Cl_2 \rightarrow 2HCl$

    (b) $2NaCl + Pb(NO_3)_2 \rightarrow 2NaNO_3 + PbCl_2$

    (c) $2Al + 3H_2SO_4 \rightarrow Al_2(SO_4)_3 + 3H_2$

    (d) $SrCO_3 \rightarrow SrO + CO_2$

21. $CaCO_3 \rightarrow CaO + CO_2$

This is the decomposition of a metal carbonate.

22. (a) $TiCl_4 + 2H_2O \rightarrow TiO_2 + 4HCl$

    (b) $P_4O_{10} + 6H_2O \rightarrow 4H_3PO_4$

23. (a) Acid + base forms salt + water

    $$Fe(OH)_3 + H_3PO_4 \rightarrow FePO_4 + 3H_2O$$

    (b) Acid + base forms salt + water

    $$Pb(OH)_2 + 2HNO_3 \rightarrow Pb(NO_3)_2 + 2H_2O$$

24. $SO_3 + H_2O \rightarrow H_2SO_4$

25. $2C_8H_{18} + 25O_2 \rightarrow 16CO_2 + 18H_2O$

26. $2C_3H_7OH + 9O_2 \rightarrow 6CO_2 + 8H_2O$

27. $CaSO_4 + Na_2CO_3 \rightarrow CaCO_3(s) + Na_2SO_4$

28. $C_{12}H_{22}O_{11} \rightarrow 12C + 11H_2O$

29. True. $2Al + 3H_2SO_4 \rightarrow 3H_2 + Al_2(SO_4)_3$

    $2 + 3 + 3 + 1 = 9$

30. False. $2NaNO_3 \rightarrow 2NaNO_2 + O_2$

    $2 + 2 + 1 \neq 4$

31. True. $Zn + H_2SO_4 \rightarrow ZnSO_4 + H_2$

    Zinc loses electrons and is oxidized; hydrogen gains electrons and is reduced.

32. True. $2Na + Cl_2 \rightarrow 2NaCl$

    Sodium loses electrons and is oxidized; chlorine gains electrons and is reduced.

33. True. $Sn + HNO_3 \rightarrow SnO_2 + NO_2 + H_2O$

    Sodium loses electrons and is oxidized. It acts as the reducing agent. Nitrogen gains electrons and is reduced. It acts as the oxidizing agent.

34. True. $K_2Cr_2O_7 + 6FeCl_2 + 14HCl \rightarrow 2CrCl_3 + 2KCl + 6FeCl_3 + 7H_2O$

The sum of the coefficients is 38.

35. $C + 2H_2SO_4 \rightarrow CO_2 + 2SO_2 + 2H_2O$

36. $CuO + H_2 \rightarrow Cu + H_2O$

Here 5 moles of copper require 5 moles of hydrogen for reaction to occur.

37. $2Na \quad + \quad 2H_2O \quad \rightarrow 2NaOH + H_2$

0.46 mole   0.20 mole

Because 0.46 mole Na requires 0.46 mole of water, and only 0.20 mole of water is available for reaction, only 0.20 mole of Na can be used for reaction. This produces 0.20 mole of NaOH.

38. $C_3H_8 + 5O_2 \rightarrow \quad 3CO_2 \quad + 4H_2O$

6.0 moles

Because 3 moles of CO_2 are produced from 1 mole of C_3H_8, 6 moles of CO_2 would be produced from 2 moles of C_3H_8.

$$\text{g } C_3H_8 = 2.0 \text{ moles} \times \frac{44.0 \text{ g}}{\text{mole}} = 88 \text{ g } C_3H_8$$

39. $FeS + 2HCl \rightarrow FeCl_2 + H_2S$

$\downarrow$ $\qquad\qquad$ $\downarrow$

$\times\,10$ $\qquad\qquad$ $34\overline{0}$ g

$\downarrow$ $\qquad\qquad$ $\div\,34.1$ g/mole

19.9 moles $\qquad\qquad$ $\downarrow$

9.97 moles

$$\text{g HCl} = 19.9 \text{ moles} \times \frac{36.5 \text{ g}}{\text{mole}} = 726 \text{ g HCl needed}$$

40. $2C_2H_6 \quad + \quad 7O_2 \quad \rightarrow \quad 4CO_2 + 6H_2O$

30.0 g   16.0 g   ? g

$$\text{Moles } C_2H_6 = 30.0 \text{ g} \times \frac{1 \text{ mole}}{30.0 \text{ g}} = 1.00 \text{ mole } C_2H_6$$

$$\text{Moles } O_2 = 1.00 \text{ mole } C_2H_6 \times \frac{7 \text{ moles } O_2}{2 \text{ moles } C_2H_6} = 3.50 \text{ moles } O_2$$

1.00 mole C_2H_6 requires 3.50 moles O_2 for reaction.

$$\text{g } O_2 = 3.50 \text{ moles} \times \frac{32.0 \text{ g}}{\text{mole}} = 112 \text{ g } O_2$$

Because only 16.0 g O_2 are available, the O_2 is the limiting reactant.

$$\text{Moles } O_2 = 16.0 \text{ g} \times \frac{1 \text{ mole}}{32.0 \text{ g}} = 0.500 \text{ mole } O_2$$

$$\text{Moles } CO_2 = 0.500 \text{ mole } O_2 \times \frac{4 \text{ moles } CO_2}{7 \text{ moles } O_2} = 0.286 \text{ mole } CO_2$$

$$\text{g } CO_2 = 0.286 \text{ mole} \times \frac{44.0 \text{ g}}{\text{mole}} = 12.6 \text{ g } CO_2$$

41. $H_3PO_4 + 3LiOH \rightarrow Li_3PO_4 + 3H_2O$

    ? g   1,360 g

$$\text{Moles LiOH} = 1,360 \text{ g} \times \frac{1 \text{ mole}}{23.9 \text{ g}} = 56.9 \text{ moles LiOH}$$

$$\text{Moles } H_3PO_4 = 56.9 \text{ moles LiOH} \times \frac{1 \text{ mole } H_3PO_4}{3 \text{ moles LiOH}} = 19.0 \text{ moles } H_3PO_4$$

$$\text{g } H_3PO_4 = 19.0 \text{ moles} \times \frac{98.0 \text{ g}}{\text{mole}} = 1,860 \text{ g } H_3PO_4$$

42. $3Ca(OH)_2 + 2H_3PO_4 \rightarrow Ca_3(PO_4)_2 + 6H_2O$

               49.0 g

$$\text{Moles } H_3PO_4 = 49.0 \text{ g} \times \frac{1 \text{ mole}}{98.0 \text{ g}} = 0.500 \text{ mole } H_3PO_4$$

$$\text{Moles Ca(OH)}_2 = 0.500 \text{ mole } H_3PO_4 \times \frac{3 \text{ moles Ca(OH)}_2}{2 \text{ moles } H_3PO_4}$$

$$= 0.750 \text{ mole Ca(OH)}_2$$

$$\text{g Ca(OH)}_2 = 0.750 \text{ mole} \times \frac{74.1 \text{ g}}{\text{mole}} = 55.6 \text{ g Ca(OH)}_2$$

$$\text{Moles Ca}_3(\text{PO}_4)_2 = 0.500 \text{ mole H}_3\text{PO}_4 \times \frac{1 \text{ mole Ca}_3(\text{PO}_4)_2}{2 \text{ moles H}_3\text{PO}_4}$$

$$= 0.250 \text{ mole Ca}_3(\text{PO}_4)_2$$

$$\text{g Ca}_3(\text{PO}_4)_2 = 0.250 \text{ mole} \times \frac{310.3 \text{ g}}{\text{mole}} = 77.6 \text{ g Ca}_3(\text{PO}_4)_2$$

43. $\text{MgSO}_4 \cdot 7\text{H}_2\text{O} \rightarrow \text{MgSO}_4 + 7\text{H}_2\text{O}$

    15.0 moles

$$\text{Moles MgSO}_4 = 15.0 \text{ moles MgSO}_4\underline{}7\text{H}_2\text{O} \times \frac{1 \text{ mole MgSO}_4}{1 \text{ mole MgSO}_4\underline{}7\text{H}_2\text{O}}$$

$$= 15.0 \text{ moles MgSO}_4$$

$$\text{g MgSO}_4 = 15.0 \text{ moles} \times \frac{120.4 \text{ g}}{\text{mole}} = 1{,}806 \text{ g MgSO}_4$$

        or 1,810 g (3 significant figures)

44. $2\text{H}_2\text{O}_2 \rightarrow 2\text{H}_2\text{O} + \text{O}_2$

        63.0 g

$$\text{Moles H}_2 = 63.0 \text{ g} \times \frac{1 \text{ mole}}{18.0 \text{ g}} = 3.50 \text{ moles H}_2\text{O}$$

$$\text{Moles H}_2\text{O}_2 = 3.50 \text{ moles H}_2\text{O} \times \frac{2 \text{ moles H}_2\text{O}_2}{2 \text{ moles H}_2\text{O}} = 3.50 \text{ moles H}_2\text{O}_2$$

$$\text{g H}_2\text{O}_2 = 3.50 \text{ moles} \times \frac{34.0 \text{ g}}{\text{mole}} = 119. \text{ g H}_2\text{O}_2$$

45. $2\text{NaCl} + \text{Pb(NO}_3)_2 \rightarrow \text{PbCl}_2 + 2\text{NaNO}_3$

    5.85 g   66.4 g   ? g

$$\text{Moles NaCl} = 5.85 \text{ g} \times \frac{1 \text{ mole}}{58.5 \text{ g}} = 0.100 \text{ mole NaCl}$$

$$\text{Moles Pb(NO}_3)_2 = 0.100 \text{ mole NaCl} \times \frac{1 \text{ mole Pb(NO}_3)_2}{2 \text{ moles NaCl}}$$

$$= 0.0500 \text{ mole } Pb(NO_3)_2$$

$$g\ Pb(NO_3)_2 = 0.0500\ \cancel{mole} \times \frac{331.2\ g}{\cancel{mole}} = 16.6\ g\ Pb(NO_3)_2$$

Because 66.4 g $Pb(NO_3)_2$ equals 0.20 mole, and that would require 0.40 mole NaCl for reaction, and because we know that there is only 0.100 mole NaCl available, we can conclude that NaCl is the limiting reactant. Looking at the balanced equation, we see that 2 moles NaCl can produce 1 mole $PbCl_2$. Therefore 0.100 mole NaCl can produce 0.0500 mole $PbCl_2$.

$$g\ PbCl_2 = 0.0500\ \cancel{mole} \times \frac{278.2\ g}{\cancel{mole}} = 13.9\ g\ PbCl_2$$

46. $CO_2 + 2LiOH \rightarrow Li_2CO3 + H_2O$

$$\downarrow \qquad\qquad \downarrow$$

$$?\ g \qquad\qquad 148\ g$$

$$\text{Moles } Li_2CO_3 = 148\ \cancel{g} \times \frac{1\ mole}{73.8\ \cancel{g}} = 2.01\ \text{moles } Li_2CO_3$$

$$\text{Moles } LiOH = 2.01\ \cancel{\text{moles } Li_2CO_3} \times \frac{2\ \text{moles } LiOH}{1\ \cancel{\text{mole } Li_2CO_3}} = 4.02\ \text{moles } LiOH$$

$$g\ LiOH = 4.02\ \cancel{moles} \times \frac{23.9\ g}{1\ \cancel{mole}} = 96.1\ g\ LiOH\ \text{needed}$$

47. $2Mg + O_2 \rightarrow 2MgO$

$$?\ g \quad 48.0\ g$$

$$\text{Moles } O_2 = 48.0\ \cancel{g} \times \frac{1\ mole}{32.0\ \cancel{g}} = 1.50\ \text{moles } O_2$$

$$\text{Moles } Mg = 1.50\ \cancel{\text{moles } O_2} \times \frac{2\ \text{moles } Mg}{1\ \cancel{\text{mole } O_2}} = 3.00\ \text{moles } Mg$$

$$g\ Mg = 3.00\ \cancel{moles} \times \frac{24.3\ g}{1\ \cancel{mole}} = 72.9\ g\ Mg\ \text{needed}$$

48. $\quad Ba \quad + \quad 2H_2O \quad \rightarrow \quad Ba(OH)_2 \quad + \quad H_2$

$$137.3\ g \qquad 72.00\ g \qquad\quad ?\ g \qquad\quad ?\ g$$

$$\text{Moles H}_2\text{O} = 72.00 \text{ g} \times \frac{1 \text{ mole}}{18.0 \text{ g}} = 4.00 \text{ moles H}_2\text{O}$$

$$\text{Moles Ba} = 4.00 \text{ moles H}_2\text{O} \times \frac{1 \text{ mole Ba}}{2 \text{ moles H}_2\text{O}} = 2.00 \text{ moles Ba}$$

$$\text{Moles Ba} = 137.3 \text{ g} \times \frac{1 \text{ mole}}{137.3 \text{ g}} = 1.000 \text{ mole Ba}$$

Because 2.00 moles of Ba are needed for reaction, and only 1.000 mole is available, Ba is the limiting reactant. Therefore only 2.00 moles of water will be used, and 1.000 mole Ba(OH)$_2$ and 1.00 mole H$_2$ will be produced. There will be 2.00 moles of water in excess.

$$\text{g H}_2\text{O excess} = 2.00 \text{ moles} \times \frac{18.0 \text{ g}}{\text{mole}} = 36.0 \text{ g H}_2\text{O}$$

$$\text{g Ba(OH)}_2 \text{ produced} = 1.000 \text{ mole} \times \frac{171.3 \text{ g}}{\text{mole}} = 171.3 \text{ g Ba(OH)}_2 \text{ produced}$$

$$\text{g H}_2 \text{ produced} = 1.00 \text{ mole} \times \frac{2.0 \text{ g}}{\text{mole}} = 2.0 \text{ g H}_2 \text{ produced}$$

SOLUTIONS TO CUMULATIVE REVIEWS CHAPTERS 12–14

1. An *endothermic reaction* is one in which heat is taken in from the surroundings. An *exothermic reaction* is one in which heat is released to the surroundings.

2. Heat $= (m)(c)(\Delta t)$

$$= (500.0 \text{ g})\left(\frac{1\text{cal}}{\text{g}°\text{C}}\right)(20.0°\text{C}) = 10,\overline{0}00 \text{ cal}$$

3. Heat $= (m)(c)(\Delta t)$

$$= (25.0 \text{ g})\left(\frac{0.0920 \text{ cal}}{\text{g}°\text{C}}\right)(60.0°\text{C}) = 138 \text{ cal}$$

4. Heat $= (m)(c)(\Delta t)$

$$? \text{ g} = 25.0 \text{ mL} \times \frac{0.800 \text{ g}}{\text{mL}} = 20.0 \text{ g ethyl alcohol}$$

$$\text{Heat} = (20.0 \text{ g})\left(\frac{0.581\text{cal}}{\text{g}°\text{C}}\right)(25.0°\text{C}) = 291 \text{ cal}$$

5. We must use standard-state conditions when calculating changes in heat so that we can measure heat given up or absorbed during a thermochemical reaction (as opposed to measuring heat involved in temperature or pressure changes).

6. Heat $= (m)(c)(\Delta t)$

$$= (1,\overline{000} \text{ g})\left(\frac{1.00\text{cal}}{\text{g°C}}\right)(25.0\text{°C}) = 25,\overline{0}00 \text{ cal}$$

7. $$H_2(g) + \frac{1}{2} O_2(g) \rightarrow H_2O(l) + 68.3 \text{ kcal}$$

8. $$H_2O(l) + SO_3(g) \rightarrow H_2SO_4(aq)$$

    Use Table 12.2 to determine heats of formation at 25∞C and 1 atm pressure.

    $$(-217) - (-68.3 - 94.45) = -54 \text{ kcal/mole}$$

9. $$S + O_2 \rightarrow SO_2 + 70.96 \text{ kcal/mole}$$

    $$254 \text{ g}$$

    $$\text{Moles SO}_2 = 254 \text{ g} \times \frac{1 \text{ mole}}{64.1 \text{ g}} = 3.96 \text{ moles SO}_2$$

    If 70.96 kcal are released when 1 mole of SO_2 is formed, 281 kcal are released when 3.96 moles of SO_2 are formed.

    $$? \text{ kcal} = (3.96 \text{ moles})\left(\frac{70.96 \text{ kcal}}{1 \text{ mole}}\right) = 281 \text{ kcal}$$

10. $$H_2O_2(l) \rightarrow H_2O(l) + \frac{1}{2} O_2(g)$$

    From Table 12.2, ΔH is calculated as follows:

    $$\Delta H = (-68.3 + 0) - (-44.8)$$

    $$= -68.3 + 44.8 = -23.5 \text{ kcal/mole}$$

    $$\text{Moles H}_2O_2 = 10.2 \text{ g} \times \frac{1 \text{ mole}}{34.0 \text{ g}} = 0.300 \text{ mole H}_2O_2$$

    If 1 mole of H_2O_2 releases 23.5 kcal, the amount of heat released by 0.300 mole is found as follows:

    $$? \text{ kcal} = (0.300 \text{ mole})\left(\frac{23.5 \text{ kcal}}{1 \text{ mole}}\right) = 7.05 \text{ kcal}$$

11. $P_i \times V_i = P_f \times V_f$ or $\dfrac{P_i}{P_f} = \dfrac{V_f}{V_i}$ or $V_f = \dfrac{P_i \times V_i}{P_f}$

$$V_f = \frac{(2.0 \text{ atm})(55 \text{ mL})}{(4.5 \text{ atm})} = 24 \text{ mL}$$

12. $\dfrac{P_i}{P_f} = \dfrac{V_f}{V_i}$ or $V_f = \dfrac{P_i \times V_i}{P_f}$

$$V_f = \frac{(15.05 \text{ mL})(2.50 \text{ atm})}{(2.00 \text{ atm})} = 18.8 \text{ mL}$$

13. $\dfrac{P_i}{P_f} = \dfrac{V_f}{V_i}$ or $P_f = \dfrac{P_i V_i}{V_f}$

$$P_f = \frac{(770 \text{ torr})(0.200 \text{L})}{(0.2500 \text{L})} = 616 \text{ torr}$$

14. $\dfrac{V_i}{T_i} = \dfrac{V_f}{T_f}$ $t_i = 27 \text{°C}$ $t_f = 227 \text{°C}$

$$273 + t_i = T_i \qquad\qquad 273 + t_f = T_f$$

$$273 + 27 = 3\overline{0}0 \text{ K} \qquad 273 + 227 = 5\overline{0}0 \text{ K}$$

$$V_f = \frac{V_i T_f}{T_i} = \frac{(1{,}500.0 \text{mL})(5\overline{0}0 \text{K})}{(3\overline{0}0 \text{K})} = 2{,}5\overline{0}0 \text{ mL}$$

15. $\dfrac{V_i}{T_i} = \dfrac{V_f}{T_f}$ $t_f = 180.0 \text{°C}$

$$273 + t_f = T_f$$

$$273 + 180 = 453 \text{ K}$$

$$T_i = \frac{T_f V_i}{V_f} = \frac{(453 \text{ K})(100.0 \text{ mL})}{(55.0 \text{ mL})} = 824 \text{ K}$$

$$t_i = T_i - 273$$

$$= 824 - 273 = 551 \text{°C}$$

16. $\dfrac{P_i V_i}{T_i} = \dfrac{P_f V_f}{T_f}$ $t_i = 50.5 \text{°C}$ $t_f = 250.0 \text{°C}$

$$T_i = t_i + 273 \qquad T_f = t_f + 273$$

$$= 50.5 + 273 \qquad = 250.0 + 273$$

$$= 323.5 \text{ K} = 324 \text{ K} \qquad = 523 \text{ K}$$

$V_f = \dfrac{P_i V_i T_f}{P_f T_i}$ $P_i = 1.50 \text{ atm}$

$$\text{? torr} = 1.50 \text{ atm} \times \dfrac{760 \text{ torr}}{\text{atm}} = 1{,}140 \text{ torr}$$

$$V_f = \dfrac{(1{,}140 \text{ torr})(2.50 \text{ L})(523 \text{ K})}{(775 \text{ torr})(324 \text{ K})} = 5.94 \text{ L}$$

17. $\dfrac{P_i V_i}{T_i} = \dfrac{P_f V_f}{T_f}$ $t_i = 127 \text{°C}$ $t_f + 273 = T_f$

$$T_i = 127 + 273 \qquad\qquad 273 \text{ K} = T_f$$

$$= 40\overline{0} \text{ K}$$

$V_f = \dfrac{P_i V_i T_f}{P_f T_i}$ $P_i = 775 \text{ torr}$ $P_f = 76\overline{0} \text{ torr}$

$$V_f = \dfrac{(775 \text{ torr})(10.5 \text{ L})(273 \text{ K})}{(76\overline{0} \text{ torr})(40\overline{0} \text{ K})} = 7.31 \text{ L}$$

18. $P_{\text{gas}} = P_{\text{total}} - P_{\text{water}}$

Using Table 13.1, we find that P_{H_2O} at 20.0∞C is 17.54 torr.

$$P_{O_2} = 775 - 17.54 = 757.46 \text{ torr}$$

Therefore, $P_i = 757 \text{ torr}$.

$\dfrac{P_i V_i}{T_i} = \dfrac{P_f V_f}{T_f}$ $t_i = 20.0 \text{°C}$ $T_f = 273 + t_f$

$$T_i = 273 + t_i \qquad\qquad = 273 + 0$$

$$= 273 + 20.0 \qquad\qquad = 273 \text{ K}$$

$$= 293 \text{ K}$$

$$V_f = \frac{(757 \text{ torr})(4\overline{0}0 \text{ mL})(273 \text{ K})}{(76\overline{0} \text{ torr})(293 \text{ K})} = 371 \text{ mL} \quad \text{or} \quad 0.371 \text{ L}$$

19. $P_{H_2} = P_{total} - P_{water}$

Using Table 13.1, we find that P_{H_2O} at 28.0∞C is 28.35 torr.

$P_{H_2O} = 725 \text{ torr} - 28.35 \text{ torr} = 696.65 \text{ torr} = 697 \text{ torr}$

$$\frac{P_i V_i}{T_i} = \frac{P_f V_f}{T_f} \qquad t_i = 28.0 °C \qquad\qquad t_f = 0 °C$$

$$T_i = 273 + 28.0 \qquad\qquad T_f = 273 + 0$$

$$= 301 \text{ K} \qquad\qquad = 273 \text{ K}$$

$$V_f = \frac{P_i V_i T_f}{P_f T_i} = \frac{(697 \text{ torr})(5.00 \text{ L})(273 \text{ K})}{(76\overline{0} \text{ torr})(301 \text{ K})} = 4.16 \text{ L}$$

20. $PV = nRT$

$$n = \frac{PV}{RT} = \frac{(1.00 \text{ atm})(358.4 \text{ L})}{\left(0.0821 \frac{\text{(L)(atm)}}{\text{(mole)(K)}}\right)(273 \text{ K})} = 16.0 \text{ moles}$$

21. $V = 15.0 \text{ moles} \times \dfrac{22.4 \text{ L}}{\text{mole}} = 336 \text{ L}$

22. $PV = nRT$

$$V = \frac{nRT}{P} = \frac{(20.0 \text{ moles})\left(0.0821 \frac{\text{(L)(atm)}}{\text{(mole)(K)}}\right)(5\overline{0}0 \text{ K})}{(3.00 \text{ atm})} = 274 \text{ L}$$

23. $PV = nRT$ atm $= 550.0 \text{ torr} \times \dfrac{1 \text{ atm}}{76\overline{0} \text{ torr}} = 0.724 \text{ atm}$

$$n = \frac{PV}{RT} = \frac{(0.724 \text{ atm})(2.00 \text{ L})}{\left(0.0821 \frac{\text{(L)(atm)}}{\text{(mole)(K)}}\right)(428 \text{ K})} = 0.0412 \text{ mole}$$

24. $\text{MM} = \dfrac{gRT}{PV} = \dfrac{(3.55 \text{ g})\left(0.0821 \dfrac{\text{(L)(atm)}}{\text{(mole)(K)}}\right)(5\overline{0}0 \text{ K})}{(2.000 \text{ atm})(0.255 \text{ L})} = 286 \text{ g/mole}$

25. $2C_2H_6 + 7O_2 \rightarrow 4CO_2 + 6H_2O$

   5 L   ? L

   $\text{L CO}_2 = 5.00 \text{ L C}_2\text{H}_6 \times \dfrac{4 \text{ L CO}_2}{2 \text{ L C}_2\text{H}_6} = 10.0 \text{ L CO}_2$

26. $\text{MM} = \dfrac{(\text{mass})(R)(T)}{(P)(V)} \qquad D = \dfrac{\text{mass (g)}}{\text{volume (L)}} \qquad \dfrac{\text{mass}}{\text{volume}} = \dfrac{(\text{MM})(P)}{(R)(T)}$

   $\dfrac{\text{mass}}{\text{volume}} = \dfrac{(70.0 \text{ g/mole})(1 \text{ atm})}{\left(0.0821 \dfrac{\text{(L)(atm)}}{\text{(mole)(K)}}\right)(273 \text{ K})} = 3.12 \text{ g/L}$

27. Because the final pressure is less than the initial pressure, the final volume is greater than the initial volume.

28. $\dfrac{P_iV_i}{T_i} = \dfrac{P_fV_f}{T_f} \qquad\qquad 273 + t_i = T_i \qquad\qquad 273 + t_f = T_f$

   $273 + 25 = 298 \text{ K} \qquad\qquad 273 + 37 = 310 \text{ K}$

   $V_f = \dfrac{P_iV_iT_f}{P_fT_i} = \dfrac{(1.39 \text{ atm})(2.55 \text{ L})(310 \text{ K})}{(1.41 \text{ atm})(298 \text{ K})} = 2.62 \text{ L}$

29. $\text{MM} = \dfrac{gRT}{PV} \qquad\qquad 273 + t_i = T_i$

   $273 + 25.0 = 298 \text{ K}$

   $\text{MM} = \dfrac{(25.0 \text{ g})\left(0.0821 \dfrac{\text{(L)(atm)}}{\text{(mole)(K)}}\right)(298 \text{ K})}{(4.50 \text{ atm})(1.45 \text{ L})} = 93.7 \text{ g/mole}$

30. This phenomenon is observed because forces of attraction between gas molecules vary.

31. The volume of air in the balloon will decrease.

32. P_{total} = 815 torr
     P_{CO_2} = (0.420)(815) = 342.3 torr
     P_{H_2} = (0.400)(815) = 326 torr
     P_{N_2} = (0.169)(815) = 138 torr
     P_{CH_4} = (0.0000300)(815) = 0.0245 torr

33. 3.(a) $SO_2 + H_2O \rightarrow H_2SO_3$ is the reaction of a nonmetal oxide with water.

     2.(b) $CaO + H_2O \rightarrow Ca(OH)_2$ is the reaction of a metal oxide with water.

     1.(c) $2H_2O \rightarrow 2H_2 + O2$ is the electrolysis of water.

34. $CaCO_3 \bullet xH_2O \rightarrow CaCO_3 + xH_2O$

     20.8 g   10.0 g

        g H_2O = g $CaCO_3 \bullet xH_2O$ – g $CaCO_3$ = 20.8 g – 10.00 g = 10.8 g H_2O

        Moles $CaCO_3$ = 10.0 g $\times \dfrac{1\ mole}{100.1\ g}$ = 0.09990 mole $CaCO_3$

        Moles H_2O = 10.80 g $\times \dfrac{1\ mole}{18.0\ g}$ = 0.599 mole H_2O

     The ratio of $CaCO_3$ to H_2O is 1:6; therefore the formula of the hydrate is
     $CaCO_3 \bullet 6H_2O$.

35. $CaCl_2 \bullet 6H_2O$. $CaCl_2$ has a formula mass of 111.1 and $6H_2O$ has a formula mass of
     108.0, so $CaCl_2 \bullet 6H_2O$ has a formula mass of 219.1.

        Percent $H_2O = \dfrac{108.0}{219.1} \times 100 = 49.3\%$

36. $CaSO_4 \bullet 2H_2O$. $CaSO_4$ has a formula mass of 136.2 and $2H_2O$ has a formula mass
     of 36.0, so $CaSO_4 \bullet 2H_2O$ has a formula mass of 172.2.

        Percent $H_2O = \dfrac{36.0}{172.2} \times 100 = 20.9\%$

37. The hydrated salt $BaCl_2 \cdot xH_2O$ is 14.7% by weight water. Therefore the $BaCl_2$ portion is 85.3% by weight. For every 100 g of compound, 85.3 g are $BaCl_2$ and 14.7 g are water. Therefore the numbers of moles of each are found as follows:

$$\text{Moles } BaCl_2 = (85.3 \text{ g})\left(\frac{1 \text{ mole}}{208.3 \text{ g}}\right) = 0.410 \text{ mole } BaCl_2$$

$$\text{Moles } H_2O = (14.7 \text{ g})\left(\frac{1 \text{ mole}}{18.0 \text{ g}}\right) = 0.817 \text{ mole } H_2O$$

The ratio of moles of $BaCl_2$ to moles of water is 0.410 mole to 0.817 mole, or 1 to 2. Therefore the formula of the hydrate is $BaCl_2 \sum 2H_2O$.

38. The hydrated salt $Na_2CO_3 \cdot xH_2O$ is 63% water. Therefore the Na_2CO_3 portion is 37%. For every 100 g of compound, 37 g are Na_2CO_3 and 63 g are water. Therefore the numbers of moles of each are found as follows:

$$\text{Moles } Na_2CO_3 = (37 \text{ g})\left(\frac{1 \text{ mole}}{106.0 \text{ g}}\right) = 0.35 \text{ mole } Na_2CO_3$$

$$\text{Moles } H_2O = (63 \text{ g})\left(\frac{1 \text{ mole}}{18.0 \text{ g}}\right) = 3.5 \text{ moles } H_2O$$

The ratio of moles of Na_2CO_3 to moles of water is 0.35 mole to 3.5 mole, or 1 to 10. Therefore the formula of the hydrate is $Na_2CO_3 \cdot 10H_2O$.

39. $2H_2O \rightarrow 2H_2 + O_2$

      ↓   ↓

   ? g   25.00 g

$$\text{Moles } O_2 = 25.00 \text{ g} \times \frac{1 \text{ mole}}{32.0 \text{ g}} = 0.781 \text{ mole } O_2$$

$$\text{Moles } H_2O = 0.781 \text{ mole } O_2 \times \frac{2 \text{ moles } H_2O}{1 \text{ mole } O_2} = 1.56 \text{ moles } H_2O$$

$$\text{g } H_2O = 1.56 \text{ moles } H_2O \times \frac{18.0 \text{ g}}{1 \text{ mole}} = 28.1 \text{ g } H_2O$$

40. 3.(a) $MgSO_4 \cdot 7H_2O$ is Epsom salt.

    1.(b) $KAl(SO_4)_2 \cdot 12H_2O$ is alum.

2.(c) $CaSO_4 \cdot 2H_2O$ is gypsum.

41. (a)   A liquid has no definite shape but a definite volume.
     (b)   A gas is easily compressed.
     (c)   A solid has a definite shape and volume.

The matching pairs are 1.(c), 2.(a), and 3.(b).

42. When eggs are being cooked in boiling water, increasing the heat makes the water evaporate more quickly. Answer (b) is the correct choice.

43. This is an example of sublimation, or change from the solid state to the gaseous state.

44. A soft crystalline solid with a low melting point is most likely to be a molecular solid.

45. A hard crystalline solid that has a high melting point and is hard and brittle is most likely to be an ionic solid.

46. A solid with no definite shape is likely to be an amorphous solid.

47. When molecules gain energy, kinetic energy increases and attractive forces between molecules decrease.

48. Because benzene evaporates more easily than water, it has the higher equilibrium vapor pressure.

49. In some crystals, electrons are free to wander throughout the crystal, allowing them to conduct electricity.

50. Atomic crystals that are composed of metallic atoms are strong because the metallic lattice is composed of positive ions surrounded by a cloud of electrons. The electrons are given off by the metallic atoms, but they are considered part of the entire crystal.

SOLUTIONS TO CUMULATIVE REVIEWS CHAPTERS 15–16

1. (a) Oxygen is the solute and nitrogen is the solvent.
   (b) Sulfur dioxide is the solute and water is the solvent.
   (c) Lemon juice and sugar are the solutes and water is the solvent.

2. (a) H–F is polar; H_2O is polar. Therefore a solution forms.
   (b) Benzene is nonpolar; *trans*-dichloroethane is nonpolar. Like dissolves like; therefore solutions are formed in both cases.

3. (a) $\dfrac{50.0 \text{ g salt}}{75.0 \text{ g solution}} \times 100 = 66.7\%$ by mass salt water

   (b) $\dfrac{175 \text{ g sugar}}{1,5\overline{0}0 \text{ g solution}} \times 100 = 11.7\%$ by mass sugar water

4. (a) $\dfrac{25.0 \text{ mL alcohol}}{455 \text{ mL solution}} \times 100 = 5.49\%$ by volume alcohol in water

   (b) $\dfrac{35.0 \text{ mL benzene in carbon tetrachloride}}{95.0 \text{ mL solution}} \times 100 = 36.8\%$ by volume solution

5. $\dfrac{5.0 \text{ g benzene in CCl}_4}{75 \text{ mL solution}} \times 100 = 6.7\%$ by mass–volume benzene in CCl_4

6. $M = \dfrac{\text{moles}}{\text{L}}$

234

$$\text{Moles } C_2H_5OH = 1.84 \text{ g} \times \frac{1 \text{ mole}}{46.0 \text{ g}} = 0.0400 \text{ mole } C_2H_5OH$$

$$M = \frac{0.0400 \text{ mole}}{1.5 \text{ L}} = 0.027 \text{ M}$$

7. $\text{? moles} = M \times L = 1.33M \times 0.250 \text{ L} = 0.333 \text{ mole}$

$$\text{g NaOH} = 0.333 \text{ moles} \times \frac{40.0 \text{ g}}{\text{mole}} = 13.3 \text{ g NaOH}$$

8. $L = \dfrac{\text{moles}}{M}$

$$\text{? moles} = 26.0 \text{ g} \times \frac{1 \text{ mole}}{111.1 \text{ g}} = 0.234 \text{ mole}$$

$$L = \frac{0.234 \text{ mole}}{1.00 \text{ M}} = 0.234 \text{ L} = 234 \text{ mL}$$

9. Normality is the number of equivalents of solute per liter of solution, and molarity is the number of moles of solute per liter of solution.

10. $N = \dfrac{\text{equivalents}}{L}$

$\text{? equivalents} = N \times L = (2.00 \text{ N})(1.00 \text{ L}) = 2.00 \text{ equivalents}$

The equation will be set up as follows:

$$\text{? g} = 2.00 \text{ equivalents} \times \frac{\text{g}}{\text{equivalent}} \text{ for } H_3PO_4$$

For H_3PO_4 there are 32.7 g/equivalent; therefore

$$\text{? g} = 2.00 \text{ equivalents} \times \frac{32.7 \text{ g}}{\text{equivalent}} = 65.4 \text{ g } H_3PO_4$$

11. $M = \dfrac{\text{moles}}{L}$

$$\text{? moles} = 18.5 \text{ g} \times \frac{1 \text{ mole}}{74.1 \text{ g}} = 0.250 \text{ mole Ca}$$

$$M = \frac{0.250 \text{ mole}}{0.500 \text{ L}} = 0.500 \, M$$

$$N = \frac{\text{equivalents}}{\text{L}}$$

$$\text{Equivalent} = 18.5 \, \cancel{g} \times \frac{1 \text{ equivalent}}{37.1 \, \cancel{g}} = 0.500 \text{ equivalent}$$

$$N = \frac{0.500 \text{ equivalent}}{0.500 \text{ L}} = 1.00 \, N$$

12. $N_i V_i = N_f V_f$

$$(1.33 \, N)(5.50 \text{ L}) = (36.0 \, N)(x)$$

$$x = \frac{(1.33 \, N) \, (5.50 \text{ L})}{(36.0 \, N)} = 0.203 \text{ L of } 36.0 \, N$$

needed, diluted with water to 5.50 L.

13. ? moles = $M \times$ L = $(0.150 \, M)(2.00 \text{ L}) = 0.300$ mole

$$\text{g AgNO}_3 = 0.300 \, \cancel{\text{moles}} \times \frac{169.9 \text{ g}}{\cancel{\text{mole}}} = 51.0 \text{ g AgNO}_3 \text{ needed.}$$

14. False. A solution is a homogeneous mixture.

15. ? moles = $M \times$ L = $18.0 \, M \times 0.100$ L = 1.80 moles H_2SO_4

$$\text{g H}_2\text{SO}_4 = 1.80 \, \cancel{\text{moles}} \times \frac{98.1 \text{ g}}{\cancel{\text{mole}}} = 177 \text{ g H}_2\text{SO}_4$$

16. (a) ? g solution = $2{,}\overline{0}00 \, \cancel{\text{mL}} \times \frac{1.09 \text{ g}}{\cancel{\text{mL}}} = 2{,}180$ g solution

$$\frac{25.0 \text{ g}}{100.0 \text{ g}} = \frac{x \text{ g}}{2{,}180 \text{ g}}$$

$x = 545$ g sugar in 2,180 g solution

(b) Molarity $= \dfrac{\text{moles}}{\text{L}}$

$$? \text{ moles} = 545 \text{ g} \times \frac{1 \text{ mole}}{342.0 \text{ g}} = 1.59 \text{ moles}$$

$$M = \frac{1.59 \text{ mole}}{2.00 \text{ L}} = 0.795 \, M \text{ solution}$$

17. $Percent = \dfrac{g \text{ solute}}{g \text{ solution}} \times 100$, therefore

$$? \text{ g solute} = \frac{percent \infty \text{ g solution}}{100} = \frac{(0.90)(100.0)}{100} = 0.90 \text{ g solute}$$

18. $Moles \, H_2SO_4 = 75.0 \text{ g} \times \dfrac{1 \text{ mole}}{98.1 \text{ g}} = 0.765 \text{ mole } H_2SO_4$

$$M_{H_2SO_4} = \frac{0.765 \text{ mole}}{0.400 \text{ L}} = 1.91 \, M$$

$$M_i V_i = M_f V_f$$

$$(1.91 \text{ M}) (0.400 \text{ L}) = (0.200 \text{ M } (x)$$

$$x = 3.82 \text{ L}$$

Dilute the solution to a total volume of 3.82 L.

19. $Molality = \dfrac{\text{moles solute}}{\text{kg solvent}}$

$$Moles \, C_2H_6O_2 = 100.0 \text{ g} \times \frac{1 \text{ mole}}{62.0 \text{ g}} = 1.61 \text{ moles } C_2H_6O_2$$

K_b water = 0.520°C/mole solute/kg H_2O

$\Delta t = m \, K_b$

$$m = \frac{1.61 \text{ moles}}{0.500 \text{ kg}} = 3.22 \, m$$

$\Delta t = (3.22 \, m)(0.520°C/m) = 1.67°C$

Therefore the boiling point would be 101.7°C.

20. $? \text{ moles} = 12.8 \text{ g} \times \dfrac{1 \text{ mole}}{128.0 \text{ g}} = 0.100 \text{ mole}$

Because this 0.100 mole of naphthalene is dissolved in exactly 1.00 L (1.00 kg) of water, not solution, the concentration must be 0.100 m.

21. Arrhenius acid is a substance that releases hydrogen ions (H^{1+}) when dissolved in water. Brø nsted-Lowry acid is a substance that is a proton donor.

22. False. pH 4 is not 100 times more acidic than pH 7; it is 1,000 times more acidic.

4 to 5 is 10 times, 5 to 6 is 10 times, and 6 to 7 is 10 times.

Therefore 10 x 10 x 10 is 1000 times.

23. (a) $2HC_2H_3O_2 + Ca(OH)_2 \rightarrow Ca(C_2H_3O_2)_2 + 2H_2O$

(b) $N_2O_5 + H_2O \rightarrow 2HNO_3$

24. $H_2O + SO_3 \rightarrow H_2SO_4$ or $H_2O + SO_2 \rightarrow H_2SO_3$

Sulfuric   Sulfurous

acid   acid

25. $[H^{1+}] = 1.0 \times 10^{-2}$

$pH = -\log [H^{1+}] = -\log [10^{-2}] = -(-2) = 2$

26. $[H^{1+}] = 1.0 \times 10^{-6}$

$pH = -\log [H^{1+}] = -\log [10^{-6}] = -(-6) = 6$

27. $M_i \times V_i = M_f \times V_f$

$(0.500 \ M)(x \text{ mL}) = (12.0 \ M)(75\bar{0} \text{ mL})$

$$x = \frac{(12.0 \ M)\ (75\bar{0} \text{ mL})}{(0.500 \ M)} = 18{,}\bar{0}00 \text{ mL}$$

28. $(50.0 \text{ mL})(2.00 \ M \text{ HCl}) = 0.100 \text{ mole HCl}$
$(50.0 \text{ mL})(2.00 \ M \text{ NaOH}) = 0.100 \text{ mole NaOH}$

$HCl + NaOH \rightarrow NaCl + H_2O$

Total volume = 50.0 mL + 50.0 mL = 100.0 mL, or 0.1000 L

$$M_{Cl^{1-}} = \frac{0.100 \text{ mole } Cl^{1-}}{0.1000 \text{ L}} = 1.00 \text{ } M \text{ } Cl^{1-}$$

$$M_{Na^{1+}} = \frac{0.100 \text{ mole } Na^{1+}}{0.1000 \text{ L}} = 1.00 \text{ } M \text{ } Na^{1+}$$

29.
$$M_a V_a \quad = M_b V_b$$

$$(40.0 \text{ mL})(1.50 \text{ } M) = (50.0 \text{ mL})(x)$$

$$x \quad = \frac{(40.0 \text{ mL})(1.50 \text{ } M)}{(50.0 \text{ mL})} = 1.20 \text{ } M \text{ HCl}$$

30.
$$M_a V_a \quad = M_b V_b$$

$$(0.150 \text{ } M)(1.50 \text{ mL}) = (x)(50.00 \text{ mL})$$

$$x \quad = \frac{(0.150 \text{ } M)(15.0 \text{ mL})}{(50.00 \text{ mL})} = 0.0450 \text{ } M \text{ NaOH}$$

31. *Ionization* is the process in which atoms or molecules transfer electrons and form ions. Solutions may or may not be involved in the ionization process. *Dissociation* is the breaking into ions of some substances when they dissolve in solution.

32. 1 M H_2SO_4 is more acidic than 1 N H_2SO_4, because 1 M H_2SO_4 = 1 mole H_2SO_4 (98.1 g) per liter of solution, and 1 N H_2SO_4 = 1 equivalent H_2SO_4 (49.1 g) per liter of solution.

33. 1 M HCl is more acidic than 1 M $HC_2H_3O_2$ because the HCl is ionized to a greater degree.

34.
$$0.02 \text{ } M \text{ NaCl} \rightarrow 0.02 \text{ } M \text{ } Na^{1+} + 0.02 \text{ } M \text{ } Cl^{1-}$$

Therefore

$$0.02 \text{ } M \text{ } Na^{1+} + 0.02 \text{ } M \text{ } Cl^{1-} = 0.04 \text{ } M \text{ ions}$$

35.
$$SrCl_2 \rightarrow Sr^{2+} + 2Cl^{1-}$$

If the Cl^{1-} concentration is 0.500 M, the Sr^{2+} concentration must be half of that (or 0.250 M).

36.
$$Ca(OH)_2(aq) + 2HCl(aq) \rightarrow CaCl_2(aq) + 2H_2O$$

0.1000 L	0.05000 L
x M	0.500 M

Moles HCl = (0.05000 L)(0.500 M) = 0.0250 mole HCl

$$\text{Moles Ca(OH)}_2 = 0.0250 \text{ mole HCl} \times \frac{1 \text{ mole Ca(OH)}_2}{2 \text{ moles HCl}} = 0.0125 \text{ mole Ca(OH)}_2$$

$$M = \frac{0.0125 \text{ moles}}{0.1000 \text{ L}} = 0.125 \ M$$

37. These terms refer to ionization.

38.
$$SrCl_2 \rightarrow Sr^{2+} + 2Cl^{1-}$$

There are twice as many Cl^{1-} ions as Sr^{2+} ions.

39. $[H^{1+}] = 1.0 \times 10^{-4}$

$$pH = -\log [H^{1+}] = -(-4) = 4$$

40. If $[H^{1+}] = 10^{-8}$, then $[OH^{1-}] = 10^{-6}$.